TREASURY MANAGEMENT
The Practitioner's Guide

Steven M. Bragg

WILEY

John Wiley & Sons, Inc.

For general information on our other products and services, or technical support, please contact our Customer Care Department within the United States at 800-762-2974, outside the United States at 317-572-3993 or fax 317-572-4002.

Wiley also publishes its books in a variety of electronic formats. Some content that appears in print may not be available in electronic books.

For more information about Wiley products, visit our Web site at http://*www.wiley.com*.

Library of Congress Cataloging-in-Publication Data:

Bragg, Steven M.
    Treasury management : the practitioner's guide / Steven M. Bragg.
        p. cm.
    Includes index.
    ISBN 978-0-470-49708-1 (cloth)
    1. International business enterprises–Finance–Management. 2. Banks and banking, International–Management. I. Title.
    HG4027.5.B73 2010
    658.15'99–dc22

                                                    2009035912

Printed in the United States of America
10 9 8 7 6 5 4 3

Contents

Contents

Preface

A treasurer has a broad range of responsibilities in the modern corporation, ranging from cash management to risk management. Further, the treasurer is responsible for the proper movement of potentially large amounts of funds and the construction of hedges, which call for the integration of a comprehensive set of controls into a broad-based procedural framework. *Treasury Management: The Practitioner's Guide* shortens the treasurer's learning curve for all aspects of the position, with chapters clustered into the general categories of cash management, financing, risk management, and treasury systems.

The book is divided into four sections. In Part One, we address the various methods by which a company transfers cash, both on paper and by electronic means, and then show how to create a cash forecast and monitor its accuracy. We then cover several methods for aggregating cash from a multitude of locations, so that funds can be more effectively dispositioned. Finally, a separate chapter addresses the components of working capital and how they may be altered, thereby impacting cash flow planning.

In Part Two, we cover what the treasurer does to raise debt and equity, as well as how to invest funds. This includes a discussion of the various kinds of debt and key characteristics of each one, how to deal with credit rating agencies, and the intricacies of equity offerings. The coverage of investments includes investment criteria, types of available investments, and investment and risk reduction strategies.

Part Three addresses an increasingly important aspect of the treasurer's responsibilities, which is risk management. This includes the objectives and strategies of both interest rate and foreign exchange risk management, as well as the available risk mitigation tools that are available to the treasurer.

Finally, Part Four describes the technology that drives many treasury transactions. This includes an overview of the clearing and settlement systems used in the United States, the functions of a treasury management system, and a discussion of how corporations can access the Society for Worldwide Interbank Financial Telecommunication (SWIFT) network.

These chapters are liberally sprinkled with examples to clarify concepts. Particular attention has also been paid to the specific accounting requirements of key treasury transactions, as well as related controls, policies, and procedures, with the intent of providing a treasurer with a complete framework for setting up and operating the treasury department.

The book answers a multitude of questions involved in running a treasury department, such as:

- How do I calculate the cost-effectiveness of a lockbox?

- How do I create a cash forecast?

- How do I set up a cross-border cash pool?

- How does notional pooling work?

- What policy changes can I implement to alter the investment in working capital?

- How can I securitize my accounts receivable?

- What types of exemptions are available from the stock registration rules?

- How do I set up a tranched cash flow strategy?

- How do I integrate risk mitigation into my investment strategy?

- How do I use forwards, futures, swaps, and options within my hedging strategy?

- How does the continuous link settlement system reduce settlement risk?

- What features should I look for in a treasury management system?

In short, *Treasury Management: The Practitioner's Guide* is the ideal sourcebook for the mechanics of how to run all aspects of the modern treasury department.

February 2010
Centennial, Colorado

About the Author

Steven Bragg, CPA, has been the chief financial officer or controller of four companies, as well as a consulting manager at Ernst & Young and auditor at Deloitte & Touche. He received a master's degree in finance from Bentley College, an MBA from Babson College, and a bachelor's degree in economics from the University of Maine. He has been the two-time president of the Colorado Mountain Club and is an avid alpine skier, mountain biker, and certified master diver. Mr. Bragg resides in Centennial, Colorado. He has written the following books:

Accounting and Finance for Your Small Business

Accounting Best Practices

Accounting Control Best Practices

Accounting Policies and Procedures Manual

Advanced Accounting Systems

Billing and Collections Best Practices

Business Ratios and Formulas

Controller's Guide to Costing

Controller's Guide to Planning and Controlling Operations

Controller's Guide: Roles and Responsibilities for the New Controller

Controllership

Cost Accounting

Essentials of Payroll

Fast Close

Financial Analysis

GAAP Guide

GAAP Policies and Procedures Manual

GAAS Guide

Inventory Accounting

Inventory Best Practices

Investor Relations

Just-in-Time Accounting

Management Accounting Best Practices

Managing Explosive Corporate Growth

Mergers and Acquisitions

Outsourcing

Payroll Accounting

Payroll Best Practices

Revenue Recognition

Run the Rockies

Running a Public Company

Sales and Operations for Your Small Business

The Controller's Function

The New CFO Financial Leadership Manual

The Ultimate Accountants' Reference

Throughput Accounting

FREE ONLINE RESOURCES BY STEVE BRAGG

Steve issues a free accounting best practices podcast. You can sign up for it at www.accountingtools.com, or access it through iTunes.

PART ONE

CASH MANAGEMENT

1

Treasury Department

The treasury department is responsible for a company's liquidity. The treasurer must monitor current and projected cash flows and special funding needs, and use this information to correctly invest excess funds, as well as be prepared for additional borrowings or capital raises. The department must also safeguard existing assets, which calls for the prudent investment of funds, while guarding against excessive losses on interest rates and foreign exchange positions. The treasurer needs to monitor the internal processes and decisions that cause changes in working capital and profitability, while also maintaining key relationships with investors and lenders. This chapter explores these and other responsibilities of the treasury department, as well as such key issues as treasury centralization, bank relations, outsourcing, and performance metrics.

ROLE OF THE TREASURY DEPARTMENT

Ultimately, the treasury department ensures that a company has sufficient cash available at all times to meet the needs of its primary business operations. However, its responsibilities range well beyond that single goal. It also has significant responsibilities in the following areas:

- *Cash forecasting.* The accounting staff generally handles the receipt and disbursement of cash, but the treasury staff needs to compile this information from all subsidiaries into short-range and long-range cash forecasts. These forecasts are needed for investment purposes, so the treasury staff can plan to use investment vehicles that are of the correct duration to match scheduled cash outflows. The staff also uses the forecasts to determine when more cash is needed, so that it can plan to acquire funds either through the use of debt or equity. Cash forecasting is also needed at the individual currency level, which the treasury staff uses to plan its hedging operations. This topic is covered in Chapter 3, Cash Forecasting.

- *Working capital management.* A key component of cash forecasting and cash availability is working capital, which involves changes in the levels of current assets and current liabilities in response to a company's general level of sales and various internal policies. The treasurer should be aware of working capital levels and trends, and advise management on the impact of proposed policy changes on working capital levels. This topic is addressed in Chapter 5, Working Capital Management.

- *Cash management.* The treasury staff uses the information it obtained from its cash forecasting and working capital management activities to ensure that sufficient cash is available for operational needs. The efficiency of this area is significantly improved by the use of cash pooling systems. This topic is addressed in Chapter 4, Cash Concentration.

- *Investment management.* The treasury staff is responsible for the proper investment of excess funds. The maximum return on investment of these funds is rarely the primary goal. Instead, it is much more important to not put funds at risk, and also to match the maturity dates of investments with a company's projected cash needs. This topic is addressed in Chapter 8, Investment Management.

- *Treasury risk management.* The interest rates that a company pays on its debt obligations may vary directly with market rates, which present a problem if market rates are rising. A company's foreign exchange positions could also be at risk if exchange rates suddenly worsen. In both cases, the treasury staff can create risk management strategies and implement hedging tactics to mitigate the company's risk. This topic is addressed in Chapter 9, Foreign Exchange Risk Management, and in Chapter 10, Interest Risk Management.

- *Management advice.* The treasury staff monitors market conditions constantly, and therefore is an excellent in-house resource for the management team should they want to know about interest rates that the company is likely to pay on new debt offerings, the availability of debt, and probable terms that equity investors will want in exchange for their investment in the company.

- *Credit rating agency relations.* When a company issues marketable debt, it is likely that a credit rating agency will review the company's financial condition and assign a credit rating to the debt. The treasury staff responds to information requests from the credit agency's review team and provides it with additional information over time. This topic is addressed in Chapter 6, Debt Management.

- *Bank relationships.* The treasurer meets with the representatives of any bank that the company uses to discuss the company's financial condition, the bank's fee structure, any debt granted to the company by the bank, and other services such as foreign exchange transactions, hedges, wire transfers, custodial services, cash pooling, and so forth. A long-term and open relationship can lead to some degree of bank cooperation if a company is having financial difficulties, and may sometimes lead to modest reductions in bank fees. This topic is addressed further in the Bank Relations section of this chapter.

- *Fund raising.* A key function is for the treasurer to maintain excellent relations with the investment community for fund-raising purposes. This community is composed of the *sell side*, which are those brokers and investment bankers who sell the company's debt and equity offerings to the *buy side*, which are the investors, pension funds, and other sources of cash, who buy the company's debt and equity. While all funds ultimately come from the buy side, the sell side is invaluable for its contacts with the buy side, and therefore is frequently worth the cost of its substantial fees associated with fund raising. This topic is addressed in Chapter 6, Debt Management, and Chapter 7, Equity Management.

- *Credit granting.* The granting of credit to customers can lie within the purview of the treasury department, or may be handed off to the accounting staff. This task is useful for the treasury staff to manage, since it allows the treasurer some control over the amount of working capital locked up in accounts receivable. This topic is addressed in Chapter 5, Working Capital Management.

- *Other activities.* If a company engages in mergers and acquisitions on a regular basis, then the treasury staff should have expertise in integrating the treasury systems of acquirees into those of the company. For larger organizations, this may require a core team of acquisition integration experts. Another activity is the maintenance of all types of insurance on behalf of the company. This chore may be given to the treasury staff on the grounds that it already handles a considerable amount of risk management through its hedging activities, so this represents a further centralization of risk management activities.

Clearly, the original goal of maintaining cash availability has been expanded by the preceding points to encompass some types of asset management, risk management, working capital management, and the lead role in dealing with banks and credit rating agencies. Thus, the treasury department occupies a central role in the finances of the modern corporation.

TREASURY CONTROLS

Given the large sums of cash involved in many treasury transactions, it is important to have a broad set of controls that help to ensure that transactions are appropriate. The following chapters contain sections on controls related to those chapter topics. At a more general level, it is critical that duties be properly *segregated* among the treasury staff, so that anyone concluding a deal never controls or accounts for the resulting cash flows. For example, trading activities should be separated from confirmation activities, so that someone fraudulently conducting illicit trades cannot waylay the confirmation arriving from the counterparty. In addition, a senior-level treasury manager should approve all trades, yet another person (possibly in the accounting department, in order to be positioned out of the departmental chain of command) should reconcile and account for all transactions.

It is also useful for someone outside of the trading function to regularly compare brokerage fees or commissions to reported transactions, to see if there are any unauthorized and unrecorded trades for which the company is paying fees.

Treasury is also an excellent place to schedule internal audits, with the intent of matching actual transactions against company policies and procedures. Though these audits locate problems only after they have occurred, an adverse audit report frequently leads to procedural changes that keep similar problems from arising in the future.

In addition to segregation controls and internal auditing, the treasurer should impose *limit controls* on a variety of transactions. These limits can prohibit or severely restrict the treasury staff from investing in certain types of financial instruments (such as some types of financial derivatives) that present an unduly high risk of capital loss. Another limitation is on the amount of business a company chooses to do with a specific counterparty, which is designed to reduce company losses in the event of a counterparty failure. Limitations can also apply to certain currencies if there appears to be some risk that a country's leaders may impose currency controls in the near future. Finally, there should be monetary caps on the transaction totals to which anyone in the treasury department can commit the company. Even the treasurer should have such a limitation, with some major transactions requiring the approval of the company president or board of directors.

The controls noted here are only general concepts. For more detailed itemizations of specific controls, please refer to the Controls sections of each of the following chapters.

Exhibit 1.1   Treasurer Job Description

Reports to: CFO

    Basic function: This position is responsible for corporate liquidity, investments, and risk management related to the company's financial activities.

    Principal accountabilities:

1. Forecast cash flow positions, related borrowing needs, and available funds for investment.

2. Ensure that sufficient funds are available to meet ongoing operational and capital investment requirements.

3. Use hedging to mitigate financial risks related to the interest rates on the company's borrowings, as well as on its foreign exchange positions.

4. Maintain banking relationships.

5. Maintain credit rating agency relationships.

6. Arrange for equity and debt financing.

7. Invest funds.

8. Invest pension funds.

9. Monitor the activities of third parties handling outsourced treasury functions on behalf of the company.

10. Advise management on the liquidity aspects of its short- and long-range planning.

11. Oversee the extension of credit to customers.

12. Maintain a system of policies and procedures that impose an adequate level of control over treasury activities.

TREASURER JOB DESCRIPTION

Within the organizational hierarchy, the treasurer usually reports to the chief financial officer (CFO). The treasurer's job description, as noted in Exhibit 1.1, essentially establishes responsibility for the tasks noted in the preceding sections.

POSITION OF TREASURY WITHIN THE CORPORATE STRUCTURE

In a small company, there is no treasury department at all, nor is there a treasurer. Instead, treasury responsibilities are handled by the accounting department and are under the supervision of the controller. This is an adequate situation if there are just a few bank accounts, foreign exchange exposures are minor, and there is not an excessive need for investment or borrowing expertise. However, as a company grows, the need for a specialized treasury staff increases. This typically begins with a treasurer, who personally handles all of the responsibilities of the department, and gradually includes specialized staff to handle more complex transactions, such as cash pooling and hedging. Personnel are added either as transaction volume increases or when management decides to centralize more activities under the treasurer, as described in the next section.

Once the treasurer position is created, the treasurer usually reports directly to the CFO, and may also be asked to deliver occasional reports to the board of directors or its various committees.

TREASURY CENTRALIZATION

The treasury department deals with a number of highly regimented processes, which are noted in the Procedures sections of each of the following chapters. Given the very large amounts of funds that the treasury incorporates into its transactions, it is critical that all procedures be performed precisely as planned and incorporating all controls. Procedural oversight is much easier when the treasury function is highly centralized and progressively more difficult when it is distributed over a large number of locations. Centralization is easier, because transactions are handled in higher volumes by a smaller number of highly skilled staff. There is generally better management oversight, and the internal audit staff can review operations in a single location more easily than in a distributed environment. Further, treasury activities frequently involve complicated terminology that is incomprehensible to nontreasury specialists, so it makes sense to centralize operations into a small, well-trained group.

Another reason for using treasury centralization is the presence of an enterprise resources planning (ERP) system that has been implemented throughout a company. An ERP system processes all of the transactions used to run all key operations of a company, so all of the information needed to derive cash forecasts and foreign exchange positions can be derived from a single system. If this system is available, then a centralized treasury group will find that all of the in-house information it requires is available through the nearest computer terminal. Conversely, if a company has many subsidiaries, each of which uses its own ERP or accounting system, then it becomes increasingly difficult for a centralized treasury staff to access information. Instead, it may make more sense to assign a small treasury staff to each subsidiary that is an expert in using the local system to extract information.

Exhibit 1.2   Stages in Treasury Centralization

Stage 1: Complete decentralization	Individual locations manage their own bank accounts, foreign exchange transactions, customer credit, payables, borrowings, and investments.
Stage 2: Centralized netting and hedging	A central staff nets payments between subsidiaries and hedges major foreign exchange and interest rate risks. Local locations still manage their own bank accounts, customer credit, payables, borrowings, and investments.
Stage 3: Centralized investments	In addition to prior centralization, a central treasury staff consolidates and manages all bank accounts, including pooling of funds and investment of those funds. Local locations still manage customer credit and payables.
Stage 4: Centralized working capital management	In addition to prior centralization, the central treasury staff centralizes credit granting and uses a payment factory for centralized payables management.

If a company operates in just one or a small number of countries, then banking relationships are relatively few, and can be handled by a centralized staff. However, if it operates in a multitude of countries, especially in developing countries where there may be currency controls, then there is a greater need for local treasury staff that can maintain local banking relationships and monitor local regulations that may impact treasury operations.

The preceding discussion certainly favors a centralized treasury function. However, in a company's early years, it is common to pass through a series of phases, where centralization gradually occurs over time. Exhibit 1.2 shows some typical stages in the gradual transition from dispersed to centralized treasury functions.

The transition from Stage 1 to Stage 2 may be triggered by a large loss on a foreign exchange position that could have been prevented by a proper hedge transaction, while the additional transition to Stage 3 usually arises when it becomes apparent that the increased scale of company operations has resulted in so many bank accounts that cash is not being effectively pooled and invested. In Stage 3, it is common to first create local cash pools by country, then to progress to an international cash pool in order to further aggregate cash for investment purposes. Stage 4 involves the complete integration of the accounts receivable and payable portions of working capital into the treasury department. In many companies, there is considerable resistance to Stage 4, on the grounds that working capital should remain under the control of local managers, and that centralization calls for the prior installation of an enterprise resources planning system. Thus, many companies stop at Stage 3 and do not fully centralize their treasury activities.

Even a fully centralized treasury department may find that it needs to maintain a regional treasury center in the major time zones in which it operates, so that some treasury personnel are always available during the business hours of subsidiaries located in their regions. This typically means that a company operates a regional treasury center in one of the major money center cities of the European time zones, such as Amsterdam, Brussels, London, or Zurich. Similarly, a treasury center in Chicago or New York can cover the American time zones, while an office in Singapore or Tokyo can address the needs of the Asian time zones.

Consequently, treasury centralization is usually a gradual process that progresses through several decision points as a company increases the geographic scope and scale of its operations.

TREASURY COMPENSATION

The treasury staff should not operate under a bonus plan that issues compensation based on unusually high rates of return on investment, nor for gains from active speculation in other currencies. A company's board of directors should be much more interested in conserving a company's excess cash than in putting it at risk in exchange for the possibility of improving returns by a few percentage points. Thus, it makes considerably more sense to create a compensation plan that rewards the treasury staff for its exact adherence to a detailed set of investment guidelines.

If anything, risky investment activities should result in the *opposite* of a bonus—censure and possibly termination—even if the activities resulted in outsized earnings for the company.

BANK RELATIONS

A key part of the treasury's responsibilities includes the management of a company's banking relationships. A large company may deal with dozens of banks, so it makes sense for the treasurer to gradually reduce the total number of banks with which the treasury department transacts business. By doing so, the relationship task can be refined down to only a core group of key banks. The following subsections note key aspects of bank relations.

Relationship Bank Relations

The treasurer is responsible for maintaining relations with a company's banks. There may be a number of banks to deal with, but the most critical one is a company's *relationship bank*. This is a company's designated long-term partner, with whom the company does the bulk of its business. The bank maintains its checking and zero-balance accounts there, and may have negotiated overdraft privileges, cash pooling, and a line of credit and possibly long-term debt. A company may rely heavily on a high-quality relationship bank, so the treasurer should maintain frequent and open discussions with his counterpart at this bank.

The treasurer should be thoroughly familiar with the monthly account analysis statement that is provided by the company's bank, since it itemizes the company's transactions with the bank and the cost of the bank's processing of those transactions and other services.

Bank Account Analysis

The treasurer should receive an account analysis statement from each of the company's banks shortly after the end of each month. The statement contains a summarization of the bank's fees for services rendered and the company's usage volume for each of those fees. Fee structure will vary by bank. Exhibit 1.3 shows a rough breakdown of the types of fees to be expected.

Exhibit 1.3 Types of Fees

General Category	Services Provided
General account services	Monthly account fees for checking, zero-balance, and concentration accounts, as well as the account analysis statement fee.
Depository services	Fees on an individual basis for domestic deposits, international deposits, scanned checks, electronic payment direct sends, and fees for the electronic clearing agent. If a check scanner is used, there is also a monthly fee for that service.
Paper disbursement services	Fees on an individual basis for paper checks paid.
General ACH services	Fees on an individual basis for ACH debit and credit transactions.
Wire and other funds transfer services	Fees on an individual basis for both incoming and outbound wire transfers. There may also be a monthly fee to maintain an on-line wire transfer capability.
Information services	Monthly fee to provide reporting services, to which may be added line item fees for each transaction listed in the reports.
Investment/custody services	Monthly investment sweep fee.

In addition, the account analysis statement contains an analysis of an *earnings credit allowance*, which is used to offset service charges. It is calculated using a monthly earnings credit rate, multiplied by the average collected balance in the account for the month. Because the earnings credit rate is low, the amount of credit earned to offset service charges will be minimal, unless the treasurer chooses to retain large cash balances in the account. Also, the earnings credit allowance can be used only to offset service charges incurred in the reporting period. If the earnings credit is higher than the service charges, then the company loses any unused earnings credit. Since any other type of investment carries a higher interest rate than the earnings credit allowance, it is generally better to shift funds to an investment account elsewhere and simply pay the bank its service charges.

The treasurer should compile the per-unit and per-month charges listed in the account analysis statement, and use this information to periodically conduct a comparison to the fees charged by other competing banks. While it is quite time-consuming to switch a company's account-level banking business to a new bank, the analysis can be useful for negotiating down those existing fees having the largest impact on the company's total service charges.

Bank Account Management

One of the most inefficient activities in bank relations is maintaining up-to-date lists of bank account signatories—that is, authorized check signers. The typical bank requires not only a signature card containing the signatures of all signatories, but also a board resolution approving the check signers. Further, each bank wants the same information, but in a different format, so there is no way to standardize the reporting required by each bank. This can be a real problem when a company has hundreds of bank accounts that are spread among multiple banks, since ongoing personnel turnover is bound to result in a continuing authorization updating process. There are more efficient methods being discussed for electronic bank account management (eBAM), but these discussions have only just begun to translate into commercial products. In the meantime, the treasury staff should have a quarterly procedure to review and update authorized signatories.

In addition to signatory management, the treasury staff must integrate information from bank accounts into its treasury management system, so that it has immediate access to bank transactional information. This integration process can take months to set up communication channels, exchange encryption and signing keys, configure formats, and test the interface. Given the large number of bank accounts used by larger companies, and ongoing account turnover, a treasury staff is constantly monitoring the progress of these integration efforts by its information technology staff.

Loan Covenants

The treasurer should have an excellent knowledge of the loan covenants imposed on the company by its banks, and be in frequent communication with them regarding any approaching covenant violations. A treasurer who spends considerable time with his banking counterparts is much more likely to be granted a waiver of a covenant violation than one who suddenly springs a violation on bankers whom he barely knows. However, a prolonged violation is likely to yield additional covenants, higher fees, or an interest rate increase. Also, if a loan was originally priced below the market rate, a lender will more likely impose fees in response to a covenant breach, simply to improve its rate of return on the loan.

Another factor related to covenant violations is the length of a company's relationship with a lender. If the treasurer dropped the offer of a relationship bank in favor of lower-priced offer from a new lender, he may find later that the new lender set tight covenants in hope of a violation, so that it could ratchet up its fees.

Collateral

When dealing with lenders, the treasurer should use great caution in allowing company assets to be used as collateral on various loans. A lender will always attempt to maximize its access to company assets through broad-based collateral provisions, but this leaves little room for the use of those assets for additional loans at some point in the future. If a treasurer allows this situation to occur, then the result is a senior lender who has a collateral position in virtually all company assets, and any number of junior lenders whose collateral positions fall behind the senior lender's and who accordingly charge much higher rates of interest to offset their increased risk. A better scenario is to fight off demands for broad-based collateral agreements, instead of apportioning out specific assets, so that the corporate asset base can be stretched as far as possible among multiple loans. This approach requires considerable negotiation skill with bankers and is more achievable if a company is reporting excellent financial results.

TREASURY OUTSOURCING

There are several levels of outsourcing that can be applied to the treasury department, ranging from relatively minimal technology outsourcing to a broad transfer of the bulk of the department's activities to a third party.

It is possible to shift a company's treasury management system (TMS) to a third party under an application service provider (ASP) arrangement. Not only does this allow a company to eliminate the capital cost of acquiring the software and hardware needed for a TMS, but it also eliminates the need for in-house maintenance staff to operate the system. Further, the ASP should have a considerable array of controls installed around its system to limit access, provide disaster recovery services, and so on. Many companies consider these added controls to be of considerable value, especially those public companies whose managers must personally certify their systems of internal control. Under this outsourcing scenario, the in-house treasury staff is retained, but the computer systems it uses are now accessed through the Internet, rather than through a local server.

A more expansive form of outsourcing is to retain a treasurer on the corporate staff, while shifting most other treasury functions to a third party. This means that functions such as cash flow management, foreign exchange deal execution and confirmation, cash pool management, netting, and reporting are provided by the third party. The treasurer reviews the performance of the third party against the benchmarks itemized in a service-level agreement, and sets up policies, conducts bank relations, acquires new funding, and develops the strategic direction of the department. The problem is that nearly all expertise has now left the company, which can be a problem if the company chooses to end the outsourcing arrangement and reconstitute the department in-house.

Outsourcing cannot always be proven to provide significant cost savings since the third party must also build an adequate profit into its service fee. Thus, a key reason for shifting to outsourcing may simply be that a company has experienced problems in the past with controls, transactional errors, or fraud, and so prefers to shift the function to a group of outside professionals who are presumably more competent.

Outsourcing is an especially viable option for smaller companies having smaller cash balances, banking relationships, and foreign exchange transactions. For these companies, it can be expensive to maintain a group of specialists to engage in and monitor a relatively low volume of transactions. However, as a company and its financing activities grow, it may become more cost-effective to transition the treasury function back in-house.

Treasury Metrics

Many treasury departments find that their performance falls outside of a company's normal set of performance metrics. The standard of performance is earnings before interest, taxes, depreciation and amortization (EBITDA), which essentially focuses on operational results. However, since the treasury department's primary impact is on interest expense, foreign exchange exposure, and liquidity, it does not fall within the EBITDA metric. Thus, even a stellar treasury performance may go unnoticed! The treasury department needs to look outside of EBITDA for performance measures that reveal its true effectiveness. The following subsections describe possible metrics for the treasury function.

Earnings Rate on Invested Funds

A company's investments can include interest income or an increase in the market value of securities held. The *earnings rate on invested funds* is a good measurement for tracking investment performance. To calculate it, summarize the interest earned on investments, as well as the change in market value of securities held, and divide by the total amount of funds invested. Since the amount of funds invested may fluctuate substantially over the measurement period, this can be an average value. The amount of interest earned should not be based on the actual interest paid to the company, but rather on the accrued amount (since the date of actual payment may fall outside of the measurement period). The formula is as follows:

$$\frac{\text{Interest Earned} + \text{Increase in Market Value of Securities}}{\text{Total Funds Invested}}$$

Example

The Rake and Mow Garden Centers corporate parent is earning a considerable return from its chain of small-town garden centers. Its treasurer wants to know its earnings rate on invested funds during the past year. It had $5,500,000 of invested funds at the beginning of the year and $6,200,000 at the end of the year. It earned $75,000 in interest income, and had a net gain of $132,000 on its short-term equity investments. Its total earnings rate on invested funds was as follows:

$$\frac{\text{Interest Earned} + \text{Increase in Market Value of Securities}}{\text{Total Funds Invested}}$$

$$= \frac{\$75,000 \text{ Interest Earned} + \$132,000 \text{ Increase in Market Value of Securities}}{(\$5,500,000 + \$6,200,000)/2}$$

$$= \underline{3.5\%} \text{ Earnings Rate on Invested Funds}$$

A company can place too great a degree of reliance on this measurement, resorting to increasingly risky investments in order to achieve a higher earnings rate. The board of directors must realize that a reasonable, but not spectacular, amount of return is perfectly acceptable, because a company should also focus its investment strategy on other goals, such as liquidity and minimal loss of principal, which tend to result in lower rates of return. Thus, the rate of return metric must be evaluated alongside a summary of the *types* of investments that the treasury staff engaged in to achieve the calculated results.

Borrowing Base Usage Percentage

The *borrowing base usage percentage* is an excellent measure for keeping track of the amount of debt that a company can potentially borrow, based on that portion of its accounts receivable, inventory, and fixed assets that are not currently being used as collateral for an existing loan. A treasurer should have this information available on all standard internal accounting reports, so that the company's available debt capacity is easily available. It is particularly useful when employed within a cash budget, so that one can see at a glance not only the amount of any potential cash shortfalls, but also the ability of the company to cover those shortfalls with collateralized debt from existing assets.

To calculate the borrowing base usage percentage, multiply the current amount of accounts receivable, less those invoices that are more than 90 days old, by the allowable borrowing base percentage (as per the loan document). Then multiply the current amount of inventory, less the obsolescence reserve, by the allowable borrowing base percentage (as per the loan document). Add the results of these two calculations together and divide the sum into the amount of debt outstanding. It is also possible to include in the denominator the amount of fixed assets (net of a borrowing base percentage), but many lenders do not allow a company to use fixed assets as part of its collateral, on the grounds that fixed assets are too difficult to liquidate. The formula is as follows:

$$\frac{\text{Amount of Debt Outstanding}}{\begin{array}{c}(\text{Accounts Receivable} \times \text{Allowable Percentage}) \\ + (\text{Inventory} \times \text{Allowable Percentage})\end{array}}$$

Example

The Spinning Wheel Company, maker of heirloom-quality spinning wheels, has been in a breakeven cash flow situation for a number of years. The market for its products is gradually declining, and the president is searching for alternative products that will shift the company into a more profitable situation. In the meantime, she needs to know the proportion of debt available under the company's borrowing arrangement, in order to see how much funding is available to start new lines of business. Under the terms of the loan, the borrowing base percentage for accounts receivable is 70 percent, 50 percent for inventory, and 20 percent for fixed assets. According to the company's balance sheet, it has the following assets and liabilities:

Account	Amount
Accounts receivable	$350,000
Inventory	$425,000
Fixed assets	$205,000
Accumulated depreciation	-$65,000
Loans	$250,000

The borrowing base calculation for the denominator of the ratio is as follows:

$350,000 Accounts receivable × 70% borrowing base	$245,000
$425,000 Inventory × 50% borrowing base	212,500
$140,000 Net fixed assets × 20% borrowing base	28,000
Total borrowing base	$485,500

(Note that the fixed assets borrowing base calculation was net of the accumulated depreciation figure; otherwise, the borrowing base would not properly reflect the reduced resale value of older fixed assets.)

Using the preceding borrowing base calculation, the president of Spinning Wheel can complete the borrowing base usage percentage as follows:

$$\frac{\$250,000 \text{ Loans Outstanding}}{\$485,500 \text{ Total Borrowing Base}} = 51.5\% \text{ Borrowing Base Usage}$$

The president notices that about one-half of the total borrowing base has been used to collateralize existing debt levels. Also, by subtracting the numerator from the denominator, she sees that the company can borrow another $235,500 before the borrowing base is maximized.

Other Metrics

If a company is operating in a negative or neutral cash flow situation and has minimal available sources of excess cash, then the *accuracy of its cash forecast* might be a useful metric. The treasury staff needs to predict cash balances as close to actual results as possible, so that the company does not find itself running out of cash. However, it is a difficult metric to hold the treasurer responsible, because the sources of information that comprise the forecast come from all over the company, and the treasurer is not responsible for those cash flows. Thus, even if the cash forecast is inaccurate, the cause may not lie within the control of the treasury department.

Another possible metric is *bad debts as a percentage of sales*. This metric is relevant only if the treasury department is responsible for the granting of customer credit. However, if the accounting department is responsible for collections, then this percentage is really the joint responsibility of the treasurer and the controller.

A more viable metric is a *transaction error rate*, which can be subdivided by each type of transaction in which the treasury staff engages. This can be a valuable tool for upgrading controls, procedures, and training, to mitigate the risk of such errors occurring again. This metric is not easily translated into a simplified presentation report that compares error totals by period because some errors may have much worse repercussions than others, and this is not readily apparent in a simplified report.

It is also possible to track the *cost of outside services*. The most obvious one, and most easily derived, is the cost of banking services, which can be tracked on a trend line. This information can also be compared to benchmark information, or used to compare the fees of different provider banks; the comparison provides a tool for negotiating reduced service charges.

A final metric to consider is *unhedged gains and losses*. These gains and losses can be quite large, and would initially appear to be a good way to judge the hedging activity of the treasury staff. However, the amount of hedging risk that a company chooses to expose itself to is set by the board of directors (admittedly with the advice of the treasurer), and the treasury staff is supposed to follow the board's guidelines. If the board elects not to hedge, then there will be gains and losses, but they will not be the responsibility of the treasurer.

Metrics Summary

The treasury department is not easily measured, and in fact is particularly resistant to metrics. A well-run treasury department will produce unspectacular gains on its investments, and will manage to avoid outsized gains or losses on its currency positions, while ensuring that corporate cash needs are met in a steady and reliable manner. In short, the treasury department provides functions that appear to be largely invisible unless something goes wrong—and it is difficult to build metrics around such a situation.

Of the two metrics fully explored here, the earnings rate on invested funds should be used with considerable caution, while the borrowing base usage percentage can provide useful information, but only in regard to what may be a limited amount of available borrowing capacity.

SUMMARY

A well-run treasury department is critical for the proper management of a company's liquidity. It is staffed by specialists in money and risk management, who are responsible for aggregating cash flow information from around the company, integrating it with current market data, and managing the ebb and flow of cash in a conservative and responsible manner that does not put the company's capital at risk.

The following chapters delve into considerably more detail regarding the mechanics of cash forecasting and cash concentration, the management of working capital, debt, equity, and investments, and how to use hedging to mitigate various financing risks. Where needed, the chapters include considerable detail regarding the policies, procedures, controls, and accounting required to ensure that treasury activities are properly enacted and accounted for.

2

Cash Transfer Methods

The treasurer should understand the implications of different methods of transferring cash to or from a company, since there are significant differences in the costs and cash flow speed of each one. Further, the level of manual processing and related controls is significantly different for each kind of transfer, which has a major impact on the long-term efficiency of the finance and accounting functions. This chapter intends to give the treasurer a thorough understanding of each form of cash transfer; when it should be used; what it will cost; and any required policies, procedures, and controls.

CHECK PAYMENTS

A *check payment* is made on a paper document, which has traditionally been physically routed from the payer to the payee, to the payee's bank, and then back to the payer's bank. The number of routings and the need for physical handling of the check results in significant delays in the transfer of cash between the principal parties.

The vast majority of checks are issued directly by companies. However, they may also be issued directly by a bank, which is called a *bank check* or *bank draft*. The bank check is a payment on behalf of the payer, which is guaranteed by the bank (and therefore of value to the payee). The bank can safely issue this guarantee because it immediately debits the payer's account for the amount of the check, and therefore has no risk. Not only is this a safe transaction for the bank, it is also beneficial to the bank, since the bank has ownership of the funds from the time when it debits the payer's account to when the money is eventually paid to the payee (which could be several weeks, depending on when the payer elects to send the check to the payee).

Mechanics of a Check Payment

Portland Cement Company creates a check to pay for a supplier invoice. It immediately adjusts its own records to reflect the reduction in available cash. However, its bank balance remains unchanged for several days because several additional events must occur. First, there is a delay while the payment is delivered through the postal service, which is the *mail float*. Second, the supplier must deposit the check at its bank; the time from when the supplier receives the check and deposits it is the *processing float*. The duration of the processing float is driven by the recipient's internal processes, staff training, and the existence of any work backlog. Third, the time between when the check is deposited and when it is available to the recipient is *availability float*. Availability float is generally no longer than two days. The time between when the check is deposited and when it is charged to the payer's account is the *presentation float*. Thus, while the check is clearing, Portland Cement retains ownership of the payment amount at its bank.

The same process works in reverse when a company receives a payment from a customer. In this instance, the company receives a payment and records the receipt in its own records, but must wait multiple days before the cash is credited to its bank account. This *availability float* works against the company, because it does not immediately have use of the funds noted on the check.

The combination of the floats associated with these inbound and outbound check payments is the *net float*. The net float should be relatively neutral, but a company can influence it with more aggressive working capital management to accelerate inbound payments and delay outbound payments (as described in Chapter 5).

The check process flow, with float periods included, is shown in Exhibit 2.1.

Investing Float-Related Funds

When a company has written a large volume of checks that have not yet cleared, the available cash balance shown by the company's bank will be larger than the company's ledger balance. If the treasurer can reliably predict how long it will take for the checks to clear, it is then possible to invest some of the cash that is available due to uncleared checks.

If a company has significant cash holdings, then it may be worthwhile to spend time investing in float-related funds. However, maintaining an abnormally small cash balance requires active float monitoring on a daily basis. If there is a gap of even a single day in float monitoring, then the company will very likely not have sufficient funds for all presented checks, and will incur expensive account overage fees.

Exhibit 2.1   Check Process Flow

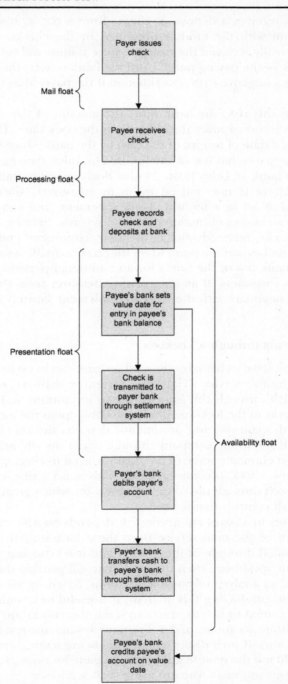

Value Dating

When a bank receives a deposit of checks from a payee, it will credit the payee's account with the funds represented by the checks. However, the bank has not really received the cash yet, since it must still collect the funds from the bank of the paying party. Until the bank collects the funds, it is at risk of having a negative cash flow situation if the payee uses the cash it has just received.

To avoid this risk, the bank posts the amount of the deposit with a *value date* that is one or more days later than the book date. This value date is the presumed date of receipt of the cash by the bank. Once the value date is reached, the payee has use of the funds. The value date may also be categorized by a bank as 1-day float, 2+-day float, or some similar term.

Value dating is not noticed by many treasurers, since it may not be mentioned at all in a monthly bank statement, and can be evaluated only through a close examination of online records. Because of this obscurity, some banks take advantage of their customers and extend the value dating out beyond the point when they have actually received the cash. This gives a bank use of the funds for an additional period of time, at the expense of its customers. If an enterprising treasurer spots this problem, it is possible to negotiate with the bank to implement shorter-duration value dating.

Check Payments through a Lockbox

A company can have its bank receive and process checks on its behalf, which is termed a *lockbox* service. The bank assigns a mailbox address to the company, which forwards this information to its customers. The customers mail their checks to the lockbox, where the bank opens the envelopes, scans all checks and accompanying documents, deposits the checks, and makes the scans available to the company through a web site. By using a lockbox, a company can eliminate some of the float involved in check processing and eliminate some check processing labor. This means that checks are no longer processed through the company's location, which greatly reduces the amount of cash controls that it needs.

How many lockboxes are needed? It depends on where customers are and the speed of the mail service from those locations. If customers are evenly distributed throughout the country and it is economically feasible to install multiple lockboxes, then the bank that will provide the lockbox can likely conduct an analysis of possible locations, based on sales by zip code. However, when conducting this analysis, it is useful to examine the larger-value checks mailed in by customers to see if the checks are being mailed from more distant locations, under a remote disbursement scheme (see the following section). If such disbursements are being made, then the lockbox analysis should use the remote disbursement bank locations, rather than the locations of the customers who are using such services.

Alternatively, if it appears that only a single lockbox is needed, then it is generally best to set up the lockbox in a large city that is roughly centrally located. For example, Chicago is an excellent location for checks being received within the United States.

Also, it is entirely possible that the company's current mail-to location yields acceptable results already. To see if this is the case, the following example shows the model results for the proposed lockboxes versus the current situation.

Example

The treasurer of Portland Cement wants to know if it would be cost-effective to open a lockbox for the collection of receivables from customers. He gathers the following information for the group of states where customers would be asked to send their payments to a lockbox:

Average number of daily payments to lockbox	165
Average size of payment	$1,450
Rate of interest per day	0.02%
Mail time savings	1.0 days
Processing time savings	0.8 days

Based on this information, the treasurer calculates the collected balance at the lockbox as follows:

$$165 \text{ items per day} \times \$1,450 \text{ each} \times (1.0 + 0.8) \text{ days saved} = \underline{\$430,650}$$

When invested at 0.02 per day, the $430,650 increase in the collected balance yields interest income of:

$$0.0002 \times \$430,650 = \underline{\$86} \text{ daily interest income}$$

The bank's lockbox fee is $0.25 per check processed, for which the daily cost calculation is:

$$165 \text{ checks} \times \$0.25 \text{ fee per check} = \underline{\$41} \text{ daily lockbox fee}$$

The treasurer finds that Portland will have a net daily gain of $45, or $11,700 over the standard number of 260 business days per year, and decides to implement the lockbox solution.

Additional factors in this calculation are the initial cost of contacting customers to have them route their payments to the new lockbox address, and the reduced cost of directly handling the checks that are now routed through the lockbox.

Remote Deposit Capture

Remote deposit capture allows a company to avoid the physical movement of received checks to its bank. Instead, one can use a special scanner and scanning software to create an electronic image of each check, which it then transmits to the bank. The bank accepts the online image, posts it to the company's account, and assigns funds availability based on a predetermined schedule.

The key benefit of remote deposit capture is the complete elimination of the transportation float that arises when shifting checks from the company to the bank—which can be a considerable delay. If the delivery person misses the bank's cutoff time, then an entire extra day is added to this float. However, since remote deposit capture typically has extended processing hours, there is far less risk of incurring this extra delay.

Another benefit is that a company no longer needs a bank that is physically located near the company location. Instead, it can consolidate its banking relationships and use just a single provider, who may be located anywhere in the country.

The system does not allow for the capture of non-U.S.-dollar checks, so they must still be deposited at a local banking institution. However, for most companies, the volume of these checks is so low that they can be mailed to a bank with minimal additional contribution to float.

Finally, the company using this system should be aware that it is financially liable for the accuracy of the information they enter into the system. This is a factor only when the system cannot correctly scan the dollar amount and the operator must manually enter the information instead. If the operator enters an incorrect check total, then the company will be liable for the variance.

Remote Disbursement

The float concept can also be applied to a company's payments. The key area that can be lengthened is the presentation float. A check written on a New York or Chicago bank will likely have a minimal lapse of a day or so before it is presented for payment. However, if a check is written on a bank in a remote location, such as Montana or Idaho, presentation may require several additional days, all of which allow a company to continue using its cash during that time. This delay is difficult for a check recipient to spot, since the check itself arrives on time, thereby triggering no late payment warnings from the accounting system.

At a more sophisticated level, a company can set up controlled disbursement accounts in different parts of the country, and then write checks on whichever banks are most distant from its check recipients.

The usefulness of remote disbursing has declined over time, as central banks have gradually driven down clearing times, with a particular emphasis on eliminating those regions where clearing intervals were unusually long.

WIRE TRANSFERS

A wire transfer sends funds to the recipient's bank account more rapidly than any other form of payment, and is the standard form of international payment. To initiate a wire, the treasury staff must send the following information to its bank:

- Sending company's name, address, and account number
- Recipient's name and account number
- Recipient bank's name and bank identification number
- Amount of the payment

To send a wire transfer, a company can access a bank's web site to enter the wiring instructions, fax the information to the bank, or call in the information. No matter what method is used, the wiring information must be received by the bank prior to its *cutoff time*. Any wiring instructions received after this time will be delayed until the beginning of the next business day.

A wire transfer between countries may not be credited to the account of the recipient for several days. Part of the problem is a bank-imposed delay in the value date. In addition, if the initiating bank does not have a direct correspondent relationship with the receiving bank, then it must route the payment through a third bank that does have a correspondent relationship with the receiving bank, which takes time. Also, some banks still manually review incoming wires and apply them to beneficiary accounts, which takes more time. Finally, the time of day when a wire is initiated can be a factor; if it begins near the close of business, then an extra day may be added to the transaction.

There are several ways to improve the situation. One is to use the same bank at both ends of a transaction. This makes the transfer a simple *book transfer*, which passes immediate value dating to the recipient. The receiving bank may be making its profits on delayed value dating; if so, specify a different receiving bank.

When a company sends funds internationally via a wire transfer, the recipient will likely be charged a stiff foreign exchange conversion fee by the receiving bank. The receiving bank can get away with a high fee (sometimes as much as 10 percent for smaller funds transfers), because it is the designated recipient, and so has a monopoly on the conversion of the funds into the local currency; the recipient cannot shop for a better exchange rate with other banks. To avoid these fees, the paying company can offer the recipient to pay in the recipient's currency in exchange for a lower price. The payer can then shop among several foreign exchange providers for the best exchange rate. At a minimum, a company should have its international customers quote in both the company's home currency and the supplier's local currency, so that the company can see if it can achieve a better exchange rate through its foreign currency provider.

Both the issuing and receiving banks in a wire transfer transaction charge high transaction fees. In particular, the payment recipient is charged a *lifting fee*, which its bank imposes for handling the transaction. This fee is deducted from the amount of the funds being transferred, which means that the amount ultimately received is always somewhat less than the amount expected, which interferes with account reconciliation.

If a company engages in a large number of wire transfer transactions, these fees can add up to a significant expense. To avoid it, some countries have created local electronic payment facilities, such as the automated clearing house (ACH) system used in the United States and Canada, which allows for low-cost electronic funds transfers. The ACH system is described in the following section.

ACH PAYMENTS

The ACH is an electronic network for the processing of both credit and debit transactions within the United States and Canada. ACH payments include direct deposit payroll, Social Security payments, tax refunds, and the direct payment of business-to-business and consumer bills. Within the ACH system, the *originator* is the entity that originates transactions, and the *receiver* is the entity that has authorized an originator to initiate a debit or credit entry to a transaction account. These transactions pass through sending and receiving banks that are authorized to use the ACH system.

The transaction costs associated with ACH payments are low, typically about 10 percent of the fees charged for wire transfers. In addition, it is easy to set up recurring payments through the ACH system, and settlements are fast. Consequently, the ACH system is the electronic payment method of choice within the geographic region where it can be used.

ACH Debits

An ACH debit allows a payee to initiate a debit of the payer's bank account, with the funds shifting into the payee's bank account. This is normally done with the written approval of the payer. The ACH debit is typically implemented between companies that plan to do business with each other for a long period of time, and who wish to avoid the expense of preparing a large amount of checks during that time. For example, ACH debits are common for lease and loan payments, as well as overnight delivery charges. The ACH debit is much less common for more complex transactions, where the payer wants to retain some control over denying payment in the event of delivery or service problems.

The ACH debit can be fraudulent, so many companies install ACH debit blocks on their accounts, preventing such debits except for those that are specifically authorized in advance, or debits that are less than a maximum cap.

The ACH debit is a boon for the initiating company, since it can predict the exact amount and timing of the incoming cash transfer. However, the transfer will not take place if there are not sufficient funds in the payer's account.

Global ACH Payments

There is no comprehensive equivalent of the ACH system that is available worldwide. Instead, similar electronic payment systems have been created in a number of countries, which are intended for payment transactions within those countries. A few large international banks have created links between these systems, which simulate a global ACH system. Under their systems, a company enters payment information, which the banks then reformat into the standard format of the country where the payment will be made. As such integrated systems become more common, there will likely be a decline in wire transfers in favor of global ACH payments. Such payments will be especially popular among recipients, who are not charged the lifting fees that are common for wire transfers.

The existing global ACH payment system is not perfect. Here are two limitations that are of particular concern:

- *Limited coverage.* Global ACH systems are by no means truly global. National ACH systems have been built in parts of Europe, North America, India, Singapore, Hong Kong, New Zealand, and Australia, and these systems can be linked into the ACH systems of other countries. However, outside of these regions, wire transfers remain the most reliable method of funds transfer.

- *Limited remittance information.* Some national ACH systems do not allow for the inclusion of remittance information with a payment, so the payer needs to send this information by some alternative method, or make the information available on a web site.

Letters of Credit

When dealing with counterparties in other countries, it is difficult to evaluate their financial condition, and the legal systems in their countries make it more difficult to collect overdue receivables. For these reasons, exporters are more concerned with using cash transfer methods that have a high probability of payment.

A well-established method for doing so is the *letter of credit*. This is an arrangement where the importer's bank (the *issuing bank*) formally authorizes an obligation to pay the exporter's bank during a specific period of time, assuming that several documented conditions have been met. The documents that must be presented to the issuing bank include an invoice and proof of delivery. In addition, a certificate of insurance may be required, as well as a quality certificate. The issuing bank creates the letter of credit, and therefore has control over its terms.

When all terms of the letter of credit have been completed, the exporter presents all required documents to its bank, which pays the exporter the amount noted in the letter of credit. If the exporter's bank is unwilling to make this payment, then it is called the *advising bank*, and merely passes along the documentation to the issuing bank, which is now designated as the *nominated bank*, and makes the payment. If the exporter is uncertain of the reliability of the nominated bank, it may ask its own bank to confirm the letter of credit. If the bank agrees, then it is designated as the *confirming bank*, and enters into an agreement to pay the exporter immediately following receipt of the required documents. Upon completion of this step, the letter of credit is said to be a *confirmed* letter of credit. A bank will charge a fee in exchange for being the confirming bank. This fee can be quite high if a banker feels that there is a significant risk of the issuing bank's failing to pay, and a banker may refuse confirmation entirely if the risk is perceived to be excessively high.

The key party in making a letter of credit work is the issuing bank, which is guaranteeing the credit. In order to do so, this bank may block out

---

Example

Portland Cement, based in Portland, Maine, is contemplating a sale of its masonry cement to Amsterdam Architectural Consultants (AAC), a firm located in the Netherlands. The contract has a total value of $500,000. Delivery will be at Amsterdam, with an expected shipment date of June 15. Payment under a letter of credit is to be through the nominated bank, which is ABN AMRO. Portland's bank, which is the advising bank, is Citibank. The steps in the letter of credit payment process are as follows:

1. AAC asks ABN AMRO to issue a letter of credit to be confirmed by Citibank.

2. ABN AMRO reviews AAC's application and issues the letter of credit. It also requests that Citibank confirm the letter of credit.

3. Citibank confirms the letter of credit and sends the letter of credit, along with a confirmation advice, to Portland.

4. Portland ships the cement to AAC.

5. Portland presents all required letter of credit documentation to Citibank, which reviews and approves them, and pays Portland $500,000, less transaction costs.

6. Citibank sends the documents to ABN AMRO, which reviews and approves them. ABN AMRO sends $500,000 to Citibank.

7. ABN AMRO sends the letter of credit documents to AAC, while also charging its account for the euro equivalent of $500,000, plus transaction costs.

8. AAC takes delivery of the masonry cement at Amsterdam on June 15.

a portion of its line of credit to the importer, which it will not release until the letter of credit transaction has been completed and the bank has been paid by the importer.

The letter of credit is useful for the importer, who receives proof of title to the goods, as well as evidence that the goods have been shipped. However, the real benefit goes to the exporter, who obtains a guarantee of payment from a bank, which is a distinct improvement over a guarantee of payment from the importer.

The letter of credit requires significant administrative time and manual effort by the importer, exporter, and their banks. There is also a significant risk that a bank will refuse to pay under the terms of a letter of credit if there are any discrepancies in the submitted documents (a number of controls are provided later in the Controls section). For these reasons, there has been ongoing pressure for a number of years to use other, more streamlined ways to transfer cash.

PROCUREMENT CARDS

A company can make smaller-scale payments with a procurement card program. This can involve the use of *debit cards*, which deduct cash directly from a company's bank account, but more commonly employ *credit cards*. Under this system, the bank managing the procurement card program will bill the payer on a monthly basis for all charges made during the month, while remitting funds to the payee within a few days of each charge. If the payer pays the monthly bill late, then the bank charges interest on the open balance. A procurement card program is an excellent tool for any company making payments to its suppliers, since it circumvents the lengthy and expensive process of issuing purchase orders, matching receiving documents to supplier invoices, and making check payments.

If a company accepts payments via credit cards, then it must sign a credit card agreement with a credit card processor, under which it agrees to be charged a processing fee in exchange for being in the program. The fee charged varies considerably by type of credit card, as well as by the amount of card volume that a company transacts. Typically, the company pays 2 to 3 percent of charged amounts to the processor as a fee. This fee is significantly lower for debit card transactions.

Because of the fee charged to the recipient of funds under a credit card program, the payee is not usually willing to accept large payments—it would seriously impact profits. Instead, procurement cards are normally used for smaller, high-volume transactions, especially in a retail environment.

Procurement cards are less commonly used for international payments, because the payer is also charged a fee for any conversions of foreign currencies back into the credit card processor's home currency.

CASH PAYMENTS

Inbound cash payments tend to be for very small transactions, though possibly in very high volume, especially in retail situations. However, business-to-business cash payments are not common.

If a company receives large volumes of cash, it is usually more secure to hire a professional money transporter to move the cash to the bank on behalf of the company. To do so, the company locks the cash into a cash box, which the transporter takes to the bank. The receiving bank also has a key for the cash box; the bank staff opens the cash box and then counts and deposits the cash for the company.

Cash is bulky, requires significant controls to maintain on-site, and does not earn interest income until deposited. Given the extra cost of counting it at the bank, it is also expensive to deposit. Consequently, companies have a strong incentive to avoid both paying with or accepting cash.

FEES FOR CASH TRANSFERS

The fees charged by banks vary considerably for different types of cash transfers. Exhibit 2.2 outlines the fee arrangements for the most common types of cash transfers.

Of these types of cash transfer, the value dating delay is usually the shortest for wire transfers, though this can be delayed in some countries where wire transfer processing is still accomplished manually. The value dating delay is normally the longest for company checks, though this can vary depending on the source of checks, as well as the negotiated value dating terms between the payee company and its bank.

The key point regarding the fees associated with cash transfers is that banks now charge their clients for both the initiation and receipt of *any* type of cash—the only difference is the amount charged. For example, the wire transfer fee can easily be 50 times more expensive than an ACH payment.

A cash transfer that crosses an international border is usually processed through a correspondent bank, which introduces both additional fees and delays into the transfer process. For these reasons, multinational companies may set up in-country bank accounts, through which these transfers are routed. By doing so, transfers can take advantage of the more automated and lower-cost settlement systems of local institutions.

SUMMARY OF CASH TRANSFER METHODS

The table in Exhibit 2.3 shows the advantages and disadvantages of each of the cash transfer methods described earlier in this chapter, along with the best use of each one.

Exhibit 2.2   Comparison of Bank Fees for Cash Transfer Methods

	Initiator Charged	Recipient Charged	Fee Size
ACH	√	√	Low
Bank check	√	√	Medium
Company check	√	√	Low
Letter of credit	√		Medium
Procurement card		√	Medium
Wire transfer	√	√	Large

Exhibit 2.3   Summary of Cash Transfer Methods

	Advantages	Disadvantages	Primary Use
ACH debit	- Assured delivery on scheduled date	- Risk of fraud	- Recurring payments
ACH payment	- Low cost - Efficient processing	- Requires setup, so not as efficient for one-time pays	- Corporate payables
Bank check	- Payment requires time to clear	- Less efficient process	- Corporate payables
Book transfer	- Low cost - Fast cash transfer	- None	- Payments between accounts at the same bank
Cash	- None	- Requires strong controls - Expensive to handle	- Retail sales
Company check	- Timing is under the control of the payer - Payer takes advantage of float	- Payment may not clear - Less efficient process	- Corporate payables
Letter of credit	- Secure for the seller	- Administratively tedious	- International payments
Procurement card	- Consolidate small billings	- Significant fee for cash recipient	- Retail and small sales
Wire transfer	- Relatively fast - Assured delivery	- Can experience delays in some countries - Requires some manual processing	- Large one-time payments that are required on short notice

In general, the ACH payment is the best alternative—it is inexpensive and can transfer cash quickly. However, it requires some initial setup time for a new payee. At the other extreme is check payments—the payee must wait a number of days before the cash arrives in its bank account, and it also involves extensive manual processing by the payer. The only viable reason for continuing to use checks is that the payer can take advantage of a favorable float. All of the other types of cash transfer lie somewhere between the extremes of these two forms of cash transfer.

CASH TRANSFER CONTROLS

Cash transfers can subject a company to a considerable risk of loss, and so require a broad array of controls, which vary considerably by transfer method. This section describes both basic and enhanced controls for multiple types of cash transfer. Flowcharts are included for the more comprehensive systems of control.

Controls for Check Payments

The control system for check payments assumes that a fully documented packet of payables information has already been created, which contains receiving, purchase order, and supplier invoice information. With this information in hand, the following controls should be used to create and monitor check payments:

- *Remove check stock from locked storage.* Unused check stock should always be kept in a locked storage cabinet. In addition, the range of check numbers used should be stored in a separate location and cross-checked against the check numbers on the stored checks to verify that no checks have been removed from the locked location.

- *Restrict access to check-signing equipment.* If a company uses any form of computerized check-printing equipment, it may be necessary to lock down all access to it. This can include any printers in which check stock is maintained, signature plates, and signature stamps.

- *Require a manual signature on checks exceeding a predetermined amount.* This control is useful when signature plates are used for smaller check amounts. When signature plates are used, there is no longer a final review of payments before they are mailed. Therefore, requiring a "real" signature for large checks adds a final review point to the payment process.

- *Check signer compares voucher package to check.* The check signer must compare the backup information attached to each check to the check itself, verifying the payee name, amount to be paid, and the due date. This review is intended to spot unauthorized purchases, payments to the wrong parties, or payments being made either too early or too late. This is a major control point for companies not using purchase orders, since the check signer represents the only supervisory-level review of purchases.

- *Implement positive pay.* A strong control that virtually eliminates the risk of an unauthorized check's being cashed is "positive pay." Under this approach, a company sends a list of all checks issued to its bank, which clears only checks on this list, rejecting all others. However, this approach also calls for consistent use of the positive pay concept, since any manual checks issued that are not included on the daily payments list to the bank will be rejected by the bank.

- *Use electronic payments.* There are several types of fraud that employees can use when a company pays with checks, while outside parties can also modify issued checks or attempt to duplicate them. This problem disappears when electronic payments are made instead. In addition, the accounts payable staff no longer has to follow up with suppliers on uncashed checks, or be concerned about remitting payments to state governments under local escheat laws, since there are no checks.

- *Reconcile the checking account every day.* An excellent detective control, this approach ensures that any fraudulently modified checks or checks not processed through the standard accounting system will be spotted as soon as they clear the bank and are posted on the bank's web site.

Controls for Remote Deposit Capture

Remote deposit capture eliminates the need to physically transfer check payments to the local bank for deposit. However, the replacement process of converting the checks to an electronic format still requires some controls. They are:

- *Verify receipt by the bank.* When processing checks through a remote deposit capture system, always print out a verification statement that the image was successfully sent to and received by the bank, and attach this verification to copies of the checks for storage. This ensures that the deposit has taken place.

- *Train for handling of foreign checks.* Remote deposit capture works only for checks originating in the United States. However, if the person operating the scanning equipment were to mistakenly scan a foreign check, the system may indicate initial acceptance of the payment and then reject it a few days later. To avoid this delay in check presentation, train the staff regarding the treatment of foreign checks, and use periodic audits of scanned checks to see if any such checks were erroneously entered in the system.

Controls for Electronic Payments

Electronic payments can involve large amounts of money, and so require a stringent set of controls to mitigate the risk of loss. A baseline set of controls over the standard electronic payment process is noted in Exhibit 2.4.

The controls shown in the flowchart are described in the following bullet points, in sequence from the top of the flowchart to the bottom:

- *Restrict access to master vendor file.* For those electronic payments being made automatically by the accounting software, it is important to keep tight control over changes to the vendor master file, since someone could access the file and alter the bank account information to which payments are being sent.

- *Require signed approval document for manually initiated electronic payments.* In a high-volume payment environment, nearly all electronic payments are routed through the accounting software, which handles the payments automatically. However, since a manually initiated payment falls outside the controls already imposed on the regular accounts payable process, the addition of an approval document is mandatory, preferably requiring multiple approval signatures.

- *Verify ACH debit filter with bank.* If the business arrangement with a supplier is for the supplier to initiate an ACH debit from the company's account, rather than the company's initiating the transfer to the supplier, then the company should verify that it has authorized the bank to allow a specific supplier to debit an account.

- *Require password access to payment software.* It is necessary not only to enforce tightly limited access to the software used to initiate electronic payments, but also to ensure that passwords are replaced on a frequent basis. This is a critical control and should be rigorously enforced.

- *Require additional approvals.* Additional approvals are useful for larger payments. Another approval should be required whenever a new supplier is set up for electronic payment, since this is an excellent spot to detect the initiation of payments to a shell company. The additional approval could be linked to the generation of a credit report on the supplier, to verify its existence as a valid business entity. The highest level of control over electronic payments would be to require dual approvals for *all* such payments, though this may prove too onerous for ongoing business operations.

Exhibit 2.4   Electronic Payment Controls

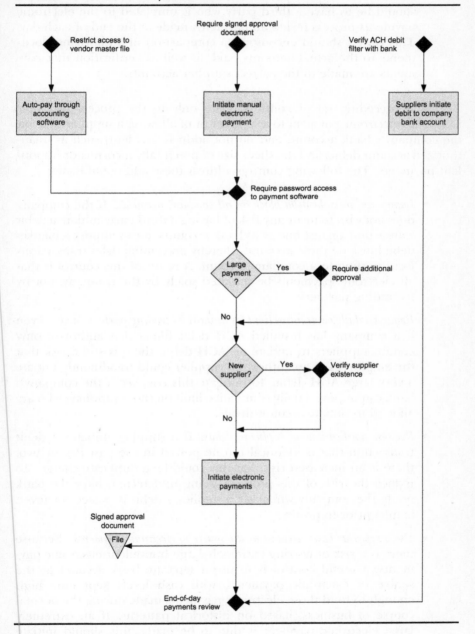

- *Require an end-of-day payments review.* A standard detection control should be to have a third party who is unrelated to the electronic payments process review all payments made at the end of each day. This review should encompass a comparison of authorizing documents to the actual amounts paid, as well as verification that payments are made to the correct supplier accounts.

The preceding set of controls relate only to the process of either issuing an electronic payment to a supplier or of allowing a supplier to debit the company's bank account, and do not address problems such as unauthorized account debits and the sheer size of potentially incorrect or fraudulent payments. The following controls address these additional issues:

- *Impose an outright debit block on all company accounts.* If the company does not wish to incur any risk of having a third party initiate a debit transaction against one of its bank accounts, it can impose a blanket debit block on those accounts, thereby preventing debit transactions from posting to a company account. A result of this control is that all electronic payments be initiated solely by the company, not by its trading partners.

- *Request a daily cumulative limit for authorized trading partner debits.* Even if a company has installed ACH debit filters that authorize only certain suppliers to initiate an ACH debit, there is still a risk that the employees of an authorized supplier could fraudulently initiate a very large ACH debit. To mitigate this risk, see if the company's bank can impose a daily cumulative limit on those suppliers who are allowed to initiate account debits.

- *Request notification of duplicate debits.* If a supplier initiates a debit transaction that is identical to one posted in the past day or two, there is an increased risk that this could be a duplicate charge. To reduce the risk of this problem going undetected, have the bank notify the company whenever a duplicate debit is posted, or (even better) prior to posting.

- *Use a separate bank account as the source of electronic payments.* Because there is a risk of making extremely large fraudulent electronic payments, a useful control is to use a separate bank account as the source of electronic payments, with cash levels kept only high enough to fund those electronic payments made during the normal course of business, based on historical patterns. If an extremely large electronic payment is due to be made, this should initiate additional perusal of the transaction before additional cash is shifted to the account from which the payment will be made. To achieve a greater level of control, the person responsible for shifting funds into the electronic payments account should not be the same person who initiates or approves electronic payments.

Controls for Letters of Credit

The greatest risk with a letter of credit is not being paid. The documents that a payee must present in order to be paid are usually prepared and controlled by other parties, and the terms of those documents may be very strictly defined, thereby delaying payment. All controls related to letters of credit are designed to improve the odds of being paid. The following controls should be implemented prior to finalizing a letter of credit:

- *Avoid approval by the buyer.* There should not be any documentation requirement under the letter of credit where the document must be signed by someone who is under the control of the buyer, since the buyer can use this requirement to effectively block payment.

- *Avoid tight dating.* The letter of credit contains dates by which goods must be shipped and documents presented. The seller should add a large margin of error to these dates to ensure that they can be met. If they cannot be met, then the seller should avoid shipping anything until the dates have been revised and agreed to in writing by all parties. In addition, the expiry date of the letter of credit should be sufficiently far off to allow for several rounds of document resubmissions.

- *Minimize presentment documents.* If there are fewer documentation requirements under the letter of credit, then it will be easier for the payee to obtain payment. This must be negotiated with the buyer prior to issuance of the letter of credit.

- *Require a financially strong issuing bank.* The issuing bank assumes the risk of the buyer's insolvency, so the payee should insist that a bank with a strong credit rating be the issuing bank.

- *Require confirmation by a U.S. bank.* If the issuing bank is in suspect financial condition, or if the political stability of the issuing bank's country is questionable, then have a U.S. bank confirm the payment obligation. This confirmation makes the U.S. bank liable for the payment. If the confirmation cost is too high or cannot be obtained at all, then try to have the letter of credit issued outside of the political area that is causing the problem.

- *Require payment prior to buyer possession.* The letter of credit should require that the seller is paid before the buyer takes possession of the goods. Otherwise, if there are discrepancies in the presented documents, a buyer that is already in possession of the goods will be less likely to waive the discrepancies, thereby delaying payment to the seller.

The following control involves the timing of shipments under a letter of credit to ensure that the buyer will pay in the event of an amendment to the letter of credit:

Complete amendments prior to shipment. If there are issues with the letter of credit that require amendment by the buyer and seller (and agreement by the issuing and confirming banks), then verify that these changes have been completed and approved in writing *prior to* shipping the goods to the buyer. Otherwise, it is possible that the bank will not allow the amendments and refuse to pay, even though the goods have shipped.

The following control involves the creation of the seller's invoice to the buyer, to ensure that it will be acceptable to the bank:

- *Match the description of goods on the invoice to the letter of credit.* A bank will not pay under the terms of a letter of credit unless the description of goods on the invoice exactly match those on the letter of credit. The invoice preparer should be well trained on this issue, and it may also be useful to have a second person verify the invoice information.

Controls for Procurement Cards

The key procurement card controls are enumerated in Exhibit 2.5, where controls are summarized next to the small black diamonds. The first control calls for card users to itemize each of their purchases in a separate log, which they then reconcile against the monthly card statement, noting missing receipts and rejected line items as part of the reconciliation. They then assemble this information into a packet of receipts and forms, and have a supervisor review it for inappropriate or split purchases, who then forwards the packet to the accounts payable department for payment.

The controls noted in the flowchart are described in the following bullet points, in sequence from the top of the flowchart to the bottom:

- *Enter receipt in procurement card transaction log.* When employees use procurement cards, there is a danger that they will purchase a multitude of items and not remember all of them when it comes time to approve the monthly purchases statement. By maintaining a log of purchases, the card user can tell which statement line items should be rejected.

- *Reconcile transaction log with monthly card statement.* Each cardholder must review his or her monthly purchases, as itemized by the card issuer on the monthly card statement.

- *Fill out missing receipt form.* Each card user should attach original receipts to the statement of account, in order to verify that they have made every purchase noted on the statement. If they do not have a receipt, they should fill out a missing receipt form, which itemizes

Exhibit 2.5   Procurement Card Controls

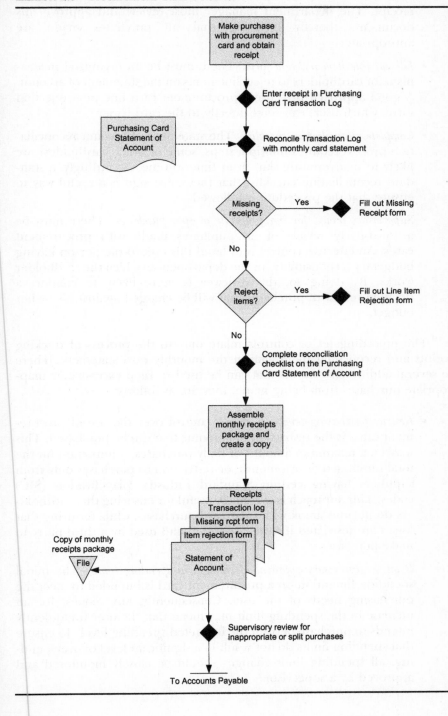

each line item on the statement of account for which there is no receipt. The department manager must review and approve this document, thereby ensuring that all purchases made are appropriate.

- *Fill out line item rejection form.* There must be an organized mechanism for cardholders to reject line items on the statement of account. A good approach is to use a procurement card line item rejection form, which users can send directly to the card issuer.

- *Complete reconciliation checklist.* The statement of account reconciliation process requires multiple steps, some of which cardholders are likely to inadvertently skip from time to time. Accordingly, a standard reconciliation checklist that they must sign is a useful way to ensure that the procedure is followed.

- *Supervisory review for inappropriate or split purchases.* There must be a third-party review of all purchases made with procurement cards. An effective control is to hand this task to the person having budgetary responsibility for the department in which the cardholder works. By doing so, the reviewer is more likely to conduct a detailed review of purchases that will be charged against his or her budget.

The preceding set of controls relate only to the process of tracking receipts and reconciling them against the monthly card statement. There are several additional controls that can be used to keep excessive or inappropriate purchases from being made; they are as follows:

- *Restrict purchasing levels.* A major control over the use of procurement cards is the restriction of amounts that can be purchased. This may be a maximum amount of daily purchases, a limitation on the total purchased over a month, or restriction to purchases only from suppliers having certain Standard Industry Classification (SIC) codes. This approach is extremely useful for ensuring that cardholders do not run amok with their card purchases, while ensuring that losses are restricted if cards are stolen and used by a third party to make purchases.

- *Require supervisory approval of changes in spending limits.* The initial spending limitation on a procurement card is intended to meet the purchasing needs of the user. Consequently, any request for an increase in the spending limit may mean that the user fraudulently intends to purchase beyond the budgeted spending level. To ensure that spending limits do not result in a significant level of overspending, all spending limit changes should be closely monitored and approved by a supervisor.

- *Verify that purchases are made through an approved supplier.* The purchasing staff may have negotiated special volume pricing deals with selected suppliers, so it may be necessary to review statements of account to ensure that card users are making purchases from those suppliers. This control can be made more robust by issuing an approved supplier "Yellow Pages" to all cardholders, so they know where they are supposed to make purchases.

Cash Transfer Policies

The policies in this section are used to designate a preferred form of funds transfer, and to define the authorizations for various transfers. They are as follows:

- *The preferred method of payment is by ACH transaction.* A company incurs the lowest transaction costs by using ACH transactions, and allows for precise cash planning, which makes ACH a good default form of cash transfer.

- *The preferred method of payment for amounts less than $___ is by procurement card.* For small-dollar payments, a single monthly payment through a procurement card program is more efficient than a large number of ACH payments.

- *The employees authorized to sign checks and approve electronic payments shall be reviewed at least annually.* This policy calls for a periodic review to see if the most appropriate people are involved in the check-signing and wire transfer approval processes.

- *All wire transfers greater than $___ must be approved by an authorized employee.* Many banks allow one person to set up a wire transfer, and then require a second person to log in separately and approve the transaction before it will be completed. This is an excellent method for maintaining oversight over wire transfers.

CASH TRANSFER PROCEDURES

The procedure shown in Exhibit 2.6 shows the basic steps required to issue a payment by check.

The procedure shown in Exhibit 2.7 shows the basic steps required to issue an electronic payment.

The procedure shown in Exhibit 2.8 shows the basic steps required to issue a letter of credit.

The procedure shown in Exhibit 2.9 shows the basic steps required to pay using a company procurement card.

Exhibit 2.6   Check Payment Procedure

Procedure Statement   Retrieval No.: TREASURY-08

Subject: Steps required to create, sign, and issue check payments.

1. PURPOSE AND SCOPE

   This procedure is used by the accounting staff to issue payments by check, and includes key control points in the process.

2. PROCEDURES

   2.1 Print Checks (Payables Clerk)

   1. Print the scheduled check payment report. Have the controller review and approve the report.
   2. If any items on the report are not scheduled for payment, designate them as such in the payables database.
   3. Unlock the cabinet containing check stock and remove a sufficient number of checks for the check run, and load the check stock into the printer.
   4. Unlock the safe containing the signature plate and load it into the printer.
   5. Access the accounting software, call up the check printing module, and print checks.
   6. Print the check register and compare it to the original scheduled payment report. Note any discrepancies.
   7. Return remaining unused check stock to the storage cabinet, and log in the range of check numbers used.
   8. Return the signature plate to the safe.

   2.2 Sign Checks (Payables Clerk)

   1. Schedule a check signing session with the controller.
   2. Attach backup documentation to each of the checks to be signed.
   3. Sit with the controller during the check signing session in order to answer questions.
   4. If the controller is not available, then use the backup check signer, and notify the controller that the backup person was used, and for which checks.
   5. If a check amount is large enough to require a second signature, then have an additional authorized person sign the check.

   2.3 Distribute Checks

   1. Detach backup documentation from each check, burst one copy of the remittance advice from each check, and staple the remittance advice to the backup documentation. File the documentation by supplier name.
   2. Stuff checks into envelopes and send to the mail room for mailing.
   3. Compile all check numbers and amounts into an electronic file and forward to the positive pay program of the company's bank.

Exhibit 2.7   Electronic Payment Procedure

Procedure Statement   Retrieval No.: TREASURY-09

Subject: Steps required to issue electronic payments.

1. PURPOSE AND SCOPE
   This procedure is used by the accounting staff to issue electronic payments, and includes key control points in the process.

2. PROCEDURES

   2.1 Authorize Payment (Payables Clerk)

   1. Print the scheduled electronic payment report. Have the controller review and approve the report.
   2. If any items on the report are not scheduled for payment, designate them as such in the payables database.
   3. Access the password-protected electronic payment module in the accounting software.
   4. Set up preliminary payment authorizations for all approved items on the scheduled electronic payment report.
   5. Print the preliminary electronic payment register and match it against the approved list. Adjust payments to match the approved list.
   6. Authorize the electronic payments.
   7. Print the final electronic payment register, staple it to the approved scheduled electronic payment report, and file the packet by date.

   2.2 Authorize Large Payments (Controller)

   1. Access the password-protected electronic payment module in the accounting software, using a supervisory password.
   2. Review and approve all electronic payments above the approval threshold that are scheduled for payment.

   2.3 Final review (Assistant Controller)

   1. At the end of each business day, match the amount of electronic payments as reported by the bank to the approved scheduled electronic payment report. Report any discrepancies to the controller.

Exhibit 2.8   Letter of Credit Procedure

Procedure Statement   Retrieval No.: TREASURY-10

Subject: Steps required for processing a letter of credit.

1. PURPOSE AND SCOPE
    This procedure is used by the treasury staff to process a letter of credit originated by a customer.

2. PROCEDURES
    2.1 Review Initial Letter of Credit Document (Treasury Clerk)

    1. Review the proposed letter of credit forwarded by the customer's bank. Review items include due dates for goods shipment and document presentation, the complexity of documents to be presented, and the credit rating of the issuing bank.
    2. Request that the company's bank confirm the letter of credit. If the confirmation fee exceeds $___, forward the confirmation proposal to the treasurer for approval.
    3. If the company's bank refuses to confirm the letter of credit, then meet with the assistant treasurer to discuss alternative financing arrangements.
    4. If amendments are required, then verify that all parties have agreed to the amendments in writing. Then issue authorization to the shipping department to ship the goods, and send the shipping manager a copy of the letter of credit.

    2.2 Submit Documentation (Treasury Clerk)

    1. Copy the exact text of the delivered goods in the letter of credit into an invoice, and print the invoice on the letterhead of the company noted in the letter of credit.
    2. Add the bill of lading for the shipment to the invoice, and forward this information to the confirming bank by overnight delivery service, along with a request for payment under the terms of the letter of credit.
    3. Contact the bank daily to determine the progress of its review of the letter of credit payment request. The review should take no longer than three days. If the letter of credit expiry date is within ___ days, then notify the treasurer.
    4. Upon receipt of funds, debit cash and credit accounts receivable for the full amount of the original invoice, and then debit the banking fees expense and credit cash for the transaction fees the bank deducted from the payment.

Exhibit 2.9 Procurement Card Payment Procedure

Procedure Statement   Retrieval No.: TREASURY-11

Subject: Steps required to pay with a procurement card.

1. PURPOSE AND SCOPE

This procedure is used by designated staff to make purchases with a procurement card, as well as to reconcile their purchases with the month-end purchasing report and to note variances.

2. PROCEDURES

2.1 Initial Payment (Authorized Procurement Card Users)

1. When first making a purchase with a procurement card, inquire if the supplier accepts credit card payments. If so, pay with the card if the purchase is less than the per-transaction purchasing maximum for the card. When making the transaction, give the supplier the address listed on the purchasing card billing statement.
2. If a purchase is declined by the supplier, refer the matter to the procurement card manager. This may call for an increase in the authorized spend limit on the card.
3. Obtain an itemized receipt for all purchases made with the procurement card. Receipts will be used at month-end to verify purchases listed on the procurement card statement.
4. Log all receipts into a procurement card transaction log.
5. Verify that items ordered are actually received. Note all items not received.

2.2 Reconcile Purchases to Statement (Authorized Procurement Card Users)

1. Upon receipt of the monthly procurement card statement, match all items on the statement to the procurement card transaction log.
2. If any receipts are missing, contact the supplier and attempt to obtain a replacement receipt.
3. If any receipts are still missing, list them on a procurement card missing receipt form, and send it to the department manager for approval.
4. If any items on the card statement are to be disputed, circle them on the statement and note "In Dispute" next to them.
5. Sign and date the billing statement, attach the missing receipt form and all receipts to it, and forward it to the procurement card manager for approval.

2.3 Review Forwarded Expense Packets (Procurement Card Manager)

1. Upon receipt of each employee's expense packet, scan the list of purchased items to determine if any inappropriate purchases were made, or if there is any evidence of split purchases being made. If so, discuss the issue with the employee's manager to see if further action should be taken.
2. Forward the expense packet to the accounts payable department for payment.

SUMMARY

A company that wants to create an efficient cash transfer system should stay away from cash, checks, and even letters of credit—they simply involve too many controls, process steps, and administrative hassles. The better forms of cash transfer are ACH payments, wire transfers, and procurement cards, because they involve fewer of the problems just noted. Of this latter group, ACH payments and procurement cards involve the least manual intervention, and so are the preferred forms of cash transfer. While a company normally deals with all of the forms of transfer noted in this chapter, the treasurer should push for a larger proportion of ACH and procurement card payments wherever possible.

3

Cash Forecasting

Cash forecasting is absolutely crucial to the operation of every organization. If there is ever a cash shortfall, payroll cannot be met, suppliers are not paid, scheduled loan payments will not be made, and investors will not receive dividend checks. Any one of these factors can either bring down a business or ensure a change in its management in short order.

Conversely, if a company is burdened by too much cash, it may be losing the opportunity to invest it in higher-yielding, longer-term investments unless it knows its projected cash balances. A quality cash forecast ideally allows the treasurer to determine how much cash is available for short-, medium-, and long-term investments, each having progressively higher returns. Since longer-term investments may have less liquidity, it is imperative that the treasurer be able to invest the correct amounts with confidence.

In order to avoid these problems, this chapter covers how to construct a cash forecast and automate the creation of some of the information contained within it, and how to create a feedback loop for gradually increasing the accuracy of the forecast. We also describe several related topics, including the bullwhip effect and the integration of business cycle forecasting into the cash forecast.

CASH FORECASTING MODEL

The core of any cash management system is the cash forecast. It is imperative for the management team to be fully appraised of any cash problems with as much lead time as possible. The sample model shown in Exhibit 3.1 is a good way to provide this information. The model is based on the *receipts and disbursements method*, which is primarily based on a combination of actual and estimated receivables and payables.

49

Exhibit 3.1 Sample Cash Forecast

Cash Forecast					
Date Last Updated	**1/4/2010**				
		For the Week Beginning on			
	1/4/2010	1/11/2010	1/18/2010	1/25/2010	2/1/2010
Beginning Cash Balance	**$ 1,037,191**	$ 1,009,796	$ 936,763	$ 957,771	$ 915,935
Receipts from Sales Projections:					
Coal Bed Drilling Corp.					
Oil Patch Kids Corp.					
Overfault & Sons Inc.					
Platte River Drillers					
Powder River Supplies Inc.					
Submersible Drillers Ltd.					
Commercial, Various					
Uncollected Invoices:					
Canadian Drillers Ltd.			$ 9,975		
Coastal Mudlogging Co.			$ 6,686		
Dept. of the Interior	$ 18,250			$ 11,629	
Drill Tip Repair Corp.				$ 5,575	
Overfault & Sons Inc.			$ 9,229		
Submersible Drillers Ltd.				$ 4,245	
U.S. Forest Service		$ 2,967	$ 8,450	$ 8,715	
Cash, Minor Invoices	$ 2,355	$ —	$ 3,668	$ —	$ 21,768
Total Cash In	$ 20,605	$ 2,967	$ 38,008	$ 30,164	$ 21,768
Cash Out:					
Payroll + Payroll Taxes		$ 62,000		$ 65,000	
Commissions		$ 7,000			
Insurance	$ 18,000				$ 18,000
Rent	$ 20,000				$ 20,000
Capital Purchases			$ 10,000		
Other Expenses	$ 10,000	$ 7,000	$ 7,000	$ 7,000	$ 10,000
Total Cash Out:	$ 48,000	$ 76,000	$ 17,000	$ 72,000	$ 48,000
Net Change in Cash	$ (27,395)	$ (73,033)	$ 21,008	$ (41,836)	$ (26,232)
Ending Cash:	$ 1,009,796	$ 936,763	$ 957,771	$ 915,935	$ 889,703

				(partial)		
Cash Forecast						
2/8/2010	2/15/2010	2/22/2010	3/1/2010	Mar-10	Apr-10	May-10
$ 889,703	$ 875,600	$ 793,600	$ 799,565	$ 816,665	$ 816,133	$ 778,883
				$ 36,937		$ 174,525
		$ 12,965		$ 48,521		$ 28,775
			$ 25,400		$ 129,000	
			$ 31,000	$ 53,000		
			$ 8,700		$ 18,500	$ 14,500
				$ 22,500	$ 16,250	$ 16,250
					$ 25,000	$ 25,000
$ 2,897			$ 18,510			
$ 2,897	$ —	$ 12,965	$ 65,100	$ 179,468	$ 188,750	$ 259,050
	$ 68,000			$ 142,000	$ 138,000	$ 138,000
	$ 7,000			$ 7,000	$ 8,000	$ 9,000
			$ 18,000		$ 18,000	$ 18,000
			$ 20,000		$ 20,000	$ 22,000
$ 10,000				$ 10,000	$ 10,000	$ 10,000
$ 7,000	$ 7,000	$ 7,000	$ 10,000	$ 21,000	$ 32,000	$ 32,000
$ 17,000	$ 82,000	$ 7,000	$ 48,000	$ 180,000	$ 226,000	$ 229,000
$ (14,103)	$ (82,000)	$ 5,965	$ 17,100	$ (532)	$ (37,250)	$ 30,050
$ 875,600	$ 793,600	$ 799,565	$ 816,665	$ 816,133	$ 778,883	$ 808,933

The cash forecast in the exhibit lists all cash activity on a weekly basis for the next nine weeks, which is approximately two months. These are followed by a partial month, which is needed in case the month that falls after the first nine weeks is also contained within the nine weeks. In the exhibit, the first week of March is listed, so the remaining three weeks of that month are described within a partial month column. There are also two more full months listed in the last two columns. By using this columnar format, the reader can see the expected cash flows for the next one-third of a year. The final two months listed in the forecast will tend to be much less accurate than the first two, but are still useful for making estimates about likely cash positions. This format can easily be extended to cover any number of additional months.

The top row of the report lists the date when the cash report was last updated. This is crucial information, for some companies will update this report every day, and the management team does not want to confuse itself with information on old reports. The next row contains the beginning cash balance. The leftmost cell in the row is encircled by heavy lines, indicating that the person responsible for the report should update this cell with the actual cash balance as of the first day of the report. The remaining cells in the row are updated from the ending cash balance for each period that is listed at the bottom of the preceding column. The next block of rows contains the expected receipt dates for sales that have not yet occurred. It is useful to break these down by specific customer and type of sale, rather than summarizing it into a single row, so that it can more easily be reviewed. The sales staff should review this information regularly to see if the timing and amount of each expected cash receipt is correct.

The next block of rows in the exhibit show the specific weeks within which accounts receivable are expected to be collected. This section can become quite large and difficult to maintain if there are many accounts receivable, so it is better to list only the largest items by customer, and then lump all others into a minor invoices row, as is the case in the exhibit. The input of the collections staff should be sought when updating these rows, since they will have the best insights into collection problems. The sum of all the rows thus far described is then listed in the "Total Cash In" row.

The next block of rows in the exhibit shows the various uses for cash. A service company is being used in this forecast, so the largest single use of cash is payroll, rather than the cost of goods sold, as would be the case in a manufacturing company. Other key cash outflows, such as monthly insurance, commission and rental payments, and capital purchases, are shown in the following rows. Being a service business, there are few other expenses, so they are lumped together in an "Other Expenses" row. In this case, cash payments have a slight tendency to be toward the beginning of the month, so the cash flows are adjusted accordingly. If the cost of goods sold had been a major component of the forecast, then it would have been listed either in aggregate and based on a percentage of total sales, or else split into a different cash outflow for each product line. The latter case is more useful when the gross margin is significantly different for each product line and when the sales by product line vary considerably over time.

The bottom of the exhibit summarizes the end-of-period cash position, which rolls forward into the beginning cash balance for the next reporting period.

There are a few other rows that could be added to the model, depending on the type of payments that a company makes. For example, there could be an annual dividend payment, quarterly income tax payment, or monthly principal and interest payments to lenders. These and other items can be added to enhance the basic model, if needed. However, the model requires considerable effort to update, so carefully consider the extra work load needed before adding more information requirements to it.

The cash forecast shown in Exhibit 3.1 relies on anticipated cash receipts and disbursements for the first month, but then gradually transitions into a greater reliance on sales forecasts and expense trend lines. To extend the forecast even further into the future, the treasurer must rely to a greater extent on the annual budget, as modified for the company's actual experience subsequent to finalization of the budget. Thus, a long-duration cash forecast draws on input from three sources—receipts and disbursements, then short-term projections, and then the budget. Since each of these sources of information is progressively less accurate, the forecasted results will be correspondingly less reliable. The impact of different sources of information on the reliability of the cash forecast is shown in Exhibit 3.2.

INFORMATION SOURCES FOR THE CASH FORECAST

The cash forecast shown in the preceding exhibit primarily includes *scheduled items*, which are specific cash inflows and outflows that can be predicted with a reasonable degree of accuracy. Examples of scheduled items are specific accounts receivable and scheduled payroll payments. If the treasurer wants an accurate cash forecast, then as much of it as possible should be comprised of scheduled items.

It is not always possible to include all of the scheduled items in the cash forecast; a company of reasonable size may have several thousand scheduled items to include in the forecast. In such cases, it is necessary to summarize many of the smaller items using the *distribution method*. Under this method, the treasurer examines historical cash flows to create an estimate of the timing and amounts of future cash flows. In the cash flow exhibit, the "Cash, Minor Invoices" and "Other Expenses" line items were generated using the distribution method. There are too many smaller incoming invoice payments to list individually, so instead we estimate the approximate arrival dates and amounts based on their occurrence in the past, possibly using the company's historical days sales outstanding. Small expenses are also quite predictable.

Exhibit 3.2   Progressive Decline in Cash Forecast Accuracy

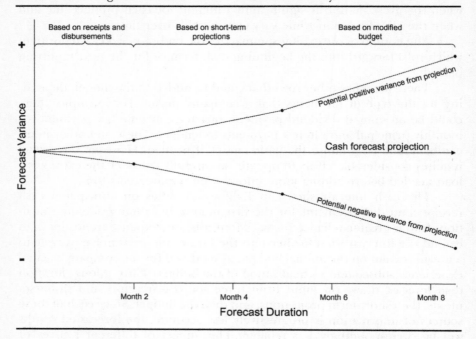

An experienced compiler of cash forecasts will consider a number of variables when constructing a forecast. For example, employee expense reports tend to arrive at the end of the month, and so will be paid during the first week of the following month. Also, the accounts payable departments of many companies operate with reduced staffing near major holidays, and are less likely to issue payments on their usual schedules; this is a particular problem during the Christmas holidays. Similarly, payroll payments will be shifted forward in time if a company holiday is scheduled for what would otherwise have been a payroll day. For these reasons, cash forecasting requires a considerable amount of experience.

MEASURING CASH FORECAST ACCURACY

A cash forecast is useless unless it can be relied upon to yield accurate cash flow information for some distance into the future. There are a number of ways to improve the forecast, all involving the continuing comparison of past forecasts to actual results and correcting the system to ensure that better information is provided for future forecasts.

A key area in which the cash forecast can be wildly incorrect is in receipts from sales forecasts. A detailed review of this area will reveal that some salespersons do not want to forecast any sales because then they will be held accountable for their predictions. This problem requires constant feedback with the sales staff to correct, and may require reinforcement by including the sales forecasting function in the annual review and compensation plan for them.

Another problem is in the accounts payable area, where actual cash outflows will typically exceed forecast cash outflows. This imbalance is caused by a faulty accounts payable data entry process, where invoices are initially mailed by suppliers to people outside of the accounts payable department, or because invoices are sent out for approval before they are logged into the accounting system, thereby resulting in their late appearance in the forecast, usually just before they need to be paid. These problems can be solved by asking suppliers to send invoices straight to the accounting department, and by entering all invoices into the accounting system before sending them out for approval. It is also possible to review open purchase orders to see if there are any missing invoices that are supposed to be currently payable, thereby proactively starting a search for the missing invoices.

A major cash flow variance will arise if a fixed asset is suddenly purchased that was not included in the cash forecast. This problem is best resolved by giving the treasury staff complete access to the capital budgeting process, so that it can tell what capital requests are in queue for approval, and when they are likely to require cash payments.

In short, the accuracy of the cash forecast requires great attention to processes that provide its source data. The treasury staff should regularly compare forecasted to actual results, and work its way back through the underlying systems to determine what issues caused the error—and then correct them.

CASH FORECASTING AUTOMATION

The steps just noted to create a cash forecast can be quite cumbersome, especially if there are multiple departments or subsidiaries spread out across many locations. When the cash forecast is generated on a regular basis, the required workload can be extraordinarily high. Automation can be used to avoid some of the most time-consuming steps.

Many off-the-shelf accounting software packages contain standard reports that itemize the daily or weekly time buckets in which payments are scheduled to be made, based on each supplier invoice date and the number of days before they are due for payment, including any requirements for early payment in order to take advantage of early payment discounts. The cash flow information provided by this report is quite reliable, but tends to be less accurate for the time period several weeks into the future, because of delays in the entry of supplier invoice information into the accounting system. This delay is usually caused by the divergence of incoming invoices to managers for approval. By first entering the invoice information and *then* sending the invoices out for approval, this time delay can be avoided, thereby improving the accuracy of the automated accounts payable payment timing report.

If there is a well-managed purchase order system in place that is stored in a purchasing database, then the accounts payable report format can be stretched further into the future with some accuracy. Since purchase orders may be issued for some months into the future, and involve specific delivery dates, this information can be compiled into a report that reveals when the payments to suppliers based on these purchase orders will be sent out. It is also useful for the purchase of fixed assets, since these orders are so large that suppliers will not normally process an order in the absence of a signed purchase order. However, a large asset purchase may require an up-front payment that will not become apparent until the purchase order is entered into the accounting system, which will result in the sudden appearance of a large cash requirement on the report in the near future.

There are some instances where invoice payments can be predicted well into the future, even in the absence of a purchase order. These are typically recurring payments in a constant amount, such as facility lease payments or maintenance payments that are prespecified under a long-term contract. If these payments are listed in the accounts payable system as recurring invoices, then it is a simple matter to extract them for use in the cash forecast.

The same report is available in many accounting software packages for accounts receivable, itemizing the day or week buckets in which invoice payments are scheduled to be received, based on their original issuance dates and the number of days before customers are required to pay for them. However, this report tends to be much less accurate, for any overdue invoice payments are scheduled for immediate payment in the current period, when in fact there may be collection problems that will delay receipt for quite some time. Also, the report does not account for the average delay in payments that varies by each customer, in accordance with each one's timeliness in making payments. Consequently, this report should be manually modified, especially for the largest outstanding invoices, to reflect the collection staff's best estimates of when payments will actually be received.

In a few cases, software packages will also extend current payroll payments into the future, by assuming that the existing salaries for current employees will continue at the same rates, and that hourly employees will be paid for a regular workweek for all future reporting periods. This is not a viable option for those companies that outsource their payroll, since the in-house software will not have any way to predict cash flows if it does not contain any information about payroll.

The preceding discussion shows that there are numerous ways in which *elements* of the cash forecast can be automated. However, there are so many variables, such as uncertain receipt dates for accounts receivable, changes in payroll levels, and the sudden purchase of fixed assets, that any automatically generated reports should be adjusted by the accounting staff's knowledge of special situations that will throw off the results of the reports. Also, the basis for automated reports is primarily very short-term accounts receivable and payable information that will rapidly become inaccurate for periods much greater than a month, so manual adjustments to the cash forecast that are derived from short-term forecasts or the budget will become increasingly necessary for later time periods.

BULLWHIP EFFECT

It is usually possible to create reasonably accurate estimates of the amounts and timing of incoming payments from customers and outgoing ones to suppliers. However, the inventory component of the forecast can be downright befuddling. Inventory levels may rise or fall so sporadically that it appears impossible to forecast accurate payables.

One element of inventory forecasting that causes so much heartburn is the *bullwhip effect*. This is when a company runs into a materials or capacity shortage and informs its customers that they are being put on an allocation basis. The customers immediately ramp up their order quantities so they can lock in a greater proportion of the company's output over a longer time horizon, which forces the company to increase its capacity to meet the unexpected demand; once the company starts meeting the larger orders and eliminates its shipment allocations, customers promptly shrink their planning horizons, find that they now have plenty of inventory for their immediate needs, and rescind most outstanding orders. The company has just been the victim of the bullwhip effect. The cash forecast has also been bullwhipped, as the payables line item alternatively skyrockets and dives. How can one avoid this problem?

The treasurer should monitor the issuance of any order allocation notices to customers and see if there is a sudden order increase that occurs subsequent to the notice. If so, the treasurer should work with the materials manager to estimate "real" order volumes based on the historical order volumes of each customer, adjusted for any seasonal effects. Inventory planning should incorporate these historical values, rather than the incremental jump in orders, until such time as the allocation notice is rescinded and order volumes return to their normal levels. This kind of proactive planning will result in a much more accurate cash forecast, and will also keep a company from suffering through the inventory and production gyrations of the bullwhip effect.

BUSINESS CYCLE FORECASTING

The cash forecasting period is generally quite short—anywhere from one to six months. The level of accuracy of this forecast declines markedly if it projects multiple months into the future. However, it is possible to incorporate longer-range business cycle forecasting into the cash forecast in order to introduce a higher degree of accuracy into the more distant parts of the cash forecast. Here are some possible actions to take to obtain, analyze, and report on business cycle forecasts. They are listed in ascending order of difficulty:

- *Report on published forecasts.* There are forecasts published by nearly every major business magazine for the economy at large. Several key advantages are that the information is fairly accurate for the entire economy, it is prepared by professional forecasters, and it is essentially free. The problem is that each company operates in a smaller industry within the national economy, and as such is subject to "mini" business cycles that may not move in lockstep with that of the national economy. For this reason, the reported information may be only generally relevant to a company's specific situation.

- *Subscribe to a forecasting service.* A company can pay a significant fee, probably in the five- to six-figure range, to a forecasting service for more specific reports that relate to the industry in which it operates. This is a good approach for those organizations that do not have the resources to gather, summarize, and interpret economic data by themselves. However, some industries are too small to be serviced by a specialized forecasting service, or the fee charged is too high in comparison to the value of the information received.

- *Develop an in-house forecasting model.* In cases where either a company wants to run its own forecasting model or there are no forecasting services available that can provide the information, it is time to try some in-house forecasting. This effort can range from a minimalist approach to a comprehensive one, with each level of effort yielding better results. The first step is to find the right kinds of data to accumulate, followed by implementing a data-gathering method that yields reliable data in a timely manner. Then arrive at a methodology for translating the underlying data into a forecast. This forecast should include the underlying assumptions and data used to arrive at the forecast, so that any changes in the assumptions are clearly laid out. Finally, there should be a methodology for comparing the results against actual data and adjusting the forecasting methodology based on that information. Though this approach is a time-consuming one, it can yield the best results if a carefully developed forecasting system is used.

Example

The treasurer of a sport rack company has elected to use the last of the preceding options for creating forecasting information. Sport racks is a very small niche market that creates and sells racks for skis, snowboards, bicycles, and kayaks that can be attached to the tops of most kinds of automobiles. The treasurer wants to derive a forecasting system that will give management an estimate of the amount by which projected sales can be expected to vary. She decides to subdivide the market into four categories, one each for skis, snowboards, bicycles, and kayaks. Based on a historical analysis, she finds that 25 percent of ski purchasers, 35 percent of snowboard purchasers, 75 percent of bicycle purchasers, and 30 percent of kayak purchasers will purchase a car-top rack system to hold their new equipment. The typical delay in these purchases from the time when they bought their sports equipment to the time they bought sport racks was six months. The treasurer finds that she can obtain new sports equipment sales data from industry trade groups every three months. Given the lag time before users purchase car-top racks, this means that she can accumulate the underlying data that predict sport rack sales and disseminate it to management with three months to go before the resulting sport rack sales will occur. Thus, she concludes that these are usable data.

The next task is to determine the company's share of the sport rack market, which is readily obtainable from the industry trade group for sport racks, though this information is at least one year old. Given the stability of sales within the industry, she feels that this information is still accurate. She then prepares the report shown in the following table. It shows total sports equipment sales for the last quarter, uses historical percentages to arrive at the amount of resulting sport rack sales, and then factors in the company's market share percentage to determine the forecasted sales of each type of sport rack. By comparing this information to the previously forecasted sales information, the report reveals that the company should significantly ramp up its production of snowboard sport racks as soon as possible.

Description	Sports Equipment Unit Sales	% Buying Sport Racks	Company Market Share	Forecasted Company Unit Sales	Original Company Forecast	Variance
Ski	3,200,000	25	40%	320,000	300,000	+20,000
Snowboard	2,700,000	35	40%	378,000	300,000	+78,000
Bicycle	2,500,000	75	30%	562,500	550,000	+16,500
Kayak	450,000	30	30%	40,500	45,000	−4,500

The example used was for an extremely limited niche market, but it does point out that a modest amount of forecasting work can yield excellent results that are much more company specific than would be the case if a company relied solely on the forecasts of experts who were concerned only with general national trends. For most companies, there will be a number of additional underlying indicators that should be factored into the forecasting model; however, the work associated with tracking these added data must be compared to the benefit of more accurate results, so that a manager arrives at a reasonable cost-benefit compromise.

Business cycle forecasting is useful for a cash flow forecast only if the forecast extends a considerable distance into the future. Such information will have a minimal impact on a cash forecast having a duration of three months or less, but can be quite useful for more extended periods.

CASH FORECASTING CONTROLS

The daily cash forecast usually is assembled quickly, using the preceding day's forecast as a template, and with only minor updates. A less frequent forecast may be assembled "from scratch," without attempting to roll forward the old forecast; this increases the risk of errors. Also, the person who prepares a cash forecast on an infrequent basis is less familiar with the process, and so is more likely to make a mistake. These characteristics allow the treasurer to mandate a reduced set of controls for a daily cash forecast and a more comprehensive one for less frequent forecasts.

If a forecast is issued on a daily basis, then the treasurer should focus controls on the incremental daily changes in the forecast. This can be achieved with the following two controls:

1. *Investigate significant variances from the preceding day's forecast.* This is a side-by-side comparison of the current day's forecast and the immediately preceding day's forecast. If there are significant changes, the preparer should verify that the changes are reasonable.

2. *Obtain the approval of a knowledgeable person.* Another person should *briefly* review the forecast, initial it, and retain a copy. The reviewer may not necessarily be the preparer's supervisor; it may make more sense to have someone else with significant and recent cash forecasting expertise review it. Alternatively, the reviewer could be someone with considerable knowledge of the information feeding into the forecast, such as the person responsible for collections, payables, payroll, or capital expenditures.

If a forecast is generated less frequently, the controls should include the preceding two controls (with some modifications), as well as additional controls. They are:

- *Match latest forecast against preceding forecasts.* It is useful to compare the new forecast against several preceding forecasts. In particular, compare the predicted ending cash balance for each time period to the same time period in the earlier forecasts. If there are significant differences in the ending balance for a specific time period as it moves closer to the present, it is likely that the forecast model needs to be changed for the periods farther in the future.

- *Match forecast against standard forecast checklist.* When a forecast is being prepared on an infrequent basis, there is an increased risk that some line items in the forecast will be inadvertently left out. It is extremely difficult to spot a missing item, so a reviewer should match the forecast against a standard checklist of forecast contents. This control is more useful when reviewing a forecast prepared by an inexperienced person who is not familiar with the company's business processes.

- *Obtain approvals.* The less frequently a forecast is prepared, the more approvals it needs, since the company is going to rely on it for a longer period of time. This may call for reviews by all of the people having provided input into the forecast, such as the managers of collections, payables, payroll, and capital expenditures. At a minimum, at least one person with extensive knowledge of the company's cash flows should review and initial the forecast, and retain a copy.

- *Retain a copy.* The best way to investigate the accuracy of a cash forecast is to compare it to the forecasts from prior periods, so retain a copy of every forecast. If the forecast is compiled on a spreadsheet, then save each forecast on a separate tab of the spreadsheet, and label each tab with the date of the forecast. It may also be useful to lock the spreadsheet, so that earlier versions are not inadvertently altered.

Finally, if the forecast is created using an electronic spreadsheet, then the departmental year-end procedure book should include a requirement to verify *every* formula in the most recent cash forecast. Any tinkering with the forecast model during the year could have caused a calculation error that no longer properly rolls up the cash forecast. This formula review should *not* be conducted by the person who prepares the cash forecast; instead, use someone who does not use the spreadsheet. This third party will be more likely to painstakingly work through all of the formulas and how they work, whereas someone who is excessively familiar with the spreadsheet is more likely to assume that it works correctly.

CASH FORECASTING POLICIES

The treasurer should implement policies that will assist in the management of two aspects of cash forecasting, which are the issuance frequency and review frequency of the forecasts. Sample policies include the following:

- *Cash forecasts shall be issued on a [daily/weekly/monthly] basis.* This policy ensures that cash forecasts are issued with sufficient frequency to match the periodic updating of a company's debt and investments. A larger company with significant transaction volume may need daily cash forecasts, while a smaller one may only require a monthly issuance.

- *Cash forecasts shall be structurally updated at least once a [month/quarter/ year].* A cash forecast may gradually become less accurate over time, due to changes in the business that are not reflected in the cash forecast model. This policy requires the treasurer to engage in a periodic updating that "fine-tunes" the forecast to make it more accurately reflect actual cash flows.

These policies should be integrated into the treasury's policies and procedures manual, and can also be integrated into the job descriptions of those responsible for the cash forecast.

CASH FORECASTING PROCEDURE

A formal cash forecasting procedure is least likely to be used if an experienced person prepares a forecast every day, but can be quite useful for more infrequent forecasting intervals or for training purposes, where there is less certainty about the various components of the forecast. The cash forecasting procedure is shown in Exhibit 3.3, and assumes the use of an electronic spreadsheet for preparation of the forecast.

The key steps in the procedure are noted in the flowchart in Exhibit 3.4. In addition, the small black diamonds on the flowchart indicate the location of key control points in the process, with descriptions next to the diamonds.

SUMMARY

Cash forecasting is an important task that deserves the utmost attention from the treasurer, since a cash shortfall can bring a company's operations to an abrupt halt in short order, or at least require the use of expensive short-term debt. The cash forecasting process is based on multiple sources of information that can yield quite inaccurate results just a few months in the future. To improve forecasting accuracy, the treasury staff should regularly compare the forecast to actual results in order to locate and root out problems. A number of controls and a rigidly followed forecasting procedure can also help improve forecasting accuracy. Only by improving forecast accuracy can a company take proper steps to mitigate its borrowing needs, as well as place excess funds in the proper types of investments.

Exhibit 3.3   Cash Forecasting Procedure

Procedure Statement   Retrieval No.: TREASURY-01

Subject: Cash Forecast

1. PURPOSE AND SCOPE
   This procedure is used by the treasury staff to create a periodic cash forecast.

2. PROCEDURES

   2.1 Create Cash Forecast (Treasury Staff)

      1. Create a new worksheet within the forecast spreadsheet.
      2. Copy the forecast model forward from the most recent worksheet into the new worksheet.
      3. Label the tab of the new version with the issuance date of the cash forecast.
      4. Lock the most recent completed worksheet.
      5. In the new worksheet, clear all numbers from the forecast model.
      6. Enter the beginning cash balance from the daily bank reconciliation.
      7. Obtain from the collections manager the best estimate of receipt dates for receivables exceeding $____. For smaller receivables, estimate the distribution of receipts based on the historical days sales outstanding metric. Enter this information in the forecast.
      8. Obtain from the payroll manager the estimated timing and amounts of scheduled wage and commission payments. Enter this information in the forecast.
      9. Obtain from the payables system the timing and amounts of scheduled payables. Enter this information in the forecast.
      10. Obtain from the financial analyst the timing and amounts of scheduled capital expenditures. Enter this information in the forecast.
      11. Obtain from the sales manager the short-term sales forecast, and estimate cash receipts from these sales based on the historical days sales outstanding.

12. Incorporate expenses into the short-term sales forecast period, based on recurring expenses and historical percentages of the cost of goods sold and administrative expenses.
13. Obtain from the financial analyst the receipts and expenditures based on the modified budget for the period beyond the short-term sales forecast. Enter this information in the forecast.
14. Review the preliminary cash forecast for reasonableness.
15. Forward the forecast to the assistant treasurer for review.

2.2 Review Cash Forecast (Assistant Treasurer)

1. Review and approve the cash forecast. This may include matching the timing and amounts of the projected collection, payables, and capital expenditures listed in the forecast to other reports, or asking for additional reviews by the managers of those functions.
2. Print two copies of the cash forecast.
3. Initial both copies to indicate approval, return one to the forecast preparer, and retain the other copy in a binder, stored by date.

2.3 Issue Cash Forecast (Treasury Staff)

1. Upon receipt of the approved forecast, issue the forecast to the treasurer, assistant treasurer, controller, and chief financial officer.

Exhibit 3.4   Procedural and Control Steps for the Cash Forecast

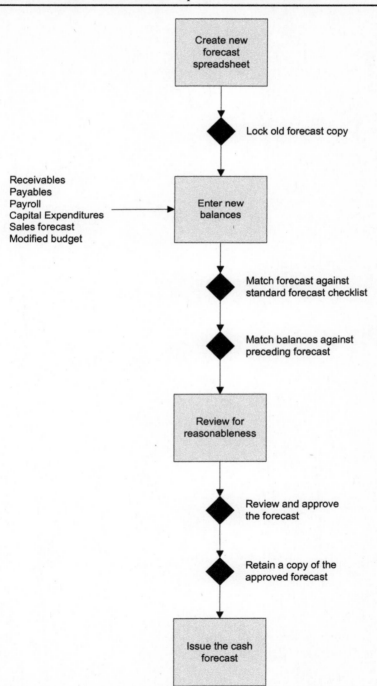

4

Cash Concentration

Larger companies with many subsidiaries, especially those with operations in multiple countries, maintain a significant number of bank accounts. This is an inefficient arrangement from the perspective of cash management, since the treasury staff must track all of the individual account balances. With such highly fragmented cash balances, it is extremely difficult to repurpose the funds for either centralized payments, debt paydown, or investments. An excellent solution is *cash concentration*, where the cash in multiple accounts is pooled. Pooling can be achieved either through *physical sweeping* (where cash is actually moved into a *concentration account* or *master account*) or *notional pooling* (where funds are not actually transferred, but balance information is reported as though physical sweeping had occurred). This chapter describes the various cash concentration strategies, the mechanics of pooling, and supporting policies, procedures, and controls.

BENEFITS OF CASH CONCENTRATION

The typical company has a number of bank accounts, each containing either a credit balance or a debit balance that is being covered by a bank overdraft. At a small-company level, and in the absence of a formal treasurer position, these balances are probably monitored by an assistant controller, with occasional cash transfers to cover debit balances. Interest income is probably minimal.

As the company becomes larger and the number of its bank accounts expands, the total volume of idle cash balances becomes too great to ignore. At this stage, the company hires a treasurer to manage the cash. The treasurer will likely advance the following list of benefits related to aggregating the cash in all of those bank accounts:

- *Elimination of idle cash.* The treasurer's best argument will be that cash idling in a multitude of accounts can be aggregated into interest-earning investments.

- *Improved investment returns.* If the company's cash can be aggregated, then it is easier to allocate the cash into short-term, low-yield investments and higher-yield, longer-term investments. The overall results should be an improved return on investment.

- *More cost-effective oversight of accounts.* When an automated sweeping arrangement is used to concentrate cash, there is no need to manually review subsidiary account balances. This can yield a significant reduction in labor costs.

- *Internal funding of debit balances.* Where a company is grappling with ongoing debit balance problems in multiple accounts, the avoidance of high-cost bank overdraft charges alone may be a sufficient incentive to use cash concentration. An example of the change in costs is shown in Exhibit 4.1. In the first part of the exhibit, ABC Company has bank accounts at four of its subsidiaries. Each of the accounts earns the same 3 percent interest rate on credit balances, while the banks all charge the same 8 percent rate on debit balances (overdrafts). In the second part of the exhibit, ABC shifts all of its funds into a cash concentration account, thereby avoiding the 8 percent overdraft charge, and realizing a significant improvement in its interest income.

Exhibit 4.1   Change in Interest Income from Cash Concentration Banking

Scenario without Cash Concentration

	Overdraft Interest Rate	Credit Balance Interest Rate	Cash Balance in Account	Annual Interest
Subsidiary 1	8%	3%	$100,000	$3,000
Subsidiary 2	8%	3%	(50,000)	(4,000)
Subsidiary 3	8%	3%	(35,000)	(2,800)
Subsidiary 4	8%	3%	75,000	2,250
		Totals	$90,000	$(1,550)

Scenario with Cash Concentration

	Overdraft Interest Rate	Credit Balance Interest Rate	Cash Balance in Account	Annual Interest
Subsidiary 1	8%	3%	—	—
Subsidiary 2	8%	3%	—	—
Subsidiary 3	8%	3%	—	—
Subsidiary 4	8%	3%	—	—
		Total	$90,000	$2,700

In the exhibit, interest income improves by $4,250, which makes cash concentration cost-effective as long as the sweeping fee charged by the bank is less than that amount.

CASH CONCENTRATION STRATEGIES

A company having multiple locations can pursue a variety of cash concentration strategies, which tend to bring larger benefits with greater centralization. The strategies are:

- *Complete decentralization.* Every subsidiary or branch office with its own bank account manages its own cash position. This is fine if balances are small, so that there is little synergy to be gained by concentrating cash in a single account. However, if large cash balances are languishing in some accounts, or other accounts are incurring overdraft charges, then a more centralized approach is called for. A more advanced version of this strategy is to centralize accounts in the country of currency (e.g., dollars are kept in the United States, and yen are kept in Japan). This alternative is transactionally efficient, but does not sufficiently centralize cash for investment purposes.

- *Centralized payments, decentralized liquidity management.* A company can implement a centralized payment factory that handles all payables for all company subsidiaries but issues payments from local accounts. This improves the overall planning for cash outflows but does not improve the management of excess cash balances, for which local managers are still responsible. Also, if investments are managed at the local level, there is a greater risk that the corporate investment policy will not be followed.

- *Centralized liquidity management, decentralized payments.* The treasury staff centralizes cash into a concentration account (either through sweeps or notional pooling) and has responsibility for investments. However, local managers are still responsible for disbursements.

- *All functions centralized.* The treasury staff pools all cash into a concentration account, invests it, and manages disbursements. This is an excellent structure for optimizing investment income and gives the treasurer considerable control over the accounts payable portion of the company's working capital. Larger companies usually follow this strategy, but may not carry it through to cross-border centralization. Instead, they may centrally manage key currencies, such as euros and dollars, while allowing regional control over other currencies.

In cases where cash is invested from a central location and multiple currencies are involved, it may be necessary for the treasury staff to invest funds locally (i.e., in the home country of the currency), because of legal or foreign exchange restrictions.

The final (and most centralized) of these strategies is the most efficient approach for cash concentration, but it may not be the most cost-effective. If a company has relatively few subsidiaries with low account balances, then creating a central treasury staff to manage the cash may add more overhead than will be offset by increased interest income or reduced interest expense.

POOLING CONCEPTS

Cash concentration requires that a company create a *cash pool*. This comprises a cluster of subsidiary bank accounts and a concentration account. Funds physically flow from the subsidiary accounts into the concentration account under a *physical sweeping* method. Alternatively, cash balances in the subsidiary accounts can be concentrated in the master account only within the bank's records, with the cash remaining in the subsidiary accounts. This later method is called *notional pooling*.

If a pooling arrangement includes accounts located in more than one country, this is known as a *cross-border cash pool*. A company may elect to pool cash within the home country of each currency (e.g., U.S. dollars are pooled in the United States), which is known as the *single-currency-center* model. If a company pools all of its foreign currency accounts in a single location, this is a *multicurrency-center* arrangement. Multicurrency centers are generally easier to manage, but transactions are more expensive than under the single-currency-center model.

PHYSICAL SWEEPING

When a company sets up a *zero-balance account*, its bank automatically moves cash from that account into a concentration account, usually within the same bank. The cash balance in the zero-balance account (as the name implies) is reduced to zero whenever a sweep occurs. If the account has a debit balance at the time of the sweep, then money is shifted from the concentration account back into the account having the debit balance. An example is shown in Exhibit 4.2.

In the example, two of three subsidiary accounts initially contain credit (positive) balances, and Account C contains a debit (negative) balance. In the first stage of the sweep transaction, the cash in the two accounts having credit balances are swept into the concentration account. In the next stage of the sweep, sufficient funds are transferred from the concentration account

Exhibit 4.2 Zero-Balance Sweep Transaction

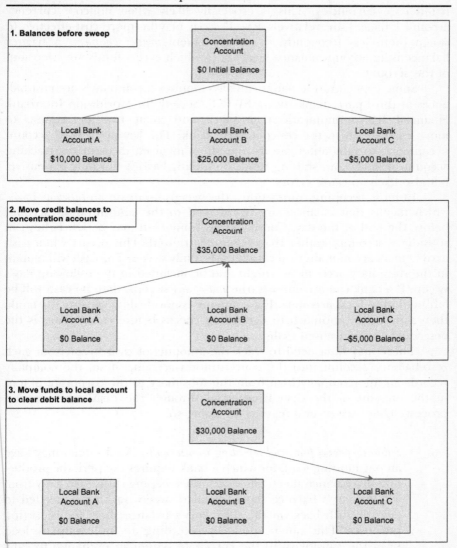

to offset the debit balance in Account C. At the end of the sweep, then, there are no credit or debit balances in the zero-balance accounts.

It is also possible to use *constant balancing* to maintain a predetermined minimum balance in a subsidiary account, which involves sweeping only those cash levels above the minimum balance, and reverse sweeping cash into the subsidiary account if the balance drops below the minimum balance.

Daily sweeping may not be necessary outside of a company's designated core currencies. This is especially likely when noncore currency
account balances are relatively low. If so, it may be more cost-effective to
sweep them less frequently, or to implement *trigger balances*. A trigger
balance is an account balance level above which excess funds are swept out
of the account.

Some concentration banks can also monitor a company's account balances at third-party banks using SWIFT (Society for Worldwide Interbank
Financial Telecommunication) messages, and create transfer requests to
move excess cash to the concentration bank. The key point with account
sweeping is to fully automate it—the effort involved in manually tracking
account balances and shifting funds on a daily basis is not only expensive,
but also likely to cause errors.

In most sweeping transactions, the sweeps occur on an *intraday* basis,
which means that balances are transferred to the concentration account
before the end of the day. Consequently, some cash may be left behind in
subsidiary accounts, rather than being centralized. This occurs when cash
arrives in an account after execution of the daily sweep. The cash will remain
in the subsidiary account overnight and be included in the following day's
sweep. If a bank can accomplish true *end-of-day* sweeps, then no cash will be
left behind in local accounts. If a company is not dealing with such a bank,
then a proactive approach to depositing checks before cutoff times is the
best way to avoid unused cash.

There may be a need to track the amounts of cash swept from each
zero-balance account into the concentration account; if so, the company
records an intercompany loan from the subsidiary to the corporate parent
in the amount of the cash transferred through the cash concentration
process. There are several reasons for doing so:

- *Subsidiary-level financial reporting requirements.* A subsidiary may have
  an outstanding loan, for which a bank requires the periodic production of a balance sheet. Since account sweeping shifts cash away from
  a subsidiary's balance sheet, detailed sweep tracking is needed to
  put the cash back on the subsidiary's balance sheet for reporting
  purposes. This can be done by recording an intercompany loan
  from the subsidiary to the corporate parent in exchange for any
  swept cash, which can then be reversed to place the cash back on
  the subsidiary's balance sheet.

- *Interest income allocation.* A company may elect to allocate the interest
  earned at the concentration account level back to the subsidiaries
  whose accounts contributed cash to the concentration account. Some
  countries require that this interest allocation be done to keep a
  company from locating the concentration account in a low-tax jurisdiction, where the tax on interest income is minimized. Thus, the

amounts of cash swept into and out of a subsidiary account must be tracked in order to properly allocate the correct proportion of interest income to that account.

- *Interest expense allocation.* Some tax jurisdictions may require the parent company to record interest expense on intercompany loans associated with the transfer of cash in a physical sweeping arrangement. If so, the company must track the intercompany loan balances outstanding per day, which is then used as the principal for the calculation of interest expense. The interest rate used for these calculations should be the market rate; any other rate can be construed by local tax authorities to be transfer pricing designed to shift income into low-tax regions.

- *Central bank reporting.* Some central banks require that they be sent reports on transfers between resident and nonresident accounts. This may be handled by the company's bank but can still increase the administrative burden associated with the sweep.

Some banks have the capability to track the amount of balance sweeps from each subsidiary account on an ongoing basis, which a company can use as its record of intercompany loans.

NOTIONAL POOLING

Notional pooling is a mechanism for calculating interest on the combined credit and debit balances of accounts that a corporate parent chooses to cluster together without actually transferring any funds. This approach allows each subsidiary company to take advantage of a single, centralized liquidity position, while still retaining daily cash management privileges. Also, since it avoids the use of cash transfers to a central pooling account, there is no need to create or monitor intercompany loans, nor are there any bank fees related to cash transfers (since there are no transfers). In addition, it largely eliminates the need to arrange overdraft lines with local banks. Further, interest earnings tend to be higher than if investments were made separately for the smaller individual accounts. Also, it offers a solution for partially owned subsidiaries whose other owners may balk at the prospect of physically transferring funds to an account controlled by another entity. And finally, the use of notional pooling is not a long-term commitment; on the contrary, it is relatively easy to back out of the arrangement.

Where global notional pooling is offered (usually where all participating accounts are held within a single bank), the pool offsets credit and debit balances on a multicurrency basis without the need to engage in any foreign exchange transactions. An additional benefit of global notional pooling lies in the area of intercompany cash flows; for example, if there are charges for administrative services, the transaction can be accomplished with no net movement of cash.

Once a company earns interest on the funds in a notional account, interest income is usually allocated back to each of the accounts making up the pool. For tax management reasons, it may be useful for the corporate parent to charge the subsidiaries participating in the pool for some cash concentration administration expenses related to management of the pool. This scenario works best if the corporate subsidiaries are located in high-tax regions, where reduced reportable income will result in reduced taxes.

The main downside of notional pooling is that it is not allowed in some countries, especially in portions of Africa, Asia, and Latin America (though it is very common in Europe). In these excluded areas, physical cash sweeping is the most common alternative. Also, the precise form of the notional pooling arrangement will vary according to local laws, so that some countries allow cross-border pooling, while others do not.

In addition to the prohibition against notional pooling in some countries, it is difficult to find anything but a large multinational bank that offers cross-currency notional pooling. Instead, it is most common to have a separate notional cash pool for each currency area.

COMPARISON OF ACCOUNT SWEEPING AND NOTIONAL POOLING

Where there is a choice between account sweeping and notional pooling, notional pooling is usually the better alternative. Under notional pooling, cash does not physically leave the bank accounts of each subsidiary, which greatly reduces the amount of intercompany loans that would otherwise have to be recorded. This eliminates the treasury overhead cost that would otherwise be associated with tracking and recording the intercompany loans.

Similarly, if the parent company allocates interest earned to its various subsidiaries based on their cash balances, this requires significant accounting resources to calculate the interest income allocation based on intercompany loans and deposits. In multicurrency situations, this also involves revaluing the interest income into different currencies. However, in a notional pooling environment, the bank may be able to automate the calculation of interest, with a physical transfer of funds at month-end to pay out the interest income to each subsidiary.

Also, if the intent is to pool funds denominated in multiple currencies, account sweeps require the use of foreign exchange transactions and possibly hedging. Notional pooling eliminates these activities, since funds are not shifted from one currency to another.

When account sweeping moves cash from one entity to another, this can have adverse tax consequences in some countries. Conversely, because notional pooling requires no physical transfer of funds between legal entities, no tax problems are triggered.

Notional pooling is more likely to be supported by the managers of local subsidiaries, since it means that they retain control over their cash balances. Indeed, they may not even realize that a notional pooling arrangement has been created!

However, a major disadvantage of notional pooling is that it is illegal in some countries. Thus, notional pooling should be taken advantage of where it is offered. When not available, physical sweeping is a very acceptable alternative to conducting no cash concentration activities at all.

NONPOOLING SITUATIONS

A company may need to use a local bank that cannot be linked into its corporate account sweeping or notional pooling structures. If so, the company's account balances within that bank must be managed manually. A key focus of this activity is to prevent overdrafts, since their cost usually greatly exceeds the interest income to be earned on the same account; thus, it is cost-effective to maintain excess balances in such accounts, rather than incurring overdraft fees.

If there are to be cash transfers out of such accounts, they tend to be infrequent, since the parent company will prefer to maintain excess cash balances in order to avoid overdrafts, and so will only siphon off cash when there is a clear excess balance. Also, because account management is manual, it is more cost-effective from a labor perspective to limit the number of transfers into or out of these accounts.

BANK OVERLAY STRUCTURE

Companies operating on an international scale frequently have trouble reconciling the need for efficient cash concentration operations with the use of local banking partners with whom they may have long-standing relationships and valuable business contacts. The solution is the *bank overlay structure*.

A bank overlay structure consists of two layers. The lower layer is comprised of all in-country banks that are used for local cash transaction requirements. The higher layer is a group of networked regional banks, or even a single global bank, that maintains a separate bank account for each country or legal entity of the corporate structure. Cash balances in the lower layer of banks are zero-balanced into the corresponding accounts in the higher layer of banks on a daily basis (where possible, subject to cash flow restrictions). These sweeps are accomplished either with manual transfers, SWIFT

Exhibit 4.3   Multicountry Physical Sweeping with Bank Overlay Structure

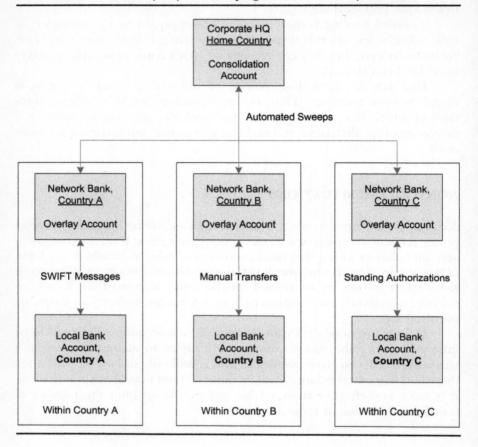

messages from the networked banks to the local banks, or with standing authorizations to the local banks. The concept is shown in Exhibit 4.3. This approach allows funds to be consolidated on either a regional or global basis for centralized cash management.

CASH CONCENTRATION CONTROLS

There is a strong argument that having a physical sweep cash concentration system in place *is* a control, since it pushes all cash balances into a single location for easier monitoring. Otherwise, the treasury staff would be faced with a large jumble of accounts, over which it might exercise little control.

Nonetheless, the following controls can improve on the inherent control of a physical sweep system:

- *Review target balances.* If a subsidiary account is allowed a target cash balance, then periodically review account usage to see if the target balance is appropriate.

- *Review excluded accounts.* Some subsidiary accounts may have been excluded from the sweep on the grounds that there are local currency restrictions, or that minimal transaction activity does not justify a periodic sweep. These factors may change over time, so schedule an annual analysis of excluded accounts.

- *Compare intercompany loan rates to market rates.* If the company uses nonmarket interest rates when calculating intercompany charges, it may run afoul of transfer pricing rules in some tax jurisdictions. Thus, create a tracking procedure to periodically compare market rates to the intercompany loan rates.

- *Verify the allocation of interest income to subsidiaries.* Depending on the circumstances, it may be necessary to allocate interest earned back to the subsidiaries. If so, verify that the calculation is consistently applied across all subsidiaries.

- *Verify the calculation of intercompany loan balances.* A company using physical sweeping may need to record intercompany loan balances to reflect the shifts in cash to the corporate consolidation account. If so, have the internal audit staff periodically verify the calculation of these balances. This review can impact the amount of interest expense or income allocated to subsidiaries.

A notional pooling system does not create an inherent control over physical cash balances, as was the case with a physical sweep, since cash is still sitting in what may be a large number of accounts in multiple locations. Thus, all controls normally exercised over a bank account would be in effect in this situation. The primary change with notional pooling is the presence of interest income distributions back to the originating bank accounts. This calls for a repetition of a preceding control, which is:

- *Verify the allocation of interest income to subsidiaries.* Depending on the circumstances, it may be necessary to allocate interest earned back to the subsidiaries. If so, verify that the calculation is consistently applied across all subsidiaries.

The receipt and disbursement of cash involve intricate controls, which are beyond the scope of this book. For detailed cash controls, refer to the author's *Accounting Control Best Practices,* 2nd edition (Wiley, 2009). The controls noted here were specific just to the cash concentration function.

CASH CONCENTRATION POLICIES

There is one key policy required for cash concentration, which is one that places responsibility for cash concentration on a specific group within the company. Otherwise, it can be extremely difficult to exert central control over far-flung accounts that are normally under the control of the managers of local subsidiaries. The policy follows:

- *All cash concentration activities shall be managed by the corporate treasury department.* This can be a surprisingly important policy in a larger firm where divisional managers may attempt to retain control over their bank accounts. The policy clearly places responsibility for cash concentration in the hands of the *corporate* treasury department.

Of course, a deliberate decentralization policy could revise the preceding policy to state that cash concentration activities are limited to a lower level within the company, such as at the division level.

It is also possible, though not necessary, to state the company's cash concentration strategy with a policy statement. Doing so certainly clarifies the company's direction in this area, but also requires a subsequent policy change if the treasurer wants to turn in a different direction. Strategies for both small and large companies are noted in the following two policies:

1. *Small-company policy.* The company shall engage in cash concentration with a "physical sweeping" strategy. All subsidiary accounts shall be designated as zero-balance, and shall sweep into a concentration account, which in turn shall also be used as a central disbursement account. The treasurer may exclude accounts from this strategy if sweeping is not cost-effective. This policy works well for smaller entities using a single currency, in locations where notional pooling is not available.

2. *Large-company policy.* The company shall engage in cash concentration with a "cross-currency notional pooling" strategy. All subsidiaries are restricted to accounts with a bank designated by the treasurer. In areas where notional pooling is not available, the treasurer may opt for physical sweeping, or no sweeping if it is not cost-effective. This policy assumes that notional pooling will be organized under a single global bank, and provides for the inevitable exceptions that will arise in some jurisdictions.

It is not necessary at the policy level to define any greater level of detail regarding cash concentration, such as the allowable methods of cash transfer for physical sweeping—these are tactical issues over which the treasury staff should have discretion.

CASH CONCENTRATION PROCEDURES

Once a cash concentration system is set up, the system should be fully auto-mated, with cash balances either shifting to a concentration account with physical sweeping or appearing in a notional account with a notional pooling arrangement. Thus, there is no need for a procedure to conduct the cash concentration. However, procedures *are* needed to track intercompany loans and related interest expense allocations (if physical sweeping is used), as well as to allocate interest income back to the subsidiaries. These procedures are noted in Exhibits 4.4 and 4.5.

Exhibit 4.4   Intercompany Loan Tracking Procedure

Procedure Statement   Retrieval No.: TREASURY-02

Subject: Tracking of Intercompany Loans and Allocation of Related Interest Expense Caused by Physical Sweeping

1. PURPOSE AND SCOPE

This procedure is used by the treasury staff to determine the amount of intercompany loans caused by the sweeping of cash from subsidiary accounts into the corporate cash concentration account, as well as the amount of inter-nal interest charges related to these loans.

2. PROCEDURES

2.1 Record Intercompany Loans (Treasury Staff)

1. At the end of each month, access the company's bank statements and calculate the amount of intercompany loans outstanding from each subsidiary to the corporate entity that was caused by physical sweeps into the corporate cash concentration account. Add to this amount the balance of any intercompany loans that were outstand-ing at the beginning of the month.
2. Subtract from the revised intercompany loan balances the amount of any expenditures related to each subsidiary for disbursements from the corporate shared services centers for payroll and disbursements.
3. Subtract from the remaining intercompany loan balances the amount of any cash flows from corporate to the subsidiaries for other purposes, such as debit balance replenishment.
4. Calculate the incremental change in intercompany loan balances, and create a journal entry to reflect the change. If there is an increase in a subsidiary's loan to corporate, then this is a debit to their notes receivable account and a credit to corporate loans payable. If there is a decrease in a subsidiary's loan to corporate, then this entry is reversed.

5. Also calculate the average loan balance outstanding during the month, which is calculated [*on a daily basis / by adding the beginning and ending balances and dividing by two*], which shall be used for subsequent allocations of interest income or expense.
6. Retain a copy of the calculations for use during the next month's calculations.
7. Forward the intercompany loan calculations to the treasurer for approval.
8. Forward the approved calculations and journal entry to the general ledger accountant for entry into the accounting system.

2.2 Allocate Interest Expense (Treasury Staff)

1. Determine the market interest rate on debt, which is the monthly interest rate charged to the company on its primary line of credit.
2. Calculate the intercompany interest expense to be charged to corporate for use of the subsidiary's funds, and credited to the subsidiaries, based on the market interest rate multiplied by their average intercompany loans outstanding during the month.
3. Create a journal entry to reflect the interest expense, which is a debit to the corporate interest expense account, and a credit to the subsidiary's interest income accounts. If there is a net flow of cash *to* a subsidiary, then this entry is reversed.
4. Retain a copy of the calculations.
5. Forward the interest expense calculations and journal entry to the treasurer for approval.
6. Forward the approved calculation and journal entry to the general ledger accountant for entry into the accounting system.

Exhibit 4.5   Interest Income Allocation from Cash Concentration Account

Procedure Statement   Retrieval No.: TREASURY-03

Subject: Calculation and Recording of Interest Income from Cash Concentration Account

1. PURPOSE AND SCOPE

This procedure is used by the treasury staff to calculate the interest income earned from the investment of cash concentration activities, less administrative charges.

2. PROCEDURES

2.1 Calculate Allocable Interest Income (Treasury Staff)

1. Summarize interest income earned for the month, as reported on investment statements.

2. Record the interest income as corporate income, with a debit to cash and credit to the interest income account. Have the entry approved by the treasurer, and forward to the general ledger accountant for entry into the accounting system.
3. Calculate the amount of administrative expense that is associated with the administration of cash concentration and subsequent investment activities. This should include bank pooling fees and loaded labor expenses. Compare this expense to the amount for previous months to establish the reasonableness of the amount.
4. Subtract the administrative expense from the total interest earned.
5. Allocate the remaining interest earned to the subsidiaries, based on the proportional average amount of intercompany loans they had outstanding to the parent company during the month. This is a debit to the corporate interest income account, and a credit to the interest income accounts of the subsidiaries.
6. Combine the interest allocation, administrative fee calculation, and copies of investment statements into a package, and retain a copy for backup purposes.
7. Forward the originals of the package to the treasurer for approval.
8. Forward the approved package to the general ledger accountant for entry into the accounting system.

SUMMARY

A company must determine if it makes sense to engage in cash concentration activities. For it to be cost-effective, the company should have large, ongoing balances in multiple accounts that are not being efficiently invested. Further, the incremental reduction in overdraft fees and increase in interest income should outweigh the incremental increase in pooling fees and administrative costs. There is also the intangible factor of whether the managers of local subsidiaries will accept corporate-level interference in their bank accounts. If this analysis is favorable, then a company should engage in cash concentration activities. While notional pooling is theoretically to be preferred over physical sweeping, either method is significantly better than having no pooling at all. Also, manual sweeping is not recommended; it involves a large volume of manually initiated transactions to transfer funds between accounts.The level of automation associated with these services mandates the use of a large bank with a broad range of automated services; a small local bank simply cannot assist a multilocation company with a cash concentration strategy.

5

Working Capital Management

When a company requires additional funding, the treasurer usually turns to either debt or an equity issuance. However, if the cost of these traditional funding sources is too high, the treasurer should take a hard look at unlocking cash that is trapped in working capital. While working capital management calls for a considerable amount of tactical work on an ongoing basis, it can be a rewarding exercise if the result is a significant source of cash. The following example shows how much cash can potentially be extracted from a company's working capital.

The following sections note how working capital tends to vary with changes in corporate sales volume, and then describe the key management aspects of each component of working capital that can impact the level of funds invested in working capital.

WORKING CAPITAL VARIABILITY

Working capital is defined as a company's current assets minus its current liabilities. While there are a number of minor asset and liability categories that can be included in this definition, the primary components of working capital are cash, accounts receivable, inventory, and accounts payable. All of these components tend to vary in proportion to the level of sales, but not at the same time. For example, if a company experiences high seasonal sales in its fourth quarter, then inventories and accounts payable will likely rise in advance of the prime selling season, while accounts receivable will increase during the fourth quarter and remain high through the early part of the first quarter of the following year. Cash will decline before the key sales season in order to pay for inventories, and will increase as receivables are collected, so that cash levels are maximized after the prime selling season is over. If a company is not profitable, the cash levels will not recover at the end of the prime selling season, but will instead remain low.

Carstensz Corporation is conducting due diligence on its possible purchase of the Hamilton Furniture Company. The acquisitions manager, Mr. Harrer, is interested in the possibility of reducing the amount of Hamilton's working capital, which can then be used to pay down the purchase price. Mr. Harrer uncovers the following information about Hamilton:

	Balances	Days Outstanding*	Industry Standard	Variance	Value of Variance
Annual revenues	$52,000,000	—	—	—	—
Annual cost of goods	26,000,000	—	—	—	—
Annual purchases	18,000,000	—	—	—	—
Average receivables	13,000,000	91	62	29	$4,143,000
Average payables	2,250,000	45	45	0	0
Average inventory	10,000,000	140	100	40	2,857,000
				Total	$7,000,000

The analysis shows that, if Carstensz were to buy Hamilton and reduce its receivable and inventory balances down to their industry averages, this would extract $7 million from working capital. Mr. Harrer is aware that the extended receivables may be caused by longer-term payment agreements with key customers, while it may take a considerable amount of time to reduce Hamilton's inventory levels, especially if it is comprised of slow-moving items. Nonetheless, it appears that careful management may unlock a considerable amount of cash.

*The formulas used in the table to calculate days outstanding are provided later in the Working Capital Metrics section of this chapter.

That example assumes that there is a sales peak during one part of a year, so that there is a natural ebb and flow to the amount of working capital needed. In that scenario, the treasurer can obtain a line of credit from a local bank, which should be sufficient to handle seasonal cash needs, and which can reliably be paid off once the peak period ends.

An alternative scenario is when a company's sales continue to increase over time, which occurs in an expanding market or as a company acquires market share from other entities. In this case, both inventory and receivable levels continually increase, while the corresponding increase in accounts payable will not be sufficient to hold down the overall level of working capital investment. All available cash will be used to pay for working capital, so that the cash balance is essentially zero, and new funds are continually needed as sales continue to increase. This is a demanding environment for the treasurer, who must look for long-term loans or equity infusions to help pay for the additional working capital.

A final scenario is when a company's sales are declining. As inventories are sold off and receivables are collected, cash may increase substantially, since there is less ongoing working capital to fund. This is the easiest scenario for the treasurer to deal with, since it is the only case where working capital becomes a net source of cash, which can then be applied to other company requirements.

The treasurer should also be aware of unusually high proportions of any one component of working capital, since this may be caused by improper management practices. For example, if the investment in inventory is usually high, this may correspond to an ongoing practice of purchasing in bulk in order to save per-unit costs. Similarly, a very high receivables balance may be caused by the use of special deals to boost sales over the short term or because revenues are being accrued but have not yet been billed. In such cases, the expanded working capital level is not related to sales, but rather to company policy. If funding sources are in short supply, the treasurer may be able to lobby for a policy change that eliminates the need for more cash.

The following five sections describe the various management practices that cause changes in working capital, and note actions the treasurer may take to control or at least monitor them.

CASH MANAGEMENT

Cash is a key component of working capital, and is thoroughly covered in Chapter 4. That chapter reveals how to concentrate cash through various pooling methods, so that the balances scattered in a multitude of bank accounts can be centrally marshaled for use by the treasurer.

CREDIT MANAGEMENT

There are no receivables unless a company elects to extend credit to its customers through a credit policy. Thus, proper credit management is key to the amount of funds that a company must invest in its accounts receivable.

A *loose credit policy* is common in companies having a certain mix of characteristics. For example, they may have high product margins, such as in the software industry, and so have little to lose if a customer defaults on payment. Also, they may be intent on gaining market share, and so will "buy" sales with a loose credit policy, which essentially means they give liberal credit to everyone. Another variation is that a company may be eliminating a product line or exiting an industry, and so is willing to take some losses on credit defaults in exchange for selling off its inventory as expeditiously as possible. In all of these cases, a company has a specific reason for extending an inordinate amount of credit, even though it knows there will be above-average credit defaults.

A *tight credit policy* is common in the reverse circumstances; product margins are small, or the industry is an old one with little room to gain market share. Also, a recessionary environment may require a firm to restrict its credit policy, on the assumption that customers will have less money available to make timely payments.

Any change in a company's credit policy can have a profound effect on the funding requirements that a treasurer must deal with. For example, if a $48 million (revenues) company has receivables with an average age of 30 days, and its wants to enact a looser credit policy that will increase the average receivable days to 45 days, then the company's investment in receivables is going to increase by 50 percent, from $4 million to $6 million. Consequently, the treasurer must be prepared to find $2 million to fund this increase in working capital.

In many companies, the treasurer has direct control over the credit policy and, indeed, over the entire credit granting function. This is a wise placement of responsibility, since the treasurer can now see both sides of the credit policy—both the resulting change in sales and the offsetting change in required working capital funds.

The treasurer can set up a considerable number of credit controls to reduce the probability of default by customers. Here are some possibilities:

- *Issue credit based on credit scoring.* There are several credit-monitoring services, such as Experian and Dun & Bradstreet, which provide online credit scores on most larger businesses. The treasury staff can create a credit-granting model that is based on a mix of the credit scores of these services, the company's history with each customer, and the amount of credit requested.

- *Alter payment terms.* If a customer requests an inordinate amount of credit, it may be possible to alter the payment terms to accommodate the customer while still reducing the level of credit risk. For example, one-half of a sale can be made with 15-day payment terms, with the remainder of the order to be shipped upon receipt of payment for the first half of the order. This results in payment of the total order in 30 days, but with half the risk.

- *Offer financing by a third party.* If the treasury department is unwilling to extend credit, then perhaps a third party is willing to do so. This can be a leasing company or perhaps even a distributor with a loose credit policy.

- *Require guarantees.* There is a variety of possible payment guarantees that can be extracted from a customer, such as a personal guarantee by an owner, a guarantee by a corporate parent, or a letter of credit from a bank.

- *Perfect a security interest in goods sold.* It may be possible to create a security agreement with a customer in which the goods being sold are listed, which the company then files in the jurisdiction where the goods reside. This gives the company a senior position ahead of general creditors in the event of default by the customer.

- *Obtain credit insurance.* Credit insurance is a guarantee by a third party against nonpayment by a customer. It can be used for both domestic and international receivables. The cost of credit insurance can exceed one-half percent of the invoiced amount, with higher costs for riskier customers and substantially lower rates for customers who are considered to be in excellent financial condition.

- *Require a credit reexamination upon an initiating event.* The treasury staff should review customer credit at regular intervals to see if they still deserve existing credit limits. These reviews can be triggered when the current credit limit is exceeded, if a customer places an order after a long interval of inactivity, if there is an unjustified late payment, or if a customer stops taking early payment discounts.

An active treasury staff that manages the credit function can use the preceding list of credit practices to retain the appropriate level of control over accounts receivable and the corresponding amount of working capital funding.

RECEIVABLES MANAGEMENT

Once credit has been granted to a customer, responsibility for billing and collecting from the customer usually passes to the accounting department. The ability of the accounting staff to reliably invoice and collect in a timely manner has a major impact on the amount of working capital invested in accounts receivable. The treasurer does not have direct control over these functions but should be aware of the following factors, which can seriously extend customer payment intervals unless carefully managed:

- *Invoicing delay.* Invoices should be issued immediately after the related goods or services have been provided. If the accounting staff is billing only at stated intervals, then receivables are being extended just because of an internal accounting work policy.

- *Invoicing errors.* If invoices are being continually reissued due to errors, then additional controls are needed to increase the accuracy of initial invoices. This can be a serious issue, since invoicing errors are usually found by the customer, which may be several weeks after they were originally issued.

- *Invoice transmission.* There is a multiday mailing delay when invoices are delivered through the postal service. Instead, the accounting system should be configured to issue invoices by email or electronic data interchange, or the accounting staff should manually email invoices.

- *Lockbox receipt.* If checks are received at the company location and then sent to the bank, this creates a delay of potentially several days before the checks are processed internally, deposited, and then clear the bank. Instead, customers should send all checks to a lockbox, so that checks are deposited in the minimum amount of time, thereby increasing the availability of funds.

- *Collection management.* There should be a well-trained collection staff that assigns responsibility for specific accounts, focuses on the largest overdue account balances first, begins talking to customers immediately after payment due dates are reached, and is supported by collection software systems. The group should use a broad array of collection techniques, including dunning letters, on-site visits, attorney letters, payment commitment letters, credit holds, and collection agencies.

- *Internal error follow-up.* If payments are being delayed due to service problems by the company or product flaws, the collection staff should have a tracking system in place that stores the details of these problems, and the accounting manager should follow up with managers elsewhere in the company to have them resolved.

The treasurer can periodically inquire of the controller if these collection issues are being managed properly. Another approach is to obtain an accounts receivable aging report and determine the reasons why overdue receivables have not yet been paid. At a minimum, the treasurer should track the days receivables outstanding on a timeline, and follow up with the controller or chief financial officer if the metric increases over time.

INVENTORY MANAGEMENT

Of all the components of working capital, inventory management is the most critical because it is the least liquid and therefore tends to be a cash trap. Once funds have been spent on inventory, the time period required to convert it back into cash can be quite long, so it is extremely important to invest in the smallest possible amount of inventory.

Responsibility for inventory resides with the materials management department, which controls purchasing, manufacturing planning, and warehousing. None of these areas are ones over which the treasurer traditionally exercises control. Nonetheless, the treasurer should be aware of activities related to inventory management, because they can have a profound impact on the level of funding needed for working capital. The following topics address a number of areas in which inventory decisions impact funding.

Inventory Purchasing

When the purchasing department orders inventory from suppliers, it asks them for the lead time they need to deliver orders and then creates a *safety stock* level to at least match the lead time. For example, if a supplier says that it needs two weeks to deliver goods, and the company uses $100,000 of its inventory per week, then the purchasing department creates a safety stock level of at least $200,000 to keep the company running while it waits for the next delivery. This lead time therefore requires $200,000 of funding. The treasurer should be aware that extremely distant foreign sourcing, such as to Asia, will drastically lengthen lead times and therefore the amount of safety stock. Conversely, if a company can source its inventory needs from suppliers located very close to the company and work with them to reduce their lead times and increase the frequency of their deliveries, this results in lowered safety stock and therefore a reduced need for funding.

Another contributor to long lead times is the manual processing of purchase orders to suppliers. If inventory needs are calculated by hand, then transferred to a purchase order, manually approved, and delivered by mail, then a company must retain more safety stock to cover for this additional delay. Conversely, if a company can install a *material requirements planning system* that automatically calculates inventory needs, creates purchase orders, and transmits them to suppliers electronically, then the ordering cycle is significantly reduced and corresponding lead times can be shortened.

The purchasing department orders inventory based on its estimates of what customers are going to buy. No matter how sophisticated, these estimates are bound to be incorrect to some extent, resulting in the purchase of excess inventory. To reduce this forecasting error, a company should attempt to *gain direct access to the inventory planning systems of key customers*. This gives the purchasing staff perfect information about what it, in turn, needs to order from its suppliers, and thereby reduces excess inventory levels.

It may also be possible to *shift raw material ownership to suppliers* so that they own the inventory located on the company's premises. Suppliers may agree to this scenario if the company sole-sources purchases from them. Under this arrangement, the company pays suppliers when it removes inventory from its warehouse, to either sell it or incorporate it into the manufacture of other goods. The resulting payment delay reduces the need for funding.

All of the preceding changes in purchasing practices can reduce a company's investment in inventory. Conversely, a purchasing practice that contributes to startling increases in funding requirements is the *bulk purchase of inventory*. If the purchasing staff is offered quantity discounts in exchange for large orders, they will be tempted to proclaim large per-unit cost reductions, not realizing that this calls for much more up-front cash and a considerable storage cost and risk of obsolescence.

Inventory Receiving

The receiving staff's procedures can have an impact on inventory-related funding. For example, a supplier may ship goods without an authorizing purchase order from the company. If the receiving staff accepts the delivery, then the company is obligated to pay for it. A better practice is to *reject all inbound deliveries that do not have a purchase order authorization*.

Another procedural issue is to require the *immediate entry of all receiving information* into the company's warehouse management system. If this is not done, the risk increases that the receipt will never be recorded due to lost or misplaced paperwork. The purchasing staff will see that the inventory never arrived and may order additional goods to compensate—which requires more funding. Similarly, a procedure should call for the immediate put-away of inventory items following their receipt, on the grounds that they can become lost in the staging area.

Inventory Storage

In a traditional system, inventory arrives from suppliers, is stored in the company warehouse, and is shipped when ordered by customers. The company is funding the inventory for as long as it sits in the warehouse waiting for a customer order. A better method is to avoid the warehouse entirely by using *drop shipping*. Under this system, a company receives an order from a customer and contacts its supplier with the shipping information, who in turn ships the product directly to the customer. This is a somewhat cumbersome process and may result in longer delivery times, but it completely eliminates the company's investment in inventory and therefore all associated funding needs. This option is available only to inventory resellers.

Another option that severely reduces the amount of inventory retention time is *cross-docking*. Under cross-docking, when an item arrives at the receiving dock, it is immediately moved to a shipping dock for delivery to the customer in a different truck. There is no put-away or picking transaction, and no long-term storage, which also reduces the risk of damage to the inventory. Cross-docking only works when there is excellent control over the timing of in-bound deliveries, so the warehouse management system knows when items will arrive. It also requires multiple extra loading docks, since trailers may have to be kept on-site longer than normal while loads are accumulated from several inbound deliveries.

Production Issues Impacting Inventory

The production process is driven by several procedural, policy, and setup issues that strongly impact the amount of inventory and therefore the level of funding.

The traditional manufacturing system is geared toward very long production runs, on the justification that this results in the spreading of fixed costs over a large number of units, which yields the lowest possible cost per unit. The logic is flawed, because such large production runs also yield too much inventory, which then sits in stock and runs the significant risk of obsolescence. To reduce the funding requirement of this excess inventory, a company should produce to demand, which is exemplified by the *just-in-time (JIT) manufacturing system*. A JIT system triggers an authorization to produce only if an order is received from a customer, so there is never any excess inventory on hand. Though a JIT system initially appears to generate higher per-unit costs, the eliminated carrying cost of inventory makes it considerably less expensive. And, from the treasurer's perspective, a JIT system can release a great deal of cash from inventory.

Another production issue is to *avoid volume-based incentive pay systems*. Some companies pay their employees more if they produce more. Not only does this result in extremely high levels of inventory, but these pay systems tend to yield lower-quality goods, since employees favor higher volume over higher quality. A reasonable alternative is an incentive to exactly meet the production plan. If the plan is derived from a JIT system, then employees are producing only to match existing customer orders, which keep funding requirements low.

A related issue is the use of complex, high-capacity machinery. Industrial engineers enjoy these machines because they feature impressively high throughput rates. However, they also require immense production volumes in order to justify their initial and ongoing maintenance costs, which once again results in the accumulation of too much inventory. Instead, the treasurer should favor the *acquisition of smaller, simpler machines having lower maintenance costs*. Such machines can be operated profitably with very small production runs, thereby making it easier to drive down inventory levels.

A simple method for reducing work-in-process inventory is to *use smaller container sizes*. Typically, an employee at a workstation fills a container and then moves it to the next downstream workstation. If the container is a large one, and if there are many workstations using the same size container, then a great deal of work-in-process inventory is being unnecessarily accumulated. By shifting to a smaller container size, the inventory invest-ment is reduced, as is the amount of scrap—because the downstream work-station operator is more likely to spot faults originating in an upstream location more quickly if containers are delivered more frequently.

When a machine requires a substantial amount of time to be switched over to a new configuration for the production of a different part, there is a natural tendency to have very long production runs of the same part in order to spread the cost of the changeover across as many parts as possible. This practice results in too much inventory, so the solution is to *reduce machine setup times* to such an extent that it becomes practicable to have production runs of as little as one unit. Setup reduction can be accomplished by using changeover consultants, process videotaping, quick-release fasten-ers, color-coded parts, standardized tools, and so forth.

A common arrangement of machines on the shop floor is by functional group, where machines of one type are clustered in one place. By doing so, jobs requiring a specific type of processing can all be routed to the same cluster of machines and loaded into whichever one becomes available for processing next. However, by doing so, there tend to be large batches of work-in-process inventory piling up behind each machine because this approach calls for the completion of a job at one workstation before the entire job is moved to the next workstation. A better layout is provided by *cellular manufacturing*, where a small cluster of machines are set up in close proximity to one another, each one performing a sequential task in complet-ing a specific type or common set of products. Usually, only a few employees work in each cell and walk a single part all the way through the cell before moving on to the next part. By doing so, there is obviously only the most minimal work-in-process inventory in the cell.

The Bill of Materials

A bill of materials is the record of the materials used to construct a product. It is exceedingly worthwhile to examine the bills of material with the objec-tive of reducing inventory. For example, a bill may contain an excess quan-tity of a part. If so, and the underlying purchase order system automatically places orders for parts, the bill will be used to order too many parts, thereby increasing inventory levels. A *periodic audit of all bills*, where the reviewer compares each bill to a disassembled product, will reveal such errors. For the same reason, the estimated scrap listed in all bills of material should be compared to actual scrap levels; if the estimated scrap level is too high, then the bill will call for too much inventory to be ordered for the next produc-tion run.

A significant bill of materials issue from the perspective of inventory reduction is the *substitution of parts*. This may occur when the engineering staff issues an engineering change order, specifying a reconfiguration of the parts that form a product. Ideally, the materials management staff should draw down all remaining inventory stocks under the old bill of materials before implementing the new change order. If this is not done, then the company will have a remainder stock of raw materials inventory for which there are no disposition plans.

Product Design

There are a number of design decisions that have a considerable impact on the size of a company's investment in inventory. A key factor is the *number of product options* offered. If there are a multitude of options, then a company may find it necessary to stock every variation on the product, which calls for a substantial inventory investment. If, however, it is possible to limit the number of options, then inventory volumes can be substantially reduced. A similar issue is the *number of products* offered. If there is an enormous range of product offerings, it is quite likely that only a small proportion of the total generate a profit; the remainder requires large inventory holdings in return for minimal sales volume.

Customer Service

A company may feel that its primary method of competition is to provide excellent customer service, which requires it to never have a stockout condition for any inventory item. This may require an inordinate amount of finished goods inventory. This policy should be reviewed regularly, with an analysis of the inventory cost required to maintain such a high level of order fulfillment.

Inventory Disposition

Even if a company has built up a large proportion of obsolete inventory, continuing attention to an *inventory disposition program* can result in the recovery of a substantial amount of cash. The first step in this program is to create a materials review board, which is comprised of members of the materials management, engineering, and accounting departments. This group is responsible for determining which inventory items can be used in-house and the most cost-effective type of disposition for those items that cannot be used. This may involve sending inventory back to suppliers for a restocking charge, sales to salvage contractors, sales as repair parts through the service department, or even donating them to a nonprofit in exchange for a tax credit. Throwing out inventory is frequently better than keeping it, since retention requires the ongoing use of valuable warehouse space.

Payables Management

The processing and payment policies of the accounts payable function can have a resounding impact on the amount of funds invested in working capital. Payables processing is managed by the accounting department, and payment terms by the purchasing department. The treasurer does not have control over either function but should be aware of the following issues that can impact funding requirements.

Payment Terms

As part of its negotiations with suppliers, the purchasing staff may try to extend payment terms. This is certainly an advantage for the treasurer, since extended terms equate to free funding by suppliers. However, extended terms may be at the cost of higher per-unit prices, which the controller may not favor at all.

The reverse situation also arises, where suppliers negotiate for more rapid payment terms. This is particularly common for large and powerful suppliers that have near-monopoly control over their industries. It is also common when a company's financial condition is poor enough that suppliers insist on short payment terms or even cash in advance. While the treasurer may not be able to mitigate such onerous terms, he or she should certainly be made aware of them, so that the resulting decline in cash flows from working capital can be properly planned for.

Payment Processing

The accounting department may pay suppliers only at stated intervals, such as once a week. If so, an internal policy likely governs whether payments that are not quite due will be covered in the current payment period or the next one. This is of some importance, since paying anything prior to its due date will shrink the funding normally made available through accounts payable.

The accounting staff may also have a policy of taking all early payment discounts. Such discounts normally equate to a significant rate of interest, and so are highly favorable to the company and should be taken. Nonetheless, paying a very large supplier invoice early in order to take advantage of a discount may significantly impact the borrowing activities of the treasurer. Consequently, there should be a system in place to notify the treasury staff in advance of the amount and timing of unusually large discounts.

Intercompany Netting

If a company has multiple subsidiaries, it is possible that they do a significant amount of business with each other. If so, there could be a substantial volume of billings between them. The best way to deal with these intercompany payments is to net them out through the accounting system so that actual cash transfers are minimized. If each subsidiary uses a separate accounting system, then intercompany netting can be quite a chore. However, if they all operate under a single accounting system, then the software can automatically handle this task.

Supply Chain Financing

Under supply chain financing, a company sends its approved payables list to its bank, specifying the dates on which invoice payments are to be made. The bank makes these payments on behalf of the company. However, in addition to this basic payables function, the bank contacts the company's suppliers with an offer of early payment, in exchange for a financing charge for the period until maturity. If a supplier agrees with this arrangement and signs a receivables sale contract, then the bank delivers payment from its own funds to the supplier, less its fee. Once the company's payment dates are reached, the bank removes the funds from the company's account, transferring some of the cash to those customers electing to be paid on the prearrangement settlement date and transferring the remaining funds to its own account to pay for those invoices that it paid early to suppliers at a discount.

This arrangement works very well for suppliers, since they may be in need of early settlement. In addition, they receive a much higher percentage of invoice face value than would be the case if they opted for a factoring arrangement with a third party, where 80 percent of the invoice is typically the maximum amount that will be advanced. The amount of the discount offered by the bank may be quite small if the company is a large and well-funded entity having excellent credit. Finally, the arrangement is usually nonrecourse for the supplier, since the arrangement with the bank is structured as a receivables assignment.

The arrangement also works well for the bank, which has excellent visibility into the company's bank balances and cash flow history, and so knows when it can offer such financing. Also, it obtains fees from the company in exchange for disbursing funds on behalf of the company.

This is also a good deal for the company, whose suppliers now have ready access to funds. Further, since the bank is contacting suppliers with payment dates, they will no longer make inquiries of the company regarding when they will be paid.

Supply chain financing is less useful when payment terms are relatively short, since there is not much benefit for suppliers in being paid just a few days early. However, it is an excellent tool when standard payment terms are quite long.

Since supply chain financing is arranged with the company's primary bank, and the treasurer is in charge of banking relations, this is one payables area in which the treasurer can provide a considerable amount of value to the company and its suppliers.

WORKING CAPITAL METRICS

This section contains four metrics for working capital, which the treasurer can use to form an opinion regarding the amount of receivables, inventory, and payables that a company is maintaining. There is no right or wrong result of these metrics, since they are tied to a company's policies for granting credit, order fulfillment, and so on. Nonetheless, the treasurer should track these metrics on a trend line to see if working capital levels are changing. The same trend line will reveal the results of the working capital improvement tactics noted earlier in this chapter.

Average Receivable Collection Period

This measurement expresses the average number of days that accounts receivable are outstanding. This format is particularly useful when it is compared to the standard number of days of credit granted to customers. For example, if the average collection period is 60 days and the standard days of credit is 30, then customers are taking much too long to pay their invoices. A sign of good performance is when the average receivable collection period is only a few days longer than the standard days of credit.

To calculate the average receivable collection period, divide annual credit sales by 365 days, and divide the result into average accounts receivable. The formula is as follows:

$$\frac{\text{Average Accounts Receivable}}{\text{Annual Sales}/365}$$

Example

The new controller of the Flexo Paneling Company, makers of modularized office equipment, wants to determine the company's accounts receivable collection period. In the June accounting period, the beginning accounts receivable balance was $318,000, and the ending balance was $383,000. Sales for May and June totaled $625,000. Based on this information, the controller calculates the average receivable collection period as follows:

$$\frac{\text{Average Accounts Receivable}}{\text{Annual Sales}/365}$$

$$= \frac{(\$318,000 \text{ Beginning Receivables} + \$383,000 \text{ Ending Receivables})/2}{(\$625,000 \times 6)/365}$$

$$= \frac{\$350,500 \text{ Average Accounts Receivable}}{\$10,273 \text{ Sales per Day}}$$

$$= \underline{\underline{34.1}} \text{ Days}$$

Note that the controller derived the annual sales figure used in the denominator by multiplying the two-month sales period in May and June by six. Since the company has a stated due date of 30 days after the billing date, the 34.1 day collection period appears reasonable.

The main issue with this calculation is what figure to use for annual sales. If the total sales for the year are used, this may result in a skewed measurement, since the sales associated with the current outstanding accounts receivable may be significantly higher or lower than the average level of sales represented by the annual sales figure. This problem is especially common when sales are highly seasonal. A better approach is to annualize the sales figure for the period covered by the bulk of the existing accounts receivable.

Inventory Turnover

Inventory is frequently the largest component of a company's working capital; in such situations, if inventory is not being used up by operations at a reasonable pace, then a company has invested a large part of its cash in an asset that may be difficult to liquidate in short order. Accordingly, keeping close track of the rate of inventory turnover is a significant function of management. There are several variations on the inventory turnover measurement, which may be combined to yield the most complete turnover reporting for management to peruse. In all cases, these measurements should be tracked on a trend line in order to see if there are gradual reductions in the rate of turnover, which can indicate to management that corrective action is required in order to eliminate excess inventory stocks.

The simplest turnover calculation is to divide the period-end inventory into the annualized cost of sales. One can also use an *average* inventory figure in the denominator, which avoids sudden changes in the inventory level that are likely to occur on any specific period-end date. The formula is as follows:

$$\frac{\text{Cost of Goods Sold}}{\text{Inventory}}$$

A variation on the preceding formula is to divide it into 365 days, which yields the number of days of inventory on hand. This may be more understandable to the layman; for example, 43 days of inventory is more clear than 8.5 inventory turns, even though they represent the same situation. The formula is as follows:

$$365 \div \frac{\text{Cost of Goods Sold}}{\text{Inventory}}$$

The preceding two formulas use the entire cost of goods sold in the numerator, which includes direct labor, direct materials, and overhead. However, only direct materials costs directly relate to the level of raw materials inventory. Consequently, a cleaner relationship is to compare the value of direct materials expense to raw materials inventory, yielding a raw materials turnover figure. This measurement can also be divided into 365 days in

order to yield the number of days of raw materials on hand. The formula
is as follows:

$$\frac{\text{Direct Materials Expense}}{\text{Raw Materials Inventory}}$$

The preceding formula does not yield as clean a relationship between
direct materials expense and work-in-process or finished goods, since these
two categories of inventory also include cost allocations for direct labor and
overhead. However, if these added costs can be stripped out of the work-in-
process and finished goods valuations, then there are reasonable grounds
for comparing them to the direct materials expense as a valid ratio.

Example

The Rotary Mower Company, maker of the only lawnmower driven by a
Wankel rotary engine, is going through its annual management review of
inventory. Its treasurer has the following information:

Balance Sheet Line Item	Amount
Cost of goods sold	$4,075,000
Direct materials expense	1,550,000
Raw materials inventory	388,000
Total inventory	815,000

To calculate total inventory turnover, the treasurer creates the following
calculation:

$$\frac{\text{Cost of Goods Sold}}{\text{Inventory}}$$

$$= \frac{\$4,075,000 \text{ Cost of Goods Sold}}{\$815,000 \text{ Inventory}} = \underline{\underline{5}} \text{ Turns per Year}$$

To determine the number of days of inventory on hand, the treasurer
divides the number of turns per year into 365 days, as follows:

$$365 \div \frac{\text{Cost of Goods Sold}}{\text{Inventory}}$$

$$= 365 \div \frac{\$4,075,000 \text{ Cost of Goods}}{\$815,000 \text{ Inventory}} = \underline{\underline{73}} \text{ Days of Inventory}$$

The treasurer is also interested in the turnover level of raw materials when
compared to just direct materials expenses. He determines this amount with
the following calculation:

$$\frac{\text{Direct Materials Expense}}{\text{Raw Materials Inventory}}$$

$$= \frac{\$1,550,000 \text{ Direct Materials Expense}}{\$388 \text{ Raw Materials Inventory}} = \underline{\underline{4}} \text{ Turns Per Year}$$

The next logical step for the treasurer is to compare these results to those for previous years, as well as to the results achieved by other companies in the industry. One result that is probably not good in any industry is the comparison of direct materials to raw materials inventory, which yielded only four turns per year. This means that the average component sits in the warehouse for 90 days prior to being used, which is far too long if any reliable materials planning system is used.

The turnover ratio can be skewed by changes in the underlying costing methods used to allocate direct labor, and especially overhead cost pools, to the inventory. For example, if additional categories of costs are added to the overhead cost pool, then the allocation to inventory will increase, which will reduce the reported level of inventory turnover—even though the turnover level under the original calculation method has not changed at all. The problem can also arise if the method of allocating costs is changed; for example, it may be shifted from an allocation based on labor hours worked to one based on machine hours worked, which can alter the total amount of overhead costs assigned to inventory. The problem can also arise if the inventory valuation is based on standard costs and the underlying standards are altered. In all three cases, the amount of inventory on hand has not changed, but the costing systems used have altered the reported level of inventory costs, which impacts the reported level of turnover.

A separate issue is that the basic inventory turnover figure may not be sufficient evidence of exactly where an inventory overage problem may lie. Accordingly, one can subdivide the measurement so that there are separate calculations for raw materials, work-in-process, and finished goods (and perhaps be subdivided further by location). This approach allows for more precise management of inventory-related problems.

Accounts Payable Days

A calculation of the days of accounts payable gives a fair indication of a company's ability to pay its bills on time. If the accounts payable days are inordinately long, this is probably a sign that the company does not have sufficient cash flow to pay its bills. Alternatively, a small amount of accounts payable days indicates that a company is either taking advantage of early payment discounts or is simply paying its bills earlier than it has to.

The calculation is to divide total annualized purchases by 360 days, and then divide the result into the ending accounts payable balance. An alternative approach is to use the *average* accounts payable for the reporting period, since the ending figure may be disproportionately high or low. The amount of purchases should be derived from all nonpayroll expenses incurred during the year; payroll is not included because it is not a part of the accounts payable listed in the numerator. Depreciation and amortization should be excluded from the purchases figure, since they do not involve cash payments. The formula follows:

$$\frac{\text{Accounts Payable}}{\text{Purchases}/360}$$

Example

The Drain-Away Toilet Company has beginning accounts payable of $145,000 and ending accounts payable of $157,000. On an annualized basis, its total expenses are $2,400,000, of which $600,000 is payroll and $50,000 is depreciation. To determine its accounts payable days, we plug this information into the following formula:

$$\frac{(\text{Beginning Accounts Payable} + \text{Ending Accounts Payable})/2}{(\text{Total Expenses} - \text{Payroll} - \text{Depreciation})/360}$$

$$= \frac{(\$145,000 \text{ Beginning Payables} + \$157,000 \text{ Ending Payables})/2}{(\$2,400,000 \text{ Total Expenses} - \$600,000 \text{ Payroll} - \$50,000 \text{ Depreciation})/360}$$

$$= \frac{\$151,000 \text{ Average Accounts Payable}}{\$1,750,000 \text{ Purchases}/360} = \underline{\underline{31}} \text{ Days}$$

The most difficult part of this formulation is determining the amount of annualized purchases. If a company has an irregular flow of business over the course of a year, then estimating the amount of purchases can be quite difficult. In such cases, annualizing the amount of purchases for just the past month or two will yield the most accurate comparison to the current level of accounts payable, since these purchases are directly reflected within the accounts payable in the numerator.

Days of Working Capital

A company can use a very large amount of working capital to generate a small volume of sales, which represents a poor use of assets. The inefficient asset use can lie in any part of working capital—excessive quantities of accounts receivable or inventory in relation to sales, or very small amounts of accounts payable. The days of working capital measure, when tracked on a trend line, is a good indicator of changes in the efficient use of working capital. A low number of days of working capital indicates a highly efficient use of working capital.

To calculate days of working capital, add together the current balance of accounts receivable and inventory, and subtract accounts payable. Then divide the result by sales per day (annual sales divided by 365). The formula follows:

$$\frac{(\text{Accounts Receivable} + \text{Inventory} - \text{Accounts Payable})}{\text{Net Sales}/365}$$

Example

The Electro-Therm Company, maker of electronic thermometers, has altered its customer service policy to guarantee a 99 percent fulfillment rate within one day of a customer's order. To do that, it has increased inventory levels for many stock-keeping units. Electro-Therm's treasurer is concerned about the company's use of capital to sustain this new policy; she has collected the information in the following table to prove her point to the company president:

Time Period	Accounts Receivable	Inventory	Accounts Payable	Working Capital	Net Sales	Sales per Day	Days of Working Capital
Year before policy change	602,000	1,825,000	493,000	2,920,000	5,475,000	15,000	195
Year after policy change	723,000	2,760,000	591,000	4,074,000	6,570,000	18,000	226

The table reveals that Electro-Therm's management has acquired an additional $1,095,000 of revenue (assuming that incremental sales are solely driven by the customer service policy change) at the cost of a nearly equivalent amount of investment in inventory. Depending on the firm's cost of capital, inventory obsolescence rate, and changes in customer retention rates, the new customer service policy may or may not be considered a reasonable decision.

SUMMARY

One of the largest uses of cash within a company is its working capital. Though the treasurer does not have direct control over many aspects of working capital, he should be aware of the multitude of internal policies, controls, and systems that, in large part, are responsible for changes in the size of working capital, and which he may be able to influence. Of particular importance is a company's credit policy; a suddenly loosened credit policy can spark a rapid increase in the amount of working capital. Conversely, if a company is in need of cash in the short term, a well-managed tightening of the credit policy can provide the needed funds. Inventory is the most dangerous component of working capital because it can build rapidly unless properly controlled and can be quite difficult to convert back into cash.

The treasurer should monitor all components of working capital on a trend line, in comparison to revenue levels, and against industry benchmarks. If a company's investment in working capital appears to be disproportionately high, the treasurer should bring this to the attention of senior management and recommend ways to reduce the investment.

PART TWO

FINANCING

6

Debt Management

The treasurer is usually called upon to either manage a company's existing debt or procure new debt. In either case, this calls for a knowledge of the broad variety of debt instruments available, as well as dealing with credit rating agencies. It may also be necessary to have a working knowledge of the accounting, controls, policies, and procedures used to manage debt. This chapter gives a thorough grounding in both key areas.

TYPES OF DEBT

The typical form of corporate debt is either a secured or unsecured loan, and many treasurers do not explore further than these two basic formats. However, there are quite a few alternative forms of debt that bear consideration, based on the duration of a company's cash needs, its financial condition, and the presence of various types of collateral. This section contains descriptions of more than a dozen forms of financing. In addition, please refer to Chapter 5 for a discussion of how to reduce working capital, thereby offsetting the need for debt.

Commercial Paper

Commercial paper is unsecured debt that is issued by a company and has a fixed maturity ranging from 1 to 270 days. A company uses commercial paper to meet its short-term working capital obligations. It is commonly sold at a discount from face value, with the discount (and therefore the interest rate) being higher if the term is longer. A company can sell its commercial paper directly to investors, such as money market funds, or through a dealer in exchange for a small commission.

Because there is no collateral on the debt, commercial paper is an option only for large companies having high-level credit ratings from a recognized credit rating agency (see the Credit-Rating Agencies section of this chapter). For those companies capable of issuing it, the interest rate on commercial paper is extremely low.

Factoring

Under a factoring arrangement, a finance company agrees to take over a company's accounts receivable collections and keep the money from those collections in exchange for an immediate cash payment to the company. This process typically involves having customers mail their payments to a lockbox that appears to be operated by the company but is actually controlled by the finance company. Under a true factoring arrangement, the finance company takes over the risk of loss on any bad debts, though it will have the right to pick which types of receivables it will accept in order to reduce its risk of loss. A finance company is more interested in this type of deal when the size of each receivable is fairly large, since this reduces its per-transaction cost of collection. If each receivable is quite small, the finance company may still be interested in a factoring arrangement, but it will charge the company extra for its increased processing work. The lender will charge an interest rate (at least 2 percent higher than the prime rate), as well as a transaction fee for processing each invoice as it is received. There may also be a minimum total fee charged, in order to cover the origination fee for the factoring arrangement in the event that few receivables are actually handed to the lender. A company working under this arrangement can be paid by the factor at once or can wait until the invoice due date before payment is sent. The latter arrangement reduces the interest expense that a company would have to pay the factor, but tends to go against the reason why the factoring arrangement was established, which is to get money back to the company as rapidly as possible. An added advantage is that no collections staff is required, since the lender handles this chore.

A similar arrangement is accounts receivable financing, under which a lender uses the accounts receivable as collateral for a loan and takes direct receipt of payments from customers, rather than waiting for periodic loan payments from the company. A lender will typically loan a maximum of only 80 percent of the accounts receivable balance to a company, and only against those accounts that are less than 90 days old. Also, if an invoice against which a loan has been made is not paid within the required 90-day time period, then the lender will require the company to pay back the loan associated with that invoice.

Though both variations on the factoring concept will accelerate a company's cash flow dramatically, it is an expensive financing option, and so is not considered a viable long-term approach to funding a company's operations. It is better for short-term growth situations where money is in short supply to fund a sudden need for working capital. A company's business partners may look askance at such an arrangement, since it is an approach associated with organizations that have severe cash flow problems.

Field Warehouse Financing

Under a field warehousing arrangement, a finance company (usually one that specializes in this type of arrangement) will segregate a portion of a company's warehouse area with a fence. All inventory within it is collateral for a loan from the finance company to the company. The finance company will pay for more raw materials as they are needed, and is paid back directly from accounts receivable as soon as customer payments are received. If a strict inventory control system is in place, the finance company will employ someone who will record all additions to and withdrawals from the secured warehouse. If not, then the company will be required to frequently count all items within the secure area and report this information back to the finance company. If the level of inventory drops below the amount of the loan, then the company must pay back the finance company the difference between the outstanding loan amount and the total inventory valuation. The company is also required under state lien laws to post signs around the secured area, stating that a lien is in place on its contents.

Field warehousing is highly transaction intensive, especially when the finance company employs an on-site warehouse clerk, and therefore is a very expensive way to obtain funds. This approach is recommended only for those companies that have exhausted all other less expensive forms of financing. However, lenders typically do not require any covenants in association with these loans, giving corporate management more control over company operations.

Floor Planning

Some lenders will directly pay for large assets that are being procured by a distributor or retailer (such as kitchen appliances or automobiles) and be paid back when the assets are sold to a consumer. In order to protect itself, the lender may require that the price of all assets sold be no lower than the price the lender originally paid for it on behalf of the distributor or retailer. Since the lender's basis for lending is strictly on the underlying collateral (as opposed to its faith in a business plan or general corporate cash flows), it will undertake frequent recounts of the assets, and compare them to its list of assets originally purchased for the distributor or retailer. If there is a shortfall in the expected number of assets, the lender will require payment for the missing items. The lender may also require liquidation of the loan after a specific time period, especially if the underlying assets run the risk of becoming outdated in the near term.

This financing option is a good one for smaller or underfunded distributors or retailers, since the interest rate is not excessive (due to the presence of collateral).

Lease

A lease covers the purchase of a specific asset, which is paid for by the lease provider on the company's behalf. In exchange, the company pays a fixed rate, which includes interest and principal, to the leasing company. It may also be charged for personal property taxes on the asset purchased. The lease may be defined as an *operating lease*, under the terms of which the lessor carries the asset on its books and records a depreciation expense, while the lessee records the lease payments as an expense on its books. This type of lease typically does not cover the full life of the asset, nor does the buyer have a small-dollar buyout option at the end of the lease. The reverse situation arises for a *capital lease*, where the lessee records it as an asset and is entitled to record all related depreciation as an expense. In the latter case, the lease payments are split into their interest and principal portions and recorded on the lessee's books as such.

The cost of a lease can be reduced by clumping together the purchases of multiple items under one lease, which greatly reduces the paperwork cost of the lender. If there are multiple leases currently in existence, they can be paid off and re-leased through a larger single lease, thereby obtaining a slightly lower financing cost.

The leasing option is most useful for those companies that want to establish collateral agreements only for specific assets, thereby leaving their remaining assets available as a borrowing base for other loans. Leases can be arranged for all but the most financially shaky companies, since lenders can always use the underlying assets as collateral and rarely impose any other financing restrictions. Furthermore, future operating lease payments are not listed on the balance sheet as a liability; instead, future lease obligations are listed in a footnote.

However, unscrupulous lenders can hide or obscure the interest rate charged on leases, so that less financially knowledgeable companies will pay exorbitant rates. A company is obligated to make all payments through the end of a lease term, even if it no longer needs the equipment being leased.

Line of Credit

A line of credit is a commitment from a lender to pay a company whenever it needs cash, up to a preset maximum level. It is generally secured by company assets, and for that reason bears an interest rate not far above the prime rate. The bank will typically charge an annual maintenance fee, irrespective of the amount of funds drawn down on the loan, on the grounds that it has invested in the completion of paperwork for the loan. The bank will also likely require an annual audit of key accounts and asset balances to verify that the company's financial situation is in line with the bank's assumptions. One problem with a line of credit is that the bank can cancel the line or refuse to allow extra funds to be drawn down from it if the bank feels that the company is no longer a good credit risk. Another issue is that the bank may require a company to maintain a compensating balance in an account at the bank; this increases the effective interest rate on the line of credit, since the company earns little or no interest on the funds stored at the bank.

The line of credit is most useful for situations where there may be only short-term cash shortfalls or seasonal needs that result in the line's being drawn down to zero at some point during the year. If one's cash requirements are expected to be longer term, then a term note or bond is a more appropriate form of financing.

Loans

Asset-Based Loans   A loan that uses fixed assets or inventory as its collateral is a common form of financing by banks. Loans may also be issued that are based on other forms of collateral, such as the cash surrender value of life insurance, securities, or real estate. The bank will use the resale value of fixed assets (as determined through an annual appraisal) and/or inventory to determine the maximum amount of available funds for a loan. If inventory is used as the basis for the loan, a prudent lender typically will not lend more than 50 percent of the value of the raw materials and 80 percent of the value of the finished goods, on the grounds that it may have to sell the inventory in the event of a foreclosure and may not obtain full prices at the time of sale. Lenders will be much less likely to accept inventory as collateral if it has a short shelf life, is customized, is so seasonal that its value drops significantly at certain times of the year, or if it is subject to rapid obsolescence.

Given the presence of collateral, this type of loan tends to involve a lower interest rate. Lenders typically require minimal covenants in association with these loans, giving corporate management more control over company operations. However, the cost of an annual appraisal of fixed assets or annual audit by the bank (which will be charged to the company) should be factored into the total cost of this form of financing. Lenders require frequent reports on the status of underlying assets.

Bonds   A bond is a fixed obligation to pay, usually at a stated rate of $1,000 per bond, that is issued by a corporation to investors. It may be a *registered bond*, under which a company maintains a list of owners of each bond. The company then periodically sends interest payments, as well as the final principal payment, to the investor of record. It may also be a *coupon bond*, for which the company does not maintain a standard list of bondholders. Instead, each bond contains interest coupons that the bondholders send to the company on the dates when interest payments are due. The coupon bond is more easily transferable between investors, but the ease of transferability makes them more susceptible to loss.

Bonds come in many flavors. Following is a list and short description of the most common ones:

- *Collateral trust bond.* A bond that uses as collateral a company's security investments.

- *Convertible bond.* A bond that can be converted to stock using a predetermined conversion ratio. The presence of conversion rights typically reduces the interest cost of these bonds, since investors assign some value to the conversion privilege. See the "zero coupon convertible bond" for a variation on this approach.

- *Debenture.* A bond issued with no collateral. A subordinated debenture is one that specifies debt that is senior to it.

- *Deferred interest bond.* A bond that provides for either reduced or no interest in the beginning years of the bond term, and compensates for it with increased interest later in the bond term. Since this type of bond is associated with firms having short-term cash flow problems, the full-term interest rate can be high.

- *Floorless bond.* A bond whose terms allow purchasers to convert them to common stock, as well as any accrued interest. The reason for its "death spiral" nickname is that bondholders can convert some shares and sell them on the open market, thereby supposedly driving down the price and allowing them to buy more shares, and so on. If a major bondholder were to convert all holdings to common stock, the result could be a major stock price decline, possibly resulting in a change of control to the former bondholder. However, this conversion problem can be controlled to some extent by including conversion terms that allow bondholders to convert only at certain times or with the permission of company management.

- *Guaranteed bond.* A bond whose payments are guaranteed by another party. Corporate parents will sometimes issue this guarantee for bonds issued by subsidiaries in order to obtain a lower effective interest rate.

- *Income bond.* A bond that pays interest only if income has been earned. The income can be tied to total corporate earnings or to specific projects. If the bond terms indicate that interest is cumulative, then interest will accumulate during nonpayment periods and be paid at a later date when income is available for doing so.

- *Mortgage bond.* A bond offering can be backed by any real estate owned by the company (called a *real property mortgage bond*), or by company-owned equipment (called an *equipment bond*), or by all assets (called a *general mortgage bond*).

- *Serial bond.* A bond issuance where a portion of the total number of bonds are paid off each year, resulting in a gradual decline in the total amount of debt outstanding.

- *Variable rate bond.* A bond whose stated interest rate varies as a percentage of a baseline indicator, such as the prime rate. Treasurers should be wary of this bond type because jumps in the baseline indicator can lead to substantial increases in interest costs.

- *Zero coupon bond.* A bond with no stated interest rate. Investors purchase these bonds at a considerable discount to their face value in order to earn an effective interest rate.

- *Zero coupon convertible bond.* A bond that offers no interest rate on its face but allows investors to convert to stock if the stock price reaches a level higher than its current price on the open market. The attraction to investors is that, even if the conversion price to stock is marked up to a substantial premium over the current market price of the stock, a high level of volatility in the stock price gives investors some hope of a profitable conversion to equity. The attraction to a company is that the expectation of conversion to stock presents enough value to investors that they require no interest rate on the bond at all, or at least will only purchase the bond at a slight discount from its face value, resulting in a small effective interest rate. A twist on the concept is a contingent conversion clause (or "co-co" clause) that requires the stock price to surpass the designated conversion point by some fixed amount before allowing investors to actually switch to stock, thereby making the conversion even more unlikely. This concept is least useful for company whose stock has a history of varying only slightly from its current price, since investors will then see little chance to convert and so will place little value on the conversion feature, requiring instead a higher interest rate on the bonds.

A bond is generally issued with a fixed interest rate. However, if the rate is excessively low in the current market, then investors will pay less for the face value of the bond, thereby driving up the net interest rate paid by the company. Similarly, if the rate is too high, then investors will pay extra for the bond, thereby driving down the net interest rate paid.

There may be a bond indenture document that itemizes all features of the bond issue. It contains restrictions that the company is imposing on itself, such as limitations on capital expenditures or dividends, in order to make the bond issuance as palatable as possible to investors. If the company does not follow these restrictions, the bonds will be in default.

A number of features may be added to a bond in order to make it more attractive for investors. For example, its terms may include a requirement by the company to set up a sinking fund into which it contributes funds periodically, thereby ensuring that there will be enough cash on hand at the termination date of the bond to pay off all bondholders. There may also be a conversion feature that allows a bondholder to turn in his or her bonds in exchange for stock; this feature usually sets the conversion ratio of bonds to stock at a level that will keep an investor from making the conversion until the stock price has changed from its level at the time of bond issuance, in order to avoid watering down the ownership percentages of existing shareholders. In rare instances, bonds may be backed by personal guarantees or by a corporate parent.

There are also features that bondholders may be less pleased about. For example, it may contain a *call feature* that allows the company to buy back bonds at a set price within certain future time frames. This feature may limit the amount of money that a bondholder would otherwise be able to earn by holding the bond. The company may impose a *staggered buyback feature*, under which it can buy back some fixed proportion of all bonds at regular intervals. When this feature is activated, investors will be paid back much sooner than the stated payback date listed on the bond, thereby requiring them to find a new home for their cash, possibly at a time when interest rates are much lower than what they would otherwise have earned by retaining the bond. The bondholder may also be positioned last among all creditors for repayment in the event of a liquidation (called a *subordinated debenture*), which allows the company to use its assets as collateral for other forms of debt; however, it may have to pay a higher interest rate to investors in order to offset their perceived higher degree of risk. The typical bond offering will contain a mix of these features that impact investors from both a positive and a negative perspective, depending on its perceived level of difficulty in attracting investors, its expected future cash flows, and its need to reserve assets as collateral for other types of debt.

Bonds are highly recommended for those organizations large enough to attract a group of investors willing to purchase them, since the bonds can be structured to precisely fit a company's financing needs. Bonds are also issued directly to investors, so there are no financial intermediaries to whom transactional fees must be paid. A company can issue long-maturity bonds at times of low interest rates, thereby locking in modest financing costs for a longer period than would normally be possible with other forms of financing. Consequently, bonds can be one of the lowest-cost forms of financing.

Bridge Loans   A bridge loan is a form of short-term loan that is granted by a lending institution on the condition that the company will obtain longer-term financing shortly that will pay off the bridge loan. This option is commonly used when a company is seeking to replace a construction loan with a long-term note that it expects to gradually pay down over many years. This type of loan is usually secured by facilities or fixtures in order to obtain a lower interest rate.

Economic Development Authority Loans   Various agencies of state governments are empowered to guarantee bank loans to organizations that need funds in geographic areas where it is perceived that social improvement goals can be attained. For example, projects that will result in increased employment or the employment of minorities in specific areas may warrant an application for this type of loan. It is usually extended to finance a company's immediate working capital needs. Given these restrictions, an economic development authority loan is applicable only in special situations.

Long-Term Loans

There are several forms of long-term debt. One is a long-term loan issued by a lending institution. These loans tend to be made to smaller companies that do not have the means to issue bonds. To reduce the risk to the lender, these loans typically require the company to grant the lender senior status over all other creditors in the event of liquidation. This is a standard requirement because the lender is at much greater risk of default over the multiyear term of the loan, when business conditions may change dramatically. If there is no way for a lender to take a senior position on collateral, then the company should expect to pay a higher interest rate in exchange for dropping the lender into a junior position in comparison to other creditors. If the lender also wants to protect itself from changes in long-term interest rates, it may attempt to impose a variable interest rate on the company.

A long-term loan nearly always involves the use of fixed payments on a fixed repayment schedule, which will involve either the gradual repayment of principal or the regularly scheduled payment of interest, with the bulk of the principal being due at the end of the loan as a balloon payment. In the latter case, a company may have no intention of paying back the principal, but instead will roll over the debt into a new loan and carry it forward once again. If this is the case, the treasurer may review the trend of interest rates and choose to roll over the debt to a new loan instrument at an earlier date than the scheduled loan termination date, when interest rates are at their lowest possible levels.

In summary, long-term debt is a highly desirable form of financing, since a company can lock in a favorable interest rate for a long time, and keeps it from having to repeatedly apply for shorter-term loans during the intervening years, when business conditions may result in less favorable debt terms.

Receivables Securitization

A large company can consider securitizing its accounts receivable, thereby achieving one of the lowest interest rates available for debt. To do so, it creates a special purpose entity (SPE) and transfers a selection of its receivables into the SPE. The SPE then sells the receivables to a bank conduit, which in turn pools the receivables that it has bought from multiple companies, and uses the cash flows from the receivables to back the issuance of commercial paper to investors, who in turn are repaid with the cash flows from the receivables.

Receivables securitization is clearly a complex process to initially create; the primary benefit of doing so is that a company's receivables are isolated from its other risks, so that the SPE has a higher credit rating than the company, with an attendant decline in borrowing costs. To achieve the AAA credit rating typically needed for receivables securitization, a credit-rating agency will review the performance record of receivables previously included in the pool, debtor concentrations in the pool, and the company's credit and collection policies.

A lesser reason for using receivables securitization is that a company is not required to record it as debt on its balance sheet. However, this sometimes leads to an outcry from the investing community that a company is hiding liabilities, so companies sometimes voluntarily record the transaction as debt on their balance sheets.

A key factor in preserving the stellar credit rating of the SPE is to maintain an adequate degree of separation between the company and the SPE. To do so, the transfer of receivables is supposed to be a nonrecourse sale, so that the company's creditors cannot claim the assets of the SPE if the company goes bankrupt. This means that there should be no mechanism by which the company can regain control of any receivables shifted to the SPE.

Receivables securitization is available only to large companies having a broad customer base whose receivables experience minimal defaults. Further, there must be adequate tracking systems in place to monitor the creditworthiness of those debtors whose receivables are included in the SPE, delinquency statistics, and customer concentrations, as well as frequent reporting on receivable collections.

Sale and Leaseback

Under this arrangement, a company sells one of its assets to a lender and then immediately leases it back for a guaranteed minimum time period. By doing so, the company obtains cash from the sale of the asset that it may be able to use more profitably elsewhere, while the leasing company handling the deal obtains a guaranteed lessee for a time period that will allow it to turn a profit on the financing arrangement. A sale and leaseback is most commonly used for the sale of a corporate building, but can also be arranged for other large assets, such as production machinery.

A sale and leaseback is useful for companies in any type of financial condition, for a financially healthy organization can use the resulting cash to buy back shares and prop up its stock price, while a faltering organization can use the cash to fund operations. It has the added advantage of not burdening a company's balance sheet with debt; furthermore, it puts cash back *into* the balance sheet, allowing a company to obtain additional debt. It is especially useful when market conditions make other forms of financing too expensive. Obviously, it is an option only for those organizations that have substantial assets available for sale.

Summary of Debt Types

The previous discussion shows that there is a large array of approaches available to solve the problem of obtaining financing. The various types of debt financing are summarized in Exhibit 6.1.

Exhibit 6.1 Summary of Debt Financing Types

Debt Financing Type	Features	Cost
Commercial paper	Short-term funding	Inexpensive, but only if the company can achieve a high rating from a credit rating agency
Factoring	Short-term funding based on accounts receivable	Expensive, but greatly accelerates cash flow
Field warehouse financing	Short-term funding based on inventory	Cost is somewhat higher than the prime rate, and may require detailed inventory tracking
Floor planning	Short-term funding based on retailer inventory	Cost is somewhat higher than the prime rate, and may require detailed inventory tracking
Lease	Medium-term funding that backs the purchase of specific assets	Cost can be hidden within lease agreement
Line of credit	Short-term revolving funding collateralized by a variety of assets	Cost is near the prime rate, but bank can refuse additional funding, and it must be paid off in the short term
Loan, asset based	Long-term funding with asset collateral	Cost is near the prime rate, but may require frequent reporting on collateral status
Loan, bond	Long-term funding based on obligations issued by the company	Cost varies based on market conditions and bond terms

Exhibit 6.1   (Continued)

Debt Financing Type	Features	Cost
Loan, bridge	Short-term funding used to carry a debt position until longer-term financing is found	Cost is near the prime rate, but secured by facilities
Loan, economic development authority	Short-term funding backed by a government in special social improvement situations	Cost is near the prime rate
Loan, long-term	Long-term funding issued by a lender	Cost is near the prime rate, but requires senior debt status, and can involve balloon payments
Loan, short-term	Short-term funding based on seasonal cash flow needs	Cost is near the prime rate, but can require collateral
Receivables securitization	Move receivables into a special-purpose entity, from which the related cash flows support commercial paper	Complex setup and subsequent accounting, offset by lower borrowing costs
Sale and lease back	Long-term funding from selling a building or major asset and leasing it back for a long period	Low cost, but requires a long-term lease commitment

CREDIT-RATING AGENCIES

If a publicly held company issues debt, it can elect to have that debt rated by either Moody's, Standard & Poor's, or Fitch. These are the three top-tier credit-rating agencies that the Securities and Exchange Commission SEC allows to issue debt ratings. A debt rating results in a credit score that indicates the perceived risk of default on the underlying debt, which in turn impacts the price of the debt on the open market. Having a credit score is essentially mandatory, since most funds are prohibited by their internal investment rules from buying debt that does not have a specific level of credit rating assigned to it. The rating scores used by the three credit-rating agencies are noted in Exhibit 6.2, and are in declining order of credit quality.

Exhibit 6.2 Credit Score Comparison

Definition	Fitch Rating	Moody's Rating	S&P Rating
Prime	AAA	Aaa	AAA
High grade	AA+	Aa1	AA+
	AA	Aa2	AA
	AA–	Aa3	AA–
Upper medium grade	A+	A1	A+
	A	A2	A
	A–	A3	A–
Lower medium grade	BBB+	Baa1	BBB+
	BBB	Baa2	BBB
	BBB–	Baa3	BBB–
Non–investment grade	BB+	Ba1	BB+
Speculative	BB	Ba2	BB
	BB–	Ba3	BB–
Highly speculative	B+	B1	B+
		B2	B
		B3	B–
Substantial risk	CCC	Caa1	CCC+

A company should expect to deal with a credit-rating agency through a primary analyst who has considerable credit-rating experience, and is usually ranked at the director level. The primary analyst is supported by a senior analyst having direct experience in the company's industry. The primary analyst is responsible for formulating a rating and for the ongoing monitoring of that rating.

The treasurer represents the company to the credit-rating agency. If there is a chief risk officer or similar position, then this person will also have discussions with the analyst team. It is also entirely likely that the managers of the company's operating divisions will be asked to participate in some meetings with the analyst team or to assist them with tours of key company facilities.

In order to develop a credit rating, the analyst team uses the financial statements that a company has previously filed with the SEC, but also needs detailed information about its budgets, internal operating reports, risk management strategies, and financial and operating policies. To this end, it will ask the management team to complete an initial questionnaire that usually requires five years of historical financial data, five years of forecasted financial results, a summary of the business and its objectives, a comparison of its market share and growth prospects to those of its peer companies, and the biographies of the senior management team. The focus of this analysis is forward-looking, since the analyst team is most concerned with the company's future performance. Consequently, short- and medium-range projections of a company's financial viability are considered more important than its historical performance.

A key part of the analysis will be a question-and-answer session with the management team. The treasurer will be expected to make a presentation about the company, after which the analysts will ask about any areas of weakness that could impact the nature of their eventual credit rating. The general thrust of their questioning is to compare the company's current financial situation to its strategic intentions, to see if its financial structure can support where management wants to take the company.

The analysts will use their agency's standardized rating methodology to assign a credit rating to the specific company debt for which they are being hired. It is difficult to estimate in advance what the rating may be, since the relative weighting of factors in the methodology will vary based on individual circumstances. Generally speaking, the analysts will ascribe about 50 percent of the rating to the company's business profile and future prospects, and 50 percent to its current financial profile.

If an agency issues a low credit rating or downgrades an existing rating, the best reaction by the company is to not publicly challenge it. There is no upside to a company's complaining bitterly about the perceived injustice of a low rating, since it is very unlikely that the issuing agency will change its rating. The only result of such action is that the company has drawn attention to a negative opinion issued by a qualified third party, which may very well reduce investor confidence in the debt price. However, a company may certainly appeal the rating, usually by presenting new information to the agency. Appeals are very rare, comprising only about one-half percent of all ratings changes.

If a company wants to improve its credit rating, then it must take specific steps to make its financial structure more conservative, such as by issuing more stock and using the proceeds to pay down debt. This requires the development of a plan to achieve the higher credit rating and communication of this information to the credit rating agency.

ACCOUNTING FOR DEBT

The key accounting issues related to debt are the treatment of discounts and premiums, debt issuance costs, debt extinguishment, conversion features, and attached warrants. This section addresses how to properly account for each of these items.

Bonds Sold at a Discount or Premium to Their Face Value

When bonds are initially sold, the entry is a debit to cash and a credit to bonds payable. However, this occurs only when the price paid by investors exactly matches the face amount of the bond. A more common occurrence is when the market interest rate varies somewhat from the stated interest rate on the bond, so investors pay a different price in order to achieve an effective interest rate matching the market rate. For example, if the market rate were 8 percent and the stated rate were 7 percent, investors would pay less than the face amount of the bond so that the 7 percent interest they later receive will equate to an 8 percent interest rate on their reduced investment. Alternatively, if the rates were reversed, with a 7 percent market rate and an 8 percent stated rate, investors would pay more for the bond, thereby driving down the stated interest rate to match the market rate. If the bonds are sold at a discount, the entry will include a debit to a discount on bonds payable account. For example, if $10,000 of bonds are sold at a discount of $1,500, the entry would be:

	Debit	Credit
Cash	$8,500	
Discount on bonds payable	1,500	
Bonds payable		$10,000

If the same transaction were to occur, except that a premium on sale of the bonds occurs, then the entry would be:

	Debit	Credit
Cash	$11,500	
Premium on bonds payable		$1,500
Bonds payable		10,000

Example

Sonoma Silversmiths issues $1 million of bonds at a stated rate of 8 percent in a market where similar issuances are being bought at 11 percent. The bonds pay interest once a year and are to be paid off in ten years. Investors purchase these bonds at a discount in order to earn an effective yield on their investment of 11 percent. The discount calculation requires one to determine the present value of ten interest payments at 11 percent interest, as well as the present value of $1 million, discounted at 11 percent for ten years. The result is as follows:

$$\text{Present value of ten payments of } \$80,000 = \$80,000 \times 5.8892 = \$471,136$$
$$\text{Present value of } \$1,000,000 = \$1,000,000 \times 0.3522 = \$352,200$$
$$\$823,336$$
$$\text{Less: stated bond price} \quad \$1,000,000$$
$$\text{Discount on bond} \quad \$176,664$$

In this example, the entry would be a debit to cash for $823,336, a credit to bonds payable for $1 million, and a debit to discount on bonds payable for $176,664. If the calculation had resulted in a premium (which would have occurred only if the market rate of interest was less than the stated interest rate on the bonds), then a credit to premium on bonds payable would be in order.

Effective Interest Method

The amount of a discount or premium should be gradually written off to the interest expense account over the life of the bond. The only acceptable method for writing off these amounts is through the *effective interest method*, which allows one to charge off the difference between the market and stated rate of interest to the existing discount or premium account, gradually reducing the balance in the discount or premium account over the life of the bond. If interest payment dates do not coincide with the end of financial reporting periods, a journal entry must be made to show the amount of interest expense and related discount or premium amortization that would have occurred during the days following the last interest payment date and the end of the reporting period.

Example

To continue with our example, the interest method holds that, in the first year of interest payments, Sonoma Silversmiths' accountant would determine that the market interest expense for the first year would be $90,567 (bond stated price of $1 million minus discount of $176,664, multiplied by the market interest rate of 11 percent). The resulting journal entry would be:

	Debit	Credit
Interest expense	$90,567	
Discount on bonds payable		$10,567
Cash		$80,000

The reason why only $80,000 is listed as a reduction in cash is that the company only has an obligation to pay an 8 percent interest rate on the $1 million face value of the bonds, which is $80,000. The difference is netted against the existing discount on bonds payable account. The following table shows the calculation of the discount to be charged to expense each year for the full ten-year period of the bond, where the annual amortization of the discount is added back to the bond present value, eventually resulting in a bond present value of $1 million by the time principal payment is due, while the discount has dropped to zero.

Year	Beginning Bond Present Value (4)	Unamortized Discount	Interest Expense (1)	Cash Payment (2)	Credit to Discount (3)
1	$823,336	$176,664	$90,567	$80,000	$10,567
2	$833,903	$166,097	$91,729	$80,000	$11,729

Year	Beginning Bond Present Value (4)	Unamortized Discount	Interest Expense (1)	Cash Payment (2)	Credit to Discount (3)
3	$845,632	$154,368	$93,020	$80,000	$13,020
4	$858,652	$141,348	$94,452	$80,000	$14,452
5	$873,104	$126,896	$96,041	$80,000	$16,041
6	$889,145	$110,855	$97,806	$80,000	$17,806
7	$906,951	$93,049	$99,765	$80,000	$19,765
8	$926,716	$73,284	$101,939	$80,000	$21,939
9	$948,655	$51,346	$104,352	$80,000	$24,352
10	$973,007	$26,994	$107,031	$80,000	$26,994
	$1,000,000	$0			

(1) = Bond present value multiplied by the market rate of 11 percent.
(2) = Required cash payment of 8% stated rate multiplied by face value of $1 million.
(3) = Interest expense reduced by cash payment.
(4) = Beginning present value of the bond plus annual reduction in the discount.

Debt Issued with No Stated Interest Rate

If a company issues debt that has no stated rate of interest, then the accountant must create an interest rate for it that approximates the rate that the company would likely obtain, given its credit rating, on the open market on the date when the debt was issued. The accountant then uses this rate to discount the face amount of the debt down to its present value, and then records the difference between this present value and the loan's face value as the loan balance. For example, if a company issued debt with a face amount of $1 million, payable in five years and at no stated interest rate, and the market rate for interest at the time of issuance was 9 percent, then the discount factor to be applied to the debt would be 0.6499. This would give the debt a present value of $649,900. The difference between the face amount of $1 million and the present value of $649,900 should be recorded as a discount on the note, as shown in the following entry:

	Debit	Credit
Cash	$649,900	
Discount on note payable	350,100	
Notes payable		$1,000,000

Debt Issuance Costs The costs associated with issuing bonds can be substantial. These include the legal costs of creating the bond documents, printing the bond certificates, and (especially) the underwriting costs of the investment banker. Since these costs are directly associated with the procurement of funds that the company can be expected to use for a number of years (until the bonds are paid off), the related bond issuance costs should be recorded as an asset and then written off on a straight-line basis over the period during which the bonds are expected to be used by the company. This entry is a debit to a bond issuance asset account and a credit to cash. However, if the bonds associated with these costs are subsequently paid off earlier than anticipated, one can reasonably argue that the associated remaining bond issuance costs should be charged to expense at the same time.

Notes Issued with Attached Rights   An issuing company can grant additional benefits to the other party, such as exclusive distribution rights on its products, discounts on product sales, and so on—the range of possibilities is endless. In these cases, consider the difference between the present value and face value of the debt to be the value of the additional consideration. When this occurs, the difference is debited to the discount on note payable account and is amortized using the *effective interest method* that was described earlier. The offsetting credit can be to a variety of accounts, depending on the nature of the transaction. The credited account is typically written off either ratably (if the attached benefit is equally spread over many accounting periods) or in conjunction with specific events (such as the shipment of discounted products to the holder of the debt). Though less common, it is also possible to issue debt at an above-market rate in order to obtain additional benefits from the debt holder. In this case, the entry is reversed, with a credit to the premium on note payable account and the offsetting debit to a number of possible accounts related to the specific consideration given.

Example

Sonoma Silversmiths has issued a new note for $2,500,000 at 4 percent interest to a customer, the Alaskan Pipeline Company. Under the terms of the five-year note, Alaskan obtains a 20 percent discount on all silver beading it purchases from Sonoma during the term of the note. The market rate for similar debt was 9 percent on the date the loan documents were signed.

The present value of the note at the 9 percent market rate of interest over a five-year term is $1,624,750, while the present value of the note at its stated rate of 4 percent is $2,054,750. The difference between the two present-value figures is $430,000, which is the value of the attached right to discounted silver beading granted to Alaskan. Sonoma should make the following entry to record the loan:

	Debit	Credit
Cash	$2,500,000	
Discount on note payable	430,000	
Note payable		$2,500,000
Unearned revenue		430,000

The unearned revenue of $430,000 can either be recognized incrementally as part of each invoice billed to Alaskan, or it can be recognized ratably over the term of the debt. Since Sonoma does not know the exact amount of the security services that will be contracted for by Alaskan during the term of the five-year note, the better approach is to recognize the unearned revenue ratably over the note term. The first month's entry would be as follows, where the amount recognized is one-sixtieth of the beginning balance of unearned revenue:

	Debit	Credit
Unearned revenue	$7,166.67	
Services revenue		$7,166.67

Extinguishment of Debt

A company may find it advisable to repurchase its bonds prior to their maturity date, perhaps because market interest rates have dropped so far below the stated rate on the bonds that the company can profitably refinance at a lower interest rate. Whatever the reason may be, the resulting transaction should recognize any gain or loss on the transaction, as well as recognize the transactional cost of the retirement, and any proportion of the outstanding discount, premium, or bond issuance costs relating to the original bond issuance.

Example

To return to our earlier example, if Sonoma Silversmiths were to buy back $200,000 of its $1 million bond issuance at a premium of 5 percent, and does so with $125,000 of the original bond discount still on its books, it would record a loss of $10,000 on the bond retirement ($200,000 × 5%), while also recognizing one-fifth of the remaining discount, which is $25,000 ($125,000 × $1/5$). The entry follows:

	Debit	Credit
Bonds payable	$200,000	
Loss on bond retirement	10,000	
Discount on bonds payable		$25,000
Cash		185,000

If the issuing company finds itself in the position of being unable to pay either interest or principle to its bondholders, there are two directions the accountant can take in reflecting the problem in the accounting records. In the first case, the company may only temporarily be in default and is attempting to work out a payment solution with the bondholders. Under this scenario, the amortization of discounts or premiums, as well as of bond issuance costs and interest expense, should continue as they have in the past. However, if there is no chance of payment, then the amortization of discounts or premiums, as well as of bond issuance costs, should be accelerated, being recognized in full in the current period. This action is taken on the grounds that the underlying accounting transaction that specified the period over which the amortizations occurred has now disappeared, requiring the accountant to recognize all remaining expenses.

If the issuing company has not defaulted on a debt, but rather has restructured its terms, then the accountant must determine the present value of the new stream of cash flows and compare it to the original carrying value of the debt arrangement. In the likely event that the new present value of the debt is *less than* the original present value, the difference should be recognized in the current period as a gain.

Alternatively, if the present value of the restructured debt agreement is *more than* the carrying value of the original agreement, then a loss is *not* recognized on the difference—instead, the effective interest rate on the new stream of debt payments is reduced to the point where the resulting present value of the restructured debt matches the carrying value of the original agreement. This will result in a reduced amount of interest expense being accrued for all future periods during which the debt is outstanding.

In some cases where the issuing company is unable to pay bondholders, it gives them other company assets in exchange for the interest or principal payments owed to them. When this occurs, the issuing company first records a gain or loss on the initial revaluation of the asset being transferred to its fair market value. Next, it records a gain or loss on the transaction if there is a difference between the carrying value of the debt being paid off and the fair market value of the asset being transferred to the bondholder.

Example

Sonoma Silversmiths is unable to pay off its loan from a local lender. The lender agrees to cancel the debt, with a remaining face value of $35,000, in exchange for a company truck having a book value of $26,000 and a fair market value of $29,000. There is also $2,500 of accrued but unpaid interest expense associated with the debt. Sonoma's controller first revalues the truck to its fair market value and then records a gain on the debt settlement transaction. The entries are as follows:

	Debit	Credit
Vehicles	$3,000	
Gain on asset transfer		$3,000
Note payable	$35,000	
Interest payable	2,500	
Vehicles		$29,000
Gain on debt settlement		8,500

If convertible debt is issued with a conversion feature that is already in the money, then the intrinsic value of that equity component should have been recorded as a credit to the additional paid-in capital account. If so, the intrinsic value must be remeasured as of the debt retirement date and then removed from the additional paid-in capital account. This may result in the recognition of a gain or loss, depending on the difference between the original and final intrinsic value calculations.

Scheduled Bond Retirement

A bond agreement may contain specific requirements to either create a sinking fund that is used at the maturity date to buy back all bonds, or else to gradually buy back bonds on a regular schedule, usually through a trustee. In either case, the intention is to ensure that the company is not suddenly faced with a large repayment requirement at the maturity date. In this situation, the company usually forwards funds to a trustee at regular intervals, who in turn uses it to buy back bonds. The resulting accounting is identical to that just noted under Extinguishment of Debt. In addition, if the company forwards interest payments to the trustee for bonds that the trustee now has in its possession, these payments are used to purchase additional bonds (since there is no one to whom the interest can be paid). In this case, the journal entry that would normally record this transaction as interest expense is converted into an entry that reduces the principal balance of the bonds outstanding.

Convertible Debt

The *convertible bond* contains a feature allowing the holder to turn in the bond in exchange for stock when a preset strike price for the stock is reached, sometimes after a specific date. This involves a specific conversion price per share, which is typically set at a point that makes the transaction uneconomical unless the share price rises at some point in the future.

To account for this transaction under the popular *book value method*, the principal amount of the bond is moved to an equity account, with a portion being allocated to the capital account at par value and the remainder going to the additional paid-in capital account. A portion of the discount or premium associated with the bond issuance is also retired, based on the proportion of bonds converted to equity. If the *market value method* is used instead, the conversion price is based on the number of shares issued to former bondholders, multiplied by the market price of the shares on the conversion date. This will likely create a gain or loss as compared to the book value of the converted bonds.

Examples

BOOK VALUE METHOD

A bondholder owns $50,000 of bonds and wishes to convert them to 1,000 shares of company stock that has a par value of $5. The total amount of the premium associated with the original bond issuance was $42,000, and the amount of bonds to be converted to stock represents 18 percent of the total amount of bonds outstanding. In this case, the amount of premium to be recognized will be $7,560 ($42,000 × 18 percent), while the amount of funds shifted to the capital stock at par value account will be $5,000 (1,000 shares × $5). The entry is as follows:

	Debit	Credit
Bonds payable	$50,000	
Premium on bonds payable	7,560	
Capital stock at par value		$5,000
Additional paid-in capital		52,560

MARKET VALUE METHOD

Use the same assumptions as the last example, except that the fair market value of the shares acquired by the former bondholder is $5.50 each. This creates a loss on the bond conversion of $5,000, which is added to the additional paid-in capital account. The entry is as follows:

	Debit	Credit
Bonds payable	$50,000	
Loss on bond conversion	5,000	
Premium on bonds payable	7,560	
Capital stock at par value		$5,000
Additional paid-in capital		57,560

Convertible Debt Issued in the Money

The situation becomes more complicated if convertible bonds are issued with a stock conversion strike price that is already lower than the market price of the stock. In this case, the related journal entry must assign a value to the shares that is based on the potential number of convertible shares, multiplied by the difference between the strike price and the market value of the stock. If there is a series of strike prices for different future dates in the bond agreement, then the lowest strike price should be used to determine the intrinsic value of the deal. If bonds are issued with a strike price that is in the money, but contingent on a future event, then any recognition of the intrinsic value of the equity element is delayed until the contingent event has occurred.

Examples

BOND ISSUANCE, STRIKE PRICE IS IN THE MONEY

An investor purchases $50,000 of bonds that are convertible into 10,000 shares of common stock at a conversion price of $5. At the time of issuance, the stock had a fair market value of $6.50. The intrinsic value of the conversion feature at the time of issuance is $15,000, based on the difference between the fair market value of $6.50 and the conversion price of $5, multiplied by the 10,000 shares that would be issued if a full conversion were to take place. The entry would be as follows:

	Debit	Credit
Cash	$50,000	
Bonds payable		$35,000
Additional paid-in capital		15,000

BOND ISSUANCE, A SEQUENCE OF STRIKE PRICES ARE IN THE MONEY

Use the same information as the last example, except that the bond agreement contains a lower strike price of $4.50 after three years have passed. Since this later strike price results in a greater intrinsic value being assigned to equity than the initial strike price, the later price is used for the valuation calculation. The calculation is 11,111 shares ($50,000 divided by a strike price of $4.50), multiplied by the $2 difference between the strike price and the fair market value, resulting in a debit to cash of $50,000, a credit to bonds payable of $27,778, and a credit to additional paid-in capital of $22,222.

BOND ISSUANCE, STRIKE PRICE IS IN THE MONEY BUT DEPENDENT ON A CONTINGENT EVENT

Use the same information as was used for the first example, except that conversion cannot take place until the stock of all Series A preferred shareholders has been bought back by the company. The initial journal entry is a simple debit to cash of $50,000 and a credit to bonds payable of $50,000, since there is no intrinsic value to the equity component at this time. Once the Series A shareholders are bought out, the intrinsic value of the equity is recognized by debiting the discount on bonds payable account and crediting the additional paid-in capital accounts for $15,000.

Convertible Debt—Accrued but Unpaid Interest on Converted Debt

If a convertible debt agreement's terms state that a bondholder shall forfeit any accrued interest at the time the bondholder converts to equity, the company must recognize the accrued interest expense anyway, net of income taxes. The offset to the expense is a credit to the capital account.

Example

Mr. Abraham Smith owns $25,000 of the North Dakota Railroad's convertible debt. He elects to convert it to the railroad's common stock, and forfeits the accrued $520 of interest expense that was not yet paid as of the conversion date. The railroad debits the interest expense account and credits the capital account for $520.

Convertible Debt—Subsequent Change in Offering to Induce Conversion

If a company induces its bondholders to convert their holdings to equity by subsequently improving the conversion feature of the bond agreement, it must record an expense for the difference between the consideration given to induce the conversion and the consideration originally noted in the bond agreement.

Example

Mr. Abraham Smith owns $25,000 of the North Dakota Railroad's convertible debt. The bonds were originally issued with a conversion price of $50 per share, which the railroad has subsequently lowered to $40 to induce conversion. The shares have a market value of $38 and a par value of $1. Mr. Smith elects to convert to stock, resulting in the following calculation:

	Before Change in Terms	After Change in Terms
Face amount of bonds	$25,000	$25,000
Conversion price	50	40
Total shares converted	500	625
Fair value per share	38	38
Value of converted stock	$19,000	$23,750

The difference between the total values of converted stock before and after the change in terms is $4,750, resulting in the following entry to record the entire conversion transaction:

	Debit	Credit
Bonds payable	$25,000	
Debt conversion expense	4,750	
Capital account, par value		$625
Additional paid-in capital		29,125

Debt Issued with Stock Warrants

A company may attach warrants to its bonds in order to sell the bonds to investors more easily. A warrant gives an investor the right to buy a specific number of shares of company stock at a set price for a given time interval.

To account for the presence of a warrant, the accountant must determine its value if it were sold separately from the bond, determine the proportion of the total bond price to allocate to it, and then credit this proportional amount into the additional paid-in capital account.

Example

A bond/warrant combination is purchased by an investor for $1,100. The investment banker handling the transaction estimates that the value of the warrant is $150, while the bond (with a face value of $1,000) begins trading at $975. Accordingly, the value the accountant assigns to the warrant is $146.67, which is calculated as follows:

$$\frac{\text{Warrant Value}}{\text{Bond Value} + \text{Warrant Value}} \times \text{Purchase Price} = \text{Price Assigned to Warrant}$$

$$\frac{\$150}{\$975+\$150} \times \$1,100 = \$146.67$$

The accountant then credits the $146.67 assigned to the warrant value to the additional paid-in capital account, since this is a form of equity funding, rather than debt funding, for which the investor has paid. The discount on bonds payable represents the difference between the $1,000 face value of the bond and its assigned value of $953.33. The journal entry is as follows:

	Debit	Credit
Cash	$1,100.00	
Discount on bonds payable	46.67	
Bonds payable		$1,000.00
Additional paid-in capital		146.67

The decision tree shown in Exhibit 6.3 shows the general set of decisions to be made during the life of a bond, beginning with the treatment of discounts or premiums on the initial sale price and proceeding through the presence of attached warrants and early debt extinguishment. The decisions in the top third of the tree impact nearly all bonds, since it is unusual *not* to have a discount or premium. The middle third impacts only attached warrants, with most of the action items involving in-the-money warrants.

DEBT-RELATED CONTROLS

The recordation of debt-related transactions is somewhat technical, and therefore subject to some degree of calculation error. Several of the following controls are designed to verify that the correct interest rates and calculation dates are used. In addition, there is some possibility that the deliberate timing of gain and loss recognition related to debt transactions can be used to manipulate reported earnings. Several of the following controls are used to detect such issues. Finally, controls over the approval of debt terms, borrowings, and repayments are also described.

General Debt Transaction Controls

- *Require approval of the terms of all new borrowing agreements.* A senior corporate manager should be assigned the task of reviewing all prospective debt instruments to verify that their interest rate, collateral, and other requirements are not excessively onerous or conflict with the terms of existing debt agreements. It may also be useful from time to time to see if a lending institution has inappropriate

Exhibit 6.3   Decision Points during the Lifetime of a Bond

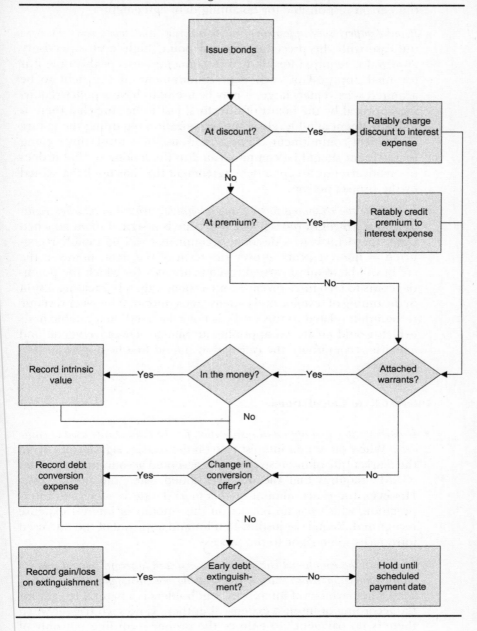

ties to the company, such as partial or full ownership in its stock by the person responsible for obtaining debt agreements.

- *Require supervisory approval of all borrowings and repayments.* As was the case with the preceding control point, high-level supervisory approval is required for all debt instruments—except this time it is for final approval of each debt commitment. If the debt to be acquired is extremely large, it may be useful to have a policy requiring approval by the board of directors, just to be sure that there is full agreement at all levels of the organization regarding the nature of the debt commitment. To be a more useful control, this signing requirement should be communicated to the lender, so that it does not inadvertently accept a debt agreement that has not been signed by the proper person.

- *Investigate the reasoning for revenue recognition related to attached rights that is not recognized ratably.* When a value is assigned to an attached right, the debit is to a discount account that will be ratably recognized as interest expense over the term of the debt; however, the credit will be to an unearned revenue account for which the potential exists to recognize revenue much sooner, thereby creating a split in the timing of revenue and expense recognition. Whenever revenue recognition related to this credit is not calculated on a ratable basis (which would create an approximate match between revenue and expense recognition), the calculation should first be approved by a manager.

Interest Rate Calculations

- *Require written and approved justification for the interest rate used to value debt.* When the stated interest rate on debt varies significantly from the market rate of interest, generally accepted accounting principles (GAAP) requires that the debt be valued using the market rate. However, the exact amount of this market rate is subject to interpretation, which has an impact on the amount of interest expense recognized. Requiring justification for and approval of the rate used introduces some rigor to the process.

- *Include in the month-end closing procedure a task to record interest expense on any bonds for which interest payments do not correspond to the closing date.* The payment of interest to bondholders is a natural trigger for the recording of interest expense, but there is no such trigger when there is no payment. To enforce the proper recording not only of unpaid interest expense but also of any amortization on related bond discounts or premiums, a specific task should be included in the closing procedure, as well as a required signoff on the task.

Extinguishment of Debt

- *Include in the debt procedure a line item to charge unamortized discounts or premiums to expense proportionate to the amount of any extinguished debt.* The general ledger accountant may not remember to write off any unamortized discount or premium when debt is extinguished, so the debt extinguishment procedure should include a line item requiring that this task be addressed. Otherwise, expense recognition could potentially be delayed until the original payment date of the debt, which may be many years in the future.

- *Report to the board of directors the repayment status of all debt.* GAAP requires that all unamortized discounts and premiums be recognized in the current period if there is no reasonable chance that the debt will be repaid. Since this acceleration has a significant impact on reported earnings in the current period, there may be some unwillingness to classify debt as unable to be paid. By requiring a standard report to the board of directors regarding the status of debt repayments at each of its meetings, the board can decide on its own when amortization must be accelerated, and can force management to do so.

Convertible Debt

- *Verify the market value of equity on conversion dates when the market value method is used.* If a company uses the market value method to record the conversion of debt to equity, it is possible to influence the gain or loss recorded, depending on fluctuations in the stock price from day to day. Accordingly, the market price of the stock should be independently matched to the date on which the conversion took place. Also, it is possible to include in the conversion procedure a fill-in blank where the stock price can be noted, dated, and initialed. This approach makes it much easier to trace transactions, and also holds accountants responsible for their entries.

- *Verify the market value of equity on debt retirement dates when offsetting equity entries are being reversed.* When a convertible bond is issued with its equity conversion feature already in the money, the intrinsic value of the equity portion of the bond must be credited to the additional paid-in capital account. If the bond is later retired, the equity portion of the bond must then be removed from the additional paid-in capital account. Any difference between the original and final intrinsic values is charged to either a gain or loss on the extinguishment of debt. The presence of a potential gain or loss on extinguishment makes it more likely for manipulation to occur in both the timing and calculation of the extinguishment transaction. One can match the date of the debt retirement to the equity valuation on that date to ensure that the proper equity value is used. Also, the correct retirement calculation can be included in the corporate accounting procedures manual to ensure that it is handled properly.

- *Include a review of accrued interest expense on all recently converted debt.* If the terms of a company's bond agreements state that bondholders must forfeit accrued interest on converted debt, then there will be a temptation to also avoid recording this accrual on the books as an expense, as is required by GAAP. Consequently, the formal procedure used to convert debt to equity should include a line item for the general ledger accountant to record this accrued interest expense, and also require a signature on the procedure to ensure its completion.

- *Verify expense calculations associated with any sweetened conversion offers.* GAAP requires the recognition of a debt conversion expense associated with any completed conversion from bonds to equity, in the incremental amount of the net increase in fair value of stock obtained through a sweetened conversion offer. Since this results in an added expense, there will be a tendency to simply process the total conversion and not recognize the incremental expense, which could be substantial. Accordingly, a copy of the relevant portions of the original bond agreement should be attached to any journal entry that records a conversion to equity, which provides documentation of the initial conversion price. When the calculation is verified by an internal auditor or senior accounting person, this provides documentation of the initial baseline conversion price.

DEBT-RELATED POLICIES

The policies set forth in this section define the issuance and buyback of debt, control the timing of expense recognition, the setting of interest rates used for expense calculations, and similar issues. The intent of the bulk of these policies is to issue and buy back debt only when it is in the best business interest of the company to do so, as well as to ensure that debt-related transactions are recorded fairly.

General Debt Transaction Policies

- *All notes and bonds shall only be issued subsequent to approval by the board of directors.* This policy gives the board control over any new debt liabilities. In reality, anyone lending money to the company will require a board motion, so this policy is likely to be imposed by the lender even if it does not exist internally.

- *Debt sinking funds shall be fully funded on scheduled dates.* This policy is designed to force the treasury staff to plan for the timely accumulation of funds needed to pay off scheduled principal payments on debt, thereby avoiding any last-minute funding crises.

• *Recognition of unearned revenue for attached rights shall match offsetting discount amortization as closely as possible.* This policy is designed to avoid the manipulation of revenue recognition for attached rights. For example, if a value is assigned to an attached right, the debit will be to a discount account that will be ratably recognized as interest expense over the term of the debt; however, the credit will be to an unearned revenue account for which the potential exists to recognize revenue much sooner, thereby creating a split in the timing of revenue and expense recognition. Though this split may be valid in some cases, an effort should be made to avoid any significant disparities, thereby avoiding any surges in profits.

Extinguishment of Debt

• *Debt shall not be extinguished early if the primary aim is to report a gain or loss on the extinguishment.* If a company buys back its bonds when the stated interest rate on the debt is lower than the current market interest rate, it will recognize a gain on the transaction, but must refinance the purchase with more expensive debt at current market rates. Thus, this policy is designed to keep company management from creating transactions that appear to increase profits when the underlying results worsen the company's financial situation.

• *When interest rates allow, the company shall repurchase its debt with less expensive debt.* Though it sounds obvious, this policy is designed to force management to make the correct decision to always use less expensive debt, even though this will result in the recognition of a loss when the older, more expensive debt is eliminated from company records.

Convertible Debt

• *Debt conversions to equity shall always be recorded using the book value method.* This policy keeps the accounting staff from switching between the book value and market value methods, whereby they could use the market value method to recognize gains and the book value method to avoid losses.

DEBT-RELATED PROCEDURES

The detailed procedures used for borrowing from a line of credit, calculating the effective interest rate, extinguishing debt, converting debt to stock, and dealing with debt that has attached warrants are shown in this section. The line of credit procedure is shown in Exhibit 6.4.

The procedure used to calculate the discount or premium to be amortized under a debt issuance is shown in Exhibit 6.5.

The procedure used to calculate debt extinguishment is shown in Exhibit 6.6.

The procedure used to convert debt to equity is shown in Exhibit 6.7.

The procedure used to issue debt with attached stock warrants is shown in Exhibit 6.8.

SUMMARY

The treasurer is regularly called upon to obtain debt financing for a company. On a simplified level, this may involve obtaining a line of credit from the

---

Exhibit 6.4   Borrow From a Line of Credit

Procedure Statement   Retrieval No.: TREASURY-12

Subject: Steps required to borrow from the corporate line of credit

1. PURPOSE AND SCOPE

This procedure is used by the treasury staff to borrow funds from a line of credit.

2. PROCEDURES

2.1 Determine Amount to Borrow (Assistant Treasurer)

1. Review the short-term cash forecast with the financial analyst and determine the immediate cash need from that report.
2. Alter the expected cash need based on any unusual cash flows not noted on the cash forecast.

2.2 Borrow Funds (Assistant Treasurer)

1. Verify that there is a sufficient amount left on the line of credit to borrow. If not, contact the treasurer at once.
2. Enter in the Loan Borrowing form the amount determined in the preceding step.
3. Have an authorized approver sign the form.
4. Fax the completed form to the bank and confirm receipt.
5. Send a copy of the completed form to the general ledger accountant for proper recording in the general ledger.
6. Follow up with the bank if it does not send a transaction confirmation within a reasonable period of time.
7. Staple the Loan Borrowing form to the bank's confirmation, and file by date.

Exhibit 6.5   Calculation of a Discount or Premium

Procedure Statement   Retrieval No.: TREASURY-13

Subject: Steps required to calculate the discount or premium associated with a bond issuance

1. PURPOSE AND SCOPE
   This procedure is used by the accounting staff to determine the amount of discount or premium to amortize in a given accounting period.

2. PROCEDURES

   2.1 Calculate Discount or Premium (Financial Analyst)

   1. Determine the present value of the outstanding bond at the beginning of the calculation period. To do this, determine the present value of all interest payments for the bond instrument, as well as the present value of the principal payment at the end of the borrowing period, using the market rate of interest as the basis for the discount factor.
   2. Calculate the interest expense in the reporting period by multiplying the market interest rate by the bond's present value for the number of days in the accounting period.
   3. Subtract from the calculated interest expense the actual cash payment made for interest expense to the bond holders, which is based on the stated interest rate rather than the market interest rate. Using the difference between the two numbers, create a journal entry offsetting the outstanding discount or premium.
   4. Add this interest rate difference to the outstanding present value of the bond if there is a discount, or subtract it from the bond if there is an outstanding premium.
   5. Store the new balance of the bond present value, as well as the newly reduced discount or premium, which will be used as the basis for the effective interest calculation in the next reporting period.

---

company's bank, or a factoring or leasing arrangement. However, larger companies with excellent credit ratings have a number of additional tools available, such as bonds, commercial paper, and receivables securitization.

Of these types of debt, bond offerings in particular present a number of challenges from the perspective of accounting and control systems because there are ways to manipulate expense recognition in a company's favor. However, for the majority of companies that are restricted to basic lines of credit and loans, the accounting and control systems are relatively straightforward, primarily involving the approval of new debt and the proper recognition of interest expense in the correct reporting periods.

Exhibit 6.6 Account for Debt Extinguishment

Procedure Statement   Retrieval No.: TREASURY-14

Subject: Steps required to determine the cost of a debt extinguishment, complete the extinguishment, and account for it

1. PURPOSE AND SCOPE

    This procedure is used by the accounting staff to summarize and account for the costs of a debt extinguishment, and is used by the treasury staff to physically withdraw the debt.

2. PROCEDURES

    2.1 Calculate the Cost of a Proposed Debt Extinguishment (Financial Analyst)

        1. Examine the bond documentation to determine the amount of any extra fees required to extinguish debt early, such as termination fees or premium payments. Calculate the full extinguishment cost including these factors, and compare it to the cost of replacement financing to see if the proposed extinguishment will result in increased cash flow for the company.

    2.2 Approve and Process the Debt Extinguishment (Treasury Staff)

        1. Obtain written approval from the Board of Directors to retire the debt, and include this document in the corporate minute book.
        2. If there is a trustee managing bondholder transactions, notify the trustee of the proposed extinguishment.
        3. Contact bond holders to notify them of the date on which conversion shall occur, and the price they will receive for each bond held. If required by the bond document, this information may require publication to the general public well in advance of the extinguishment date.

    2.3 Account for the Transaction (Accounting Staff)

        1. If the original record of the bond issuance included a recognition of the intrinsic value of its equity portion, this recognition must be reversed. To do so, determine the number of shares that could have been converted on the retirement date. Then calculate the difference between the strike price and the fair market value of the stock on that date, and multiply it by the number of shares that could have been converted. Debit the result to the Additional Paid-In Capital account.
        2. If bond issuance costs were incurred and capitalized, then any remaining unamortized amounts left in the asset account as of the date of the debt extinguishment must be recognized as expense.
        3. If there is any unamortized discount or premium related to the original bond issuance, recognize that portion of the remaining amount that equates to the proportion of debt being retired.
        4. If any premium is being paid to retire the debt, charge this premium to expense at the time of the retirement.
        5. Summarize the transaction and send this information to the general ledger accountant for entry in the general ledger.

    2.4 Retire the Debt (Treasury Staff)

        1. On the retirement date, issue settlement funding to the bondholder trustee to retire the bonds.

Exhibit 6.7 Convert Debt to Equity

Procedure Statement   Retrieval No.: TREASURY-15

Subject: Steps required to process a request by a bond holder to convert that entity's bond holdings to company stock.

1. PURPOSE AND SCOPE
    This procedure is used by the accounting staff to account for the conversion of debt to equity, as well as by the treasury staff to retire bonds and issue stock.

2. PROCEDURES

    2.1 Retire Debt and Issue Stock (Treasury Staff)

    1. Verify that a sufficient number of shares are authorized and available to fulfill the request by the bond holder.
    2. Update the bond ledger by recording the retirement of the bond serial number.
    3. Create a stock certificate for the bond holder and obtain valid signatures authorizing the certificate. Issue the certificate to the former bond holder by registered mail.
    4. Update the stock ledger by recording the stock certificate number and the number of shares issued.

    2.2 Account for the Conversion (Accounting Staff)

    1. Send documentation of the transaction to the general ledger accountant, who records any accrued but unpaid interest expense on the bond, debiting it to expense and crediting the capital account (if the bond holder forfeits the interest). The general ledger accountant should initial the step to signify its completion.
    2. If the market value method is used to record the conversion transaction, the general ledger accountant should also note in the procedure the date of the conversion, the market price of the stock on that date, and initial next to this information.

Exhibit 6.8   Issue Debt with Stock Warrants

Procedure Statement   Retrieval No.: TREASURY-16

Subject: Steps required to determine the proper valuation of each component of a debt offering that has attached warrants

1. **PURPOSE AND SCOPE**

    This procedure is used primarily by the accounting staff to determine the value of the bond and stock warrants components of a debt offering, and to account for this information.

2. **PROCEDURES**

    2.1 Obtain Approval for and Conduct Bond Offering (Treasury Staff)

    1. Obtain written approval from the Board of Directors to issue debt with attached stock warrants, and include this document in the corporate minute book.
    2. Conduct the bond offering.

    2.2 Account for the Debt Warrant Components of the Offering (Accounting Staff)

    1. Determine the value of the bond and stock warrant components of the offering. This can be obtained from the investment banker handling the transaction, who can estimated it based on the value of similar offerings for other clients. Another alternative is to wait until the bonds and warrants are publicly traded and assign values based on their initial trading prices.
    2. To assign a price to the warrants, divide the warrant value by the total of both the bond value and the warrant value, and multiply the result by the total purchase price.
    3. Have an independent party, such as the internal audit staff, review the calculations splitting the value of the offering between bonds and stock warrants.
    4. Credit the resulting warrant value to the additional paid-in capital account and credit the full face value of the bond to the bonds payable account. Debit the total cash received from the transaction to the cash account, and enter any remaining difference to either the Discount on Bonds Payable (if a debit) or to the Premium on Bonds Payable (if a credit).
    5. If bond issuance costs were incurred, capitalize them and establish an amortization schedule.

7

Equity Management

A key goal of the treasurer of a public company is to have its securities registered, so that it can more easily sell the securities, and so that its investors can freely trade them. The registration process is very time consuming and expensive, so companies attempt to circumvent it through a variety of exemptions. Regulation A provides a reduced filing requirement for small-dollar issuances, while Regulation D allows for the complete absence of registration for security sales to accredited investors, though those investors cannot resell their securities without taking additional steps. If none of these simpler methods are available, then a company must use either the Form S-1 or S-3. Form S-3 is an abbreviated registration that is available only to seasoned public companies, while Form S-1 is the "full" version that the remaining public companies must use. This chapter describes the applicability of the various forms of registration and the exemptions from registration, as well as the accounting and systems related to equity transactions.

STOCK REGISTRATION

If a treasurer wants to sell stock to investors that in turn can be immediately traded by the investors, then it is necessary to file a registration statement with the Securities and Exchange Commission (SEC). Compiling a registration statement and walking it through the SEC review process is one of the most expensive and time-consuming tasks that a treasurer can engage in. It should be avoided if one of the exemptions described in the following section is available. If not, then a Form S-1 or S-3 must be filed. The two forms are described through the remainder of this section, along with the concept of a shelf registration and the process of declaring a registration statement effective.

Form S-1

This form is the default registration form to be used if no other registration forms or exemptions from registration (such as would be applicable under Regulations A or D) are applicable.

A key factor in the preparation of a Form S-1 is whether the company can incorporate a number of required items by referencing them in the form, which can save a great deal of work. Incorporation by reference is available *only* if the company has not been for the past three years a blank check company, a shell company, or a registrant for an offering of penny stock. The company must also be current with its various filings of financial information. These requirements are a particular burden for any private company that has gone public by acquiring a shell company, since it cannot incorporate its other SEC filings by reference until three years have passed from the date of acquisition.

The main informational contents of the Form S-1 are as follows:

1. *Forepart of the registration statement.* Include the company name, the title and amount of securities to be registered, and their offering price. Also describe the market for the securities, and a cross-reference to the risk factors section. Include a legend stating that the SEC has not approved or disapproved of the securities, and then identify the underwriters and state the nature of the underwriting arrangement.

2. *Summary information.* Provide a summary of the prospectus contents that contains a brief overview of the key aspects of the offering, as well as contact information for the company's principal executive offices.

3. *Risk factors.* Discuss the most significant factors that make the offering speculative or risky, and explain how the risk affects the company or the securities being offered.

4. *Ratio of earnings to fixed charges.* If the registration is for debt securities, then show a ratio of earnings to fixed charges. If the registration is for preferred equity securities, then show the ratio of combined fixed charges and preference dividends to earnings. These ratios must be shown for the past five years and the latest interim period.

5. *Use of proceeds.* State the principal purpose for which proceeds from the offering are intended.

6. *Determination of offering price.* Describe the factors considered in determining the offering price, both for common equity and for warrants, rights, and convertible securities.

7. *Dilution.* Disclose the net tangible book value per share before and after the distribution, the amount of the change in net tangible book value per share attributable to the cash payments made by purchasers of the shares being offered, and the amount of the immediate dilution from the public offering price, which will be absorbed by these purchasers.

8. *Selling security holders.* For those securities being sold for the account of another security holder, name each security holder, as well as each person's relationship with the company within the past three years, and the before-and-after ownership percentages of each security holder.

9. *Plan of distribution.* For securities offered through an underwriter, name all underwriters involved and their relationship with the offering. Also outline the plan of distribution for any securities to be registered that are offered otherwise than through under- writers. If the securities are to be offered on an exchange, then name the exchange. Also reveal the compensation paid to the underwriters, dealers, and finders. Further, describe any stabiliza- tion transactions that the underwriter intends to conduct during the offering period, and how these transactions will affect the security's price.

10. *Description of securities to be registered.* For equity securities, state the title of the security and related rights, such as voting rights, liqui- dation rights, dividend rights, and terms of conversion. For debt securities, state their title, the principal amount being offered and terms, such as maturity, interest, conversion, amortization, and so on; the description should also address liens, rights subordination, operational and financing restrictions, default events, warrants, and so forth.

11. *Interests of named experts and counsel.* Identify any experts and counsel that are certifying or preparing the registration document, or providing a supporting valuation, and the nature of their com- pensation relating to the registration. This can be excluded if their compensation does not exceed $50,000.

12. *Information with respect to the registrant.* This section comprises the bulk of the document, and includes a description of the business and its property, any legal proceedings, the market price of the company's stock, financial statements, selected financial data, and management's discussion and analysis of the company's financial condition and its results of operations. It also requires disclosure of any disagreements with the company's auditors, market risk analysis, and several ownership and governance issues.

13. *Material changes.* Describe material changes that have occurred since the company's last-filed annual or quarterly report.

14. *Other expenses of issuance and distribution.* Itemize the expenses incurred in connection with the issuance and distribution of the securities to be registered, other than underwriting discounts and commissions.

15. *Indemnification of directors and officers.* Note the effect of any arrangements under which the company's directors and officers are insured or indemnified against liability.

16. *Recent sales of unregistered securities.* Identify all unregistered securities sold by the company within the past three years, including the names of the principal underwriters, consideration received, and the type of exemption from registration claimed. Also state the use of proceeds from registered securities until all proceeds have been applied, or the offering is terminated.

17. *Exhibits and financial statement schedules.* Provide exhibits, with a related index, for such items as the underwriting agreement, consents, and powers of attorney. A table showing the complete list of possible exhibits is noted in Item 601 of Regulation S-K.

The preceding summary addresses the essential disclosure requirements for a Form S-1, but not all; the detail for these reporting requirements is located in Regulation S-K. Clearly, the Form S-1 is a serious undertaking that will likely result in a document having the size of a small book. It requires massive internal effort, as well as substantial input by and review of the company's auditors and counsel. The result is a major expense and a diversion of management time away from operational matters. Thus, there is an excellent reason why companies use every other means at their disposal to avoid raising funds through a Form S-1. One reduced type of informational reporting is available through Form S-3.

Form S-3

Form S-3 allows a company to incorporate a large amount of information into the form by reference, which is generally not allowed in a Form S-1. Specifically, the company can incorporate the information already filed in its latest Form 10-K, subsequent quarterly 10-Q reports, and 8-K reports, thereby essentially eliminating the "information with respect to the registration" that was described in the immediately preceding section for the Form S-1. This represents a considerable time savings, so companies file a Form S-3 whenever possible. However, the Form S-3 is restricted to those companies that meet the following eligibility requirements:

1. It is organized within and has principal business operations within the United States; and

2. It already has a class of registered securities, or has been meeting its periodic reporting requirements to the SEC for at least the past 12 months; and

3. It cannot have failed to pay dividends, sinking fund installments, or defaulted on scheduled debt or lease payments since the end of the last fiscal year; and

4. The aggregate market value of the common equity held by nonaffiliates of the company is at least $75 million.

If a company has an aggregate market value of common equity held by nonaffiliates of less than $75 million, it can still use Form S-3, provided that:

1. The aggregate market value of securities sold by the company during the 12 months prior to the Form S-3 filing is no more than one-third of the aggregate market value of the voting and nonvoting common equity held by its nonaffiliated investors; and

2. It is not a shell company, and has not been one for the past 12 months; and

3. It has at least one class of common equity securities listed on a national securities exchange.

Clearly, the eligibility requirements of the Form S-3 restrict its use to larger public companies. Smaller "nano-cap" firms must search for a registration exemption, such as is provided by Regulations A and D.

Shelf Registration

Shelf registration is the registration of a new issue of securities that can be filed with the SEC up to three years in advance of the actual distribution of such securities. This allows a company to obtain funds quickly when needed, rather than compiling a registration document and then waiting for the SEC to declare the registration effective. It is especially useful for debt offerings, since a public company can wait for interest rates to decline before issuing any securities.

A shelf registration is governed by the SEC's Rule 415. It can be accomplished through a Form S-3 filing, which in turn is restricted to certain companies that meet the SEC's eligibility rules (see the preceding Form S-3 section for details). It is also possible to use a Form S-1 to initiate a shelf registration, but only if the intent is to sell the securities "on an immediate, continuous, or delayed basis," with all sales being completed within the next two years.

A shelf registration must be declared effective by the SEC before any securities sales related to it can be initiated. However, the SEC's Rule 462(e) allows for some registration statements to be declared effective immediately upon their dates of filing. This automatic shelf registration is available only to *well-known seasoned issuers* (WKSIs). A WKSI is a company whose common stock belonging to nonaffiliates has a market value of at least $700 million, or which has issued at least $1 billion of nonconvertible securities within the past three years and will register only nonconvertible securities other than common equity. In addition, such filings have reduced information filing requirements.

Declaring a Registration Statement Effective

A registration statement is reviewed by the SEC staff, and if they find that it conforms to SEC regulations and clearly states key information about the company, then they declare it *effective*. Once declared effective, either the company or those investors on whose behalf it is registering the securities can initiate selling activities.

The problem is obtaining that "effective" status. The SEC's examiners delve into registration statements with great vigor, and it is a rare document indeed that is immediately granted "effective" status. Instead, the usual situation is for the SEC to spend one month reviewing the registration document and then sending back a comment letter. The letter begins with the following boilerplate comments:

> We have reviewed your filing and have the following comments. Where indicated, we think you should revise your document in response to these comments. If you disagree, we will consider your explanation as to why our comment is inapplicable or a revision is unnecessary. Please be as detailed as necessary in your explanation. In some of our comments, we may ask you to provide us with supplemental information so we may better understand your disclosure. After reviewing this information, we may or may not raise additional questions.
>
> Please understand that the purpose of our review process is to assist you in your compliance with the applicable disclosure requirements, and to enhance the overall disclosure of your filing.

The letter then continues with potentially dozens of questions about various items of information contained within the filing. The company then sends back a response, after which the SEC spends about one month reviewing the information again, and then responds with either another (hopefully reduced) list of questions or declares the document to be effective. A new public company can reasonably expect anywhere from two to four iterations of this process, with each iteration taking an additional month. A more experienced public company whose filings have been reviewed by the SEC in the recent past will occasionally not be reviewed at all, or will only be subjected to one or two rounds of questions.

The key issues involving the effectiveness declaration are the time and expense involved. The company's attorneys and auditors are deeply involved in every question and answer iteration with the SEC, so the cost of their services builds over time. Further, being declared effective in anything under two months is an excellent achievement, with previously unreviewed companies sometimes being subjected to a half-year of effort.

EXEMPTIONS FROM STOCK REGISTRATION

Given the exceptional delay just described in having a registration statement declared effective, any treasurer will always search for a registration exemption. The most common two exemptions are Regulation A, which applies to smaller issuances, and Regulation D, which applies to accredited investors.

Regulation A Exemption

Regulation A is described in the SEC's Rules 251 through 263, and provides an exemption from the securities registration requirements of the Securities Act of 1933, on the grounds that a smaller securities issuance does not warrant registration. Regulation A allows exemption from registration if the offering is no larger than $5 million in aggregate per year. Of this amount, no more than $1.5 million can be attributed to the secondary offering of securities currently held by existing shareholders; the secondary offering cannot include resales by company affiliates if the company has not generated net income from continuing operations in at least one of the past two fiscal years. The exemption is restricted to American and Canadian companies, and it is not available to investment and development-stage (such as "blank check" companies) companies. Anyone using this exemption must also create an offering circular, similar to the one that would be required for a registered offering.

There are a number of critical advantages to the exemption provided under Regulation A. First, there is no limit on the number of investors, nor must they pass any kind of qualification test (as would be the case under Regulation D, as described below). Further, there are no restrictions on the resale of any securities sold under the Regulation. Finally, the key difference between a Regulation A offering and a registered offering is the absence of any periodic reporting requirements. This is a major reduction in costs to the company, and is the most attractive aspect of the exemption.

In addition, and unlike a registered offering, the regulation allows a company to "test the waters" with investors in advance of the offering, in order to determine the level of investor interest. To take advantage of this feature, the company must submit the materials used for this initial testing of the waters to the SEC on or before their first date of use. The materials must state that no money is being solicited or will be accepted, that no sales will be made until the company issues an offering circular, that any indication of interest by an investor does not constitute a purchase commitment, and also identify the company's chief executive officer (CEO), as well as briefly describe the business. The company can only "test the waters" until it has filed an offering circular with the SEC, and can only commence securities sales once at least 20 days have passed since the last document delivery or broadcast.

When a company is ready to notify the SEC of securities sales under this regulation, it does so using Form 1-A. Once the Form is filed, the company can conduct a general solicitation, which can include advertising the offering, as long as the solicitation states that sales cannot be completed until the SEC qualifies the company's preliminary offering circular. This preliminary document does not have to include the final security price, though it should contain an estimate of the range of the maximum offering price and the maximum number of shares or debt securities to be offered. Advertising can only state where the offering circular can be obtained, the name of the company, the price and type of security being offered, and the company's general type of business.

While a company is permitted to advertise its offering as soon as the Form 1-A is filed, it must follow a specific procedure to conduct actual security sales. Once the Form 1-A has been qualified by the SEC, the company must furnish an offering circular to each prospective purchaser at least 48 hours prior to mailing a confirmation of sale. If a broker-dealer is involved with the sale, this entity must provide a copy of the offering circular either with or prior to the confirmation of sale.

If the information in an offering circular becomes false or misleading due to changed circumstances or there have been material developments during the course of an offering, the company must revise the offering circular.

Once securities sales are under way, the company must file Form 2-A with the SEC every six months following the qualification of the offering statement, describing ongoing sales from the offering and use of proceeds. In addition, it must file a final Form 2-A within 30 calendar days following the later of the termination of the offering or the application of proceeds from the offering.

The regulation has provisions that can disqualify a company from using it. It is not available if a company has had a variety of disclosure problems with the SEC in the past five years, or if the company currently has a registration statement being reviewed by the SEC, or if any affiliates or the company's underwriter have been convicted within the past ten years of a crime related to a security transaction.

Regulation D Exemption

Securities can only be sold under Regulation D to an *accredited investor*. An accredited investor is one whom the issuing company reasonably believes falls within any of these categories at the time of the securities sale:

1. A bank, broker-dealer, insurance company, investment company, or employee benefit plan;

2. A director, executive officer, or general partner of the issuing company;

3. A person whose individual net worth (or joint net worth with a spouse) exceeds $1 million;

4. A person having individual income exceeding $200,000 or joint income with a spouse exceeding $300,000 in each of the last two years, with a reasonable expectation for reaching the same income level in the current year; and

5. Any trust with total assets exceeding $5 million.

There are several additional types of accredited investors, and some restrictions on the accredited investor types just noted; please review Rule 501 of Regulation D for more details. Nonetheless, the preceding definitions describe the primary types of accredited investors.

The information that must be sent to accredited investors as part of the financing is minimized if the issuing company is already meeting its financial reporting requirements under the Exchange Act. Additional reporting requirements are applicable if this is not the case. Please consult Rule 502 of the Regulation for further details.

The issuing company is not allowed any form of general solicitation for the sale of securities under the Regulation. This prohibits the use of advertisements and articles via any medium of publication. It also prohibits the sale of securities through seminars to which attendees were invited through any form of general solicitation. In order to avoid having a general solicitation, a company must prescreen any investor to whom an inquiry is sent, usually by using an underwriter or promoter who already has a list of qualified potential investors.

A Regulation D offering may span a number of months; if so, there may be some question about which securities sales fall within its boundaries. The consideration of a sale transaction as being integrated into a specific Regulation D offering is a judgmental one. The following factors would lead to the presumption of integration: whether the sale is part of a single financing plan; involves the issuance of the same class of securities; is being made at approximately the same time; involves the same type of consideration; and the sale is made for the same general purpose.

Securities sold under a Regulation D offering cannot be resold without registration. For this reason, the issuing company is required under Rule 502 of the Regulation to "exercise reasonable care to assure that the purchasers of the securities are not underwriters. ..." To do so, the company must take the following three steps: (1) inquire of purchasers if they are acquiring the securities for themselves or for other parties; (2) disclose to each purchaser that the securities have not been registered and therefore cannot be resold until they are registered; and (3) add a legend to each securities certificate, stating that the securities have not been registered, and stating the restrictions on their sale or transfer.

Summary of Registration Options

The preceding discussion should make it clear that a vast amount of paperwork is involved in any stock registration, even including the Regulation A exemption. Only the Regulation D exemption involves a relatively minor amount of SEC notification. Given the minimal resources available to a smaller public company, this tends to shift companies in the direction of registration exemptions. The reverse situation is true for large and well-funded public companies, whose large accounting and treasury staffs routinely file S-3 registration documents.

ACCOUNTING FOR STOCK SALES

Most types of stock contain a par value, which is a minimum price below which the stock cannot be sold. The original intent for using par value was to ensure that a residual amount of funding was contributed to the company, and which could not be removed from it until dissolution of the corporate entity. In reality, most common stock now has a par value that is so low (typically anywhere from a penny to a dollar) that its original intent no longer works. Thus, though the accountant still tracks par value separately in the accounting records, it has little meaning.

If an investor purchases a share of stock at a price greater than its par value, the difference is credited to an additional paid-in capital account. For example, if an investor buys one share of common stock at a price of $82, and the stock's par value is $1, then the entry would be:

	Debit	Credit
Cash	$82	
Common stock—par value		$1
Common stock—additional paid-in capital		81

When a company initially issues stock, there will be a number of costs associated with it, such as the printing of stock certificates, legal fees, investment banker fees, and security registration fees. These costs can be charged against the proceeds of the stock sale, rather than be recognized as expenses within the current period.

If the warrant attached to a debt instrument cannot be detached and sold separately from the debt, then it should not be separately accounted for. However, if it can be sold separately by the debt holder, then the fair market value of each item (the warrant and the debt instrument) should be determined, and then the accountant should apportion the price at which the combined items were sold amongst the two, based on their fair market values.

Example

If the fair market value of a warrant is $63.50 and the fair market value of a bond to which it was attached is $950, and the price at which the two items were sold was $1,005, then an entry should be made to an additional paid-in capital account for $62.97 to account for the warrants, while the remaining $942.03 is accounted for as debt. The apportionment of the actual sale price of $1,005 to warrants is calculated as follows:

$$\frac{\text{Fair Market Value of Warrant}}{\begin{array}{l}\text{Fair Market Value of Warrant}\\ +\text{Fair Market Value of Bond}\end{array}} \times \text{Price of Combined Instruments}$$

or,

$$\frac{\$63.50}{(\$63.50+\$950)} \times \$1,005 = \$62.97$$

If a warrant expires, then the funds are shifted from the outstanding warrants account to an additional paid-in capital account. To continue with the last example, this would require the following entry:

	Debit	Credit
Additional Paid-In Capital—Warrants	$62.97	
Additional Paid-in Capital—Expired Warrants		$62.97

If a warrant is subsequently used to purchase a share of stock, then the value allocated to the warrant in the accounting records should be shifted to the common stock accounts. To use the preceding example, if the warrant valued at $62.97 is used to purchase a share of common stock at a price of $10, and the common stock has a par value of $25, then the par value account is credited with $25 (since it is mandatory that the par value be recorded), and the remainder of the funds are recorded in the additional paid-in capital account. The entry is as follows:

	Debit	Credit
Cash	$10.00	
Additional paid-in capital—warrants	62.97	
Common stock—par value		$25.00
Common stock—additional paid-in capital		47.97

EQUITY-RELATED CONTROLS

There are a number of controls that should be used during the process of selling equity to the investment community. The following controls are listed in sequential order, from the start of an equity offering. Those applying primarily to a specific registration document or exemption are so noted.

General Stock Sale Controls

1. *Verify available authorized shares.* There must be a sufficient number of authorized and unused shares available for distribution, which can be determined by comparing the authorized number of shares listed in the articles of incorporation to the share total reported by the company's stock transfer agent.

2. *Verify board authorization.* The board minutes should reflect the approval of a stock offering that includes the minimum and maximum allowed amounts of funding, and the approximate terms of the offering.

3. *Have due diligence officer review all SEC filings.* The SEC can and will reject any registration documents if information is not presented exactly in accordance with its instructions. To avoid the delay of an SEC rejection, have a due diligence officer who specializes in SEC procedures review the filings prior to submission.

4. *Verify contents of security authorization letter.* The next step in the process is to authorize the issuance of shares to the new investors. The treasurer authorizes the issuance of shares to new investors by completing a form letter to the company's stock transfer agent, itemizing the number of shares to be issued to each investor, and noting addresses and tax identification numbers. Corporate counsel should match all information on the authorization letter to the supporting documentation prior to approving the letter.

Controls Specific to Regulation A Stock Sales

1. *Review disqualification provisions.* The SEC can use several rules to disqualify a company's Regulation A offering. Corporate counsel should review these rules in advance to determine if the regulation can be used, and advise the CEO if the offering can proceed.

2. *Submit "test the waters" documents to counsel.* The company can issue "test the waters" documents to prospective investors, but only ones that follow specific SEC guidelines, and which have been submitted to the SEC in advance. To ensure that such documents meet SEC requirements, have corporate counsel not only review them, but formally approve them and retain a copy of the approved version.

3. *Verify termination of "test the waters" documents.* A formal offering cannot begin until at least 20 days after "test the waters" materials have been distributed, so ensure that distribution is terminated as of a specific date.

4. *Control release of offering circular.* The preliminary offering circular cannot be released until the SEC qualifies it. Corporate counsel should have control over the release, so that no premature distribution occurs.

5. *Submit advertising to counsel.* The company can advertise the offering, but only include specific terminology in the advertisements. To ensure that the advertising meets SEC requirements, have corporate counsel not only review it, but formally approve it and retain a copy of the approved version.

6. *Specify an escrow cap.* Regulation A does not allow for the issuance of more than $5 million in aggregate per year, of which no more than $1.5 million can be a secondary offering. To ensure that these limitations are not exceeded, impose a cap on the amount of funds to be accepted by the escrow, beyond which funds will be returned to investors.

7. *Update offering circular.* The offering circular must be re-issued if material events occur during the offering period that would make information in the circular false or misleading. A disclosure committee, composed of at least the controller and corporate counsel, should meet regularly during the offering period to determine if such changes should be made.

8. *Ensure that Form 2-A is filed.* At least one Form 2-A must be filed within six months of the SEC's qualification of the offering statement. Responsibility for the filing lies with corporate counsel, who should note the due date on a checklist of activities associated with the funding

Controls Specific to Regulation D Stock Sales

1. *Review outgoing subscription agreement.* There is a possibility that variations on the subscription agreement will be sent to different prospective investors. To avoid this, create a master term sheet and have the CEO initial it. All subscription agreements must be compared to this master term sheet prior to being issued. Better yet, have corporate counsel initial every subscription agreement before it is issued, and retain a copy as proof of the issued terms.

2. *Review received subscription agreement.* It is possible that an investor might fraudulently modify the terms of the subscription agreement. To guard against this, compare the retained copy of the issued subscription agreement to the one returned by each investor.

3. *Review investor qualification certificate.* The company must be able to prove that it has received sufficient assurances from its investors that they are accredited investors. Accordingly, corporate counsel should verify that a signed investor qualification certificate has been received from each investor, and that it has been properly completed.

4. *Verify cash receipt.* An investor may submit signed documents indicating that he is investing, but not transfer funds to the escrow agent. To detect this, request verification of cash receipt from the escrow agent, and match the amounts received to the amounts indicated on the signed subscription agreements.

5. *Ensure that Form D is filed.* The Form D must be filed within 15 days of the receipt of funds from the escrow account. Responsibility for the filing lies with the corporate counsel, who should note the due date on a checklist of activities associated with the funding. Counsel must also obtain the signature of the chief executive officer on the Form D, and retain a copy of the completed form in storage. A subsequent audit can also verify that these tasks have been completed in a timely manner.

EQUITY-RELATED POLICIES

The policies described in this section apply to a company's use of the Regulation A or D exemptions, and so are only needed if the treasurer expects to issue stock under either exemption.

Policies Specific to Regulation A Stock Sales

A company will find itself at significant risk of having a Regulation A offering not qualified by the SEC if it either employs or is owned by an individual with an objectionable background. Accordingly, all directors, officers, share-holders owning at least 10 percent of any class of company securities, and underwriter officers should be required to complete a violations question-naire similar to the one shown later in the Procedures section, and subject the questionnaire to a review and approval process. A sample policy follows:

> **Policy:** The Company shall require all directors, officers, and shareholders owning at least 10 percent of any class of company securities to complete and sign a violations questionnaire that fully describes any convictions, court orders, and organizational suspensions to which they are subjected.

A sample violations questionnaire is shown in Exhibit 7.2. Once an individual submits this questionnaire, there should be an obligation to notify the company of any changes in the status of any responses to it. A sample policy follows:

> **Policy:** If there is a material change to the information initially submitted on the violations questionnaire, then the submitting party shall promptly notify corporate counsel of the change.

Regulation A allows for the use of "test the waters" documents, as well as advertising. Given that the Regulation restricts the content of these issu-ances, the company should channel them all past corporate counsel, who is required to review and approve them prior to issuance. A sample policy follows:

> **Policy:** All securities solicitations must be approved in advance and in writing by corporate counsel. This approval shall include a description of the solicita-tion and sample marketing materials.

Thus, the strong need for compliance with Regulation A at multiple points during an offering requires corporate counsel to be featured repeat-edly in all of the preceding policies.

Policies Specific to Regulation D Stock Sales

A key part of Regulation D is that the sale of unregistered securities can only be to accredited investors. The company must take reasonable steps to be assured that a prospective investor is indeed an accredited investor. This process begins with the following policy:

> **Policy:** The Company shall not issue unregistered securities without first obtaining a signed statement from each prospective investor, clearing stating that individual or entity's status as an accredited investor.

A procedure in the next section follows up on this policy, detailing the use of an investor qualification certificate.

All unregistered securities issued by the company must carry a restrictive legend, specifying that they cannot be traded. The following policy enumerates the precise restrictive language:

> **Policy:** All unregistered securities issued by the Company shall contain the following restrictive legend: "These securities have not been registered under the Securities Act of 1933, as amended. They may not be sold, offered for sale, pledged or hypothecated in the absence of a registration statement in effect with respect to the securities under such Act or an exemption from such registration requirements." This legend may only be modified following the recommendation of corporate counsel.

General solicitation of investors is not allowed under Regulation D, so a policy should note that prohibition. An example follows:

> **Policy:** The Company shall not use any form of general solicitation to potential investors for the sale of unregistered securities.

Better yet, require the advance approval of corporate counsel for all contemplated securities solicitations. Given the presumed expertise of counsel, it is most unlikely that a general solicitation would be approved. An example follows:

> **Policy:** All securities solicitations must be approved in advance and in writing by corporate counsel. This approval shall include a description of the solicitation and sample marketing materials.

EQUITY-RELATED PROCEDURES

There are two procedures in this section, one describing the process flow for a stock sale under the Regulation A exemption, and the other describing a sale under the Regulation D exemption.

The procedure used to sell stock under the Regulation A exemption is shown in Exhibit 7.1. It assumes that a company uses the "test the waters" option and also elects to use subsequent marketing events.

The core of the procedure surrounding stock sales under the Regulation D exemption is the issuance of a package of information to each prospective investor, and verification that it has been completed prior to accepting funds from and issuing any security certificates to the investor. The procedure shown in Exhibit 7.3 itemizes the process flow.

Please note that the investor qualification certificate shown in Exhibit 7.4 is only a *portion* of a full certificate, since it does not make reference to several additional types of accredited investors that are not commonly found. Rule 501 of Regulation D itemizes the full range of accredited investors.

Exhibit 7.1   Stock Sale Procedure Under the Regulation A Exemption

Procedure Statement   Retrieval No.: TREASURY-13

Subject: Steps required to sell stock under the filing exemption of SEC Regulation A.

1. PURPOSE AND SCOPE

This procedure is used primarily by corporate counsel to verify that the company will not be disqualified under the provisions of the exemption, as well as to file notices with the SEC, collect funds through an escrow account, and authorize the issuance of shares to investors.

2. PROCEDURES

2.1 Disqualification Investigation (Corporate Counsel)

1. Corporate counsel reviews the disqualification provisions of Regulation A to ascertain if there are any Regulation compliance issues that may prevent the company from using a Regulation A offering.
2. If there are no obvious disqualifying issues at the company level, corporate counsel distributes a questionnaire such as the sample shown in Exhibit 7.2 to the board of directors, officers, shareholders owning at least 10 percent of any class of company securities, and underwriter officers. Counsel subsequently reviews the completed questionnaires to ascertain if the activities of these individuals would disqualify the company.

2.2 Legal Requirements Review (Corporate Counsel)

1. Counsel verifies that there are a sufficient number of authorized shares available to at least match the maximum number of shares to be issued under the offering.
2. Counsel verifies that the board of directors has authorized the issuance of securities under Regulation A.

2.3 SEC Review (SEC and Corporate Counsel)

1. Submit "test the waters" documents, as well as scripts for broadcast releases, to counsel for prior approval. Counsel approves and retains copies of all such documents.
2. Counsel submits the "test the waters" documents to the SEC, and then authorizes their release to the investment community.
3. Counsel determines the final date upon which "test the waters" documents are issued to the investment community, and then authorizes the termination of such distributions.
4. Counsel reviews and approves the preliminary offering circular and submits it to the SEC for qualification, using Form 1-A.
5. Counsel responds to all SEC comment letters relating to the preliminary offering circular.

6. Upon qualification by the SEC, counsel determines the number of days that have passed since the last "test the waters" document delivery or broadcast. Once 20 days have passed, counsel authorizes commencement of a general solicitation.
7. Counsel preapproves and retains a copy of all advertising used as part of the general solicitation.

2.4 Collect Funds (Corporate Counsel and Treasurer)

1. Counsel specifies an escrow cap, so that the Regulation A maximum funding amount is not exceeded.
2. Once all funding is received, the escrow agent wires all funds to the designated corporate account. The treasurer tallies the received funds and sends a summary document to the general ledger accountant for entry in the accounting system.
2. Once funding is completed, counsel creates a security authorization letter for the stock transfer agent, specifying the number of shares to be issued.

2.5 Subsequent SEC Filings (Corporate Counsel)

1. Counsel files Form 2-A every six months following qualification, as well as a final Form 2-A within 30 calendar days following offering termination or the final application of offering proceeds.

Exhibit 7.2   Violations Questionnaire

1. Have you been convicted within ten years prior to the filing of the offering circular of any felony or misdemeanor in connection with the purchase or sale of any security, involving the making of a false filing with the SEC, or arising out of the conduct of the business of an underwriter, broker, dealer, municipal securities dealer, or investment advisor?

2. Are you subject to any order, judgment, or decree of any court, temporarily or permanently restraining you from engaging in any conduct or practice in connection with the purchase or sale of any security involving the making of a false filing with the SEC, or arising out of the conduct of the business of an underwriter, broker, dealer, municipal securities dealer, or investment advisor?

3. Have you been suspended or expelled from membership in, or barred from association with a member of, a national securities exchange for any act or omission to act constituting conduct inconsistent with just and equitable principles of trade?

4. Are you subject to a United States Postal Service false representation order within five years prior to the filing of the offering circular?

Exhibit 7.3 Stock Sale Procedure Under the Regulation D Exemption

Procedure Statement   Retrieval No.: TREASURY-14

Subject: Steps required to sell stock under the filing exemption of SEC Regulation D.

1. PURPOSE AND SCOPE

This procedure is used primarily by corporate counsel to file notices with the SEC, prepare subscription agreements and investor qualification certificates, collect funds through an escrow account, and authorize the issuance of shares to investors

2. PROCEDURES

2.1 Legal Requirements Review (Corporate Counsel)

1. Verify that there are a sufficient number of authorized shares available to at least match the maximum number of shares to be issued under the offering.
2. Verify that the board of directors has authorized the issuance of Regulation D securities.

2.2 Document Preparation (Corporate Counsel)

1. Update the subscription agreement with the minimum and maximum amount of funds to be collected, specific terms of the agreement, and wiring instructions for the escrow account.
2. Update the Investor Qualification Certificate (see Exhibit 7.4) with the dates of the last two calendar years, in the block asking whether an individual investor has earned income of at least $200,000 in each of the last two specified years.
3. Issue the documents to each prospective investor.

2.3 Collect Funds (Corporate Counsel and Treasurer)

1. Upon receipt of the documents, verify with the escrow agent that all funds have been received.
2. Once the minimum amount of funding has been received in the escrow account, authorize the transfer of funds from the escrow agent to the corporate bank account.
3. Once all funding is received, the escrow agent wires all funds to the designated corporate account. The treasurer tallies the received funds and sends a summary document to the general ledger accountant for entry in the accounting system.
4. Create a security authorization letter for the stock transfer agent, specifying the number of shares to be issued, and the restrictive legend to be placed on the back of each certificate.

2.4 Subsequent SEC Filings (Corporate Counsel)

1. Within 15 days of the initial receipt of funds, file a Form D with the SEC. The chief executive officer must manually sign this form prior to filing. Retain the original copy in storage.

Exhibit 7.4   Investor Qualification Certificate

Name of Investor:_____

This information is being furnished to _____, Inc., to determine whether securities may be issued to the undersigned pursuant to Regulation D of the Securities and Exchange Commission.

The undersigned acknowledges that the Company's evaluation of the information contained herein may preclude the Company's issuance of securities to the undersigned.

The undersigned furnishes to the Company the following representations and information:

1. Please initial in the space provided:

The undersigned has such knowledge and experience in financial and business matters as to be capable of evaluating the merits and risks of the securities. The undersigned has not relied on the advice of any representative or other persons in evaluating the merits and risks of the undersigned's acquisition of the securities.

RNC
_____

The undersigned understands that the securities cannot be transferred or sold unless they are registered under the Securities Act. The undersigned is able to bear the economic risk of the undersigned's prospective investment. In making this statement, consideration has been given to whether the undersigned could afford to hold the securities for an indefinite period and whether, at this time, the undersigned could afford a complete loss of such securities.

RNC
_____

The undersigned's overall commitment to investments which are not readily marketable is not disproportionate to the undersigned's net worth, and the undersigned's prospective investment will not cause such overall commitment to become excessive.

RNC
_____

The undersigned has adequate means of providing for the undersigned's current needs and, if applicable, possible personal contingencies. The undersigned has no need for liquidity of the prospective investment, and has no reason to anticipate any change in the undersigned's circumstances, financial or otherwise, which may cause or require any sale or distribution of the securities.

RNC
_____

The undersigned will hold the securities for the undersigned's own account for investment, and will not hold the securities for the interest of any other person and/or with a view to or for sale in connection with any distribution thereof.

RNC

The undersigned acknowledges that the undersigned has the right to ask questions of and receive answers from the company and to obtain such information concerning the terms and conditions of the securities or about the company as the company possesses or can acquire without unreasonable effort or expense. The undersigned acknowledges that prior to any purchase by the undersigned of any securities, the undersigned will have asked such questions, received such answers and obtained such information as the undersigned deems necessary to evaluate the merits and risks of the securities.

RNC

The undersigned represents to the company that: 1) the information contained in this questionnaire is complete and accurate; 2) the undersigned will notify the company immediately of any material change in any of such information occurring prior to purchase by the undersigned of any securities; and 3) if the undersigned is a corporation, partnership, trust or other entity, the person signing this Certificate on behalf of such entity has been authorized by such entity to do so.

RNC

2. Please check all appropriate spaces:

	Yes	No
The undersigned is an individual whose net worth, or joint net worth with spouse, is in excess of $1,000,000.	√	—
The undersigned is an individual whose income is each of 2008 and 2009 was in excess of $200,000, and the undersigned reasonably anticipates reaching $200,000 in income in 2010.	√	—
The undersigned is an individual whose joint income with spouse was in excess of $300,000 in each of 2008 and 2009, and the undersigned reasonably anticipates reaching $300,000 in joint income with spouse in 2010.	√	—

	Yes	No
The undersigned is a director or executive director of the Company or is a person who performs a policy-making function for the Company, or who is in charge of a principal business unit, division, or function of the Company.	___	√
The undersigned is a trust, with total assets in excess of $5,000,000, not formed for the specific purpose of acquiring the securities, the purchase of which is directed by a person having such knowledge of financial matters that he is capable of evaluating the merits and risks of the investment.	___	√
The undersigned is an employee benefit plan, and the investment plan is made by a plan fiduciary, or the plan has total assets in excess of $5,000,000, or it is a self-directed plan whose investment decisions are made by accredited investors.	___	√
The undersigned is a bank, savings and loan association, broker-dealer, insurance company, or investment company.	___	√

3. Please complete the following:

If the undersigned is a partnership, a corporation or other entity, the undersigned is organized on [date] under the laws of the State of _____, and its principal place of business is located in the State of _____.

If the undersigned is an individual, the undersigned's residence is located in the State of _____.

In witness whereof, the undersigned has caused this Investor Qualification Certificate to be executed on _____ [date].

By: *Richard N. Cladwell*
Name: Richard N. Cladwell

SUMMARY

The ability to issue high-quality registration documents to the SEC is the mark of a well-run company. It requires excellent knowledge of SEC regulations, as well as the support and direction of experienced company counsel. However, even those companies with such expertise prefer to escalate their filings from a Form S-1 to a Form S-3, simply to avoid the drudgery of preparing and defending the S-1. A filing under Regulation A involves less paperwork, but the amount of funds raised under it is quite limited, and there are a number of compliance issues to monitor. Where possible, the simplest alternative of all is a Regulation D offering, in which securities are only offered to accredited investors. The treasurer is heavily involved in stock sales, and so should be familiar with all forms of registration and related exemptions, as well as the controls and procedures needed to complete stock sales under each one.

SUMMARY

8

Investment Management

Surplus funds not needed for either operating purposes or compensating bank balances are available for investment. Prudent use of these funds can add to income, though the treasurer must consider a range of investment criteria, types of investments, and investment strategies before selecting the appropriate investment vehicle. This chapter describes these issues, as well as the accounting, controls, policies, and procedures required for an ongoing investment program.

INVESTMENT CRITERIA

When considering various forms of cash investment, the treasurer should first consider the *safety of the principal* being invested. It would not do to invest company funds in a risky investment in order to earn extraordinarily high returns if there is a chance that any portion of the principal will be lost. Accordingly, a company policy should limit investments to a specific set of low-risk investment types. Also, some consideration should be given to the *maturity* and *marketability* of an investment. For example, if an investment in a block of apartment houses appears to generate a reasonably risk-free return and a good rate of return, it is still a poor investment from a cash management perspective, because the investment probably cannot be converted to cash on short notice. Accordingly, it is best to only make investments where there is a robust market available for their immediate resale. The final consideration when making an investment is its *yield*—and this is truly the last consideration after the previous items have already been reviewed. Within the boundaries of appropriate levels of risk, maturity, and marketability, the treasurer can then pick the investment with the highest yield. Since these criteria tend to limit one to very low-risk investments, the yield will also likely be quite low.

The investment criteria for a company that finds itself in a rapid growth situation are more circumscribed. It typically burns through its cash reserves quite rapidly, so the liquidity of its investments must be extremely high in order to allow rapid access to it. Unfortunately, high liquidity is commonly associated with low investment returns, so the treasurer is forced to invest in low-yield investments. In addition, the company cannot run the risk of loss on its investments, because it is critically important to keep cash available to feed the company's growth engine. Since risk is also associated with return, the treasurer must, once again, favor low-yield investments for minimal risk.

INVESTMENT OPTIONS

Within the investment boundaries just noted, there are a number of investment options available. Here are the most common ones that have low risk levels, short maturity dates, and high levels of marketability:

- *Bankers' acceptances.* Banks sometimes guarantee (or *accept*) corporate debt, usually when they issue a loan to a corporate customer, and then sell the debt to investors. Because of the bank guarantee, they are viewed as obligations of the bank.

- *Bonds near maturity dates.* A corporate bond may not mature for many years, but one can always purchase a bond that is close to its maturity date. There tends to be a minimal risk of loss (or gain) on the principal amount of this investment, since there is a low risk that interest rates will change so much in the short time period left before the maturity date of the bond that it will impact its value. A variation on this type of investment is the municipal bond, for which there is no tax on the interest income; however, in consideration of this reduced liability, its yield also tends to be somewhat lower than on other types of bonds.

- *Certificate of deposit (CD).* These certificates are essentially term bank deposits, typically having durations of up to two years. They usually pay a fixed interest rate upon maturity, though some variable-rate CDs are available. There is a perception that they are more secure than commercial paper, since CDs are issued by banks, which are more closely regulated than companies. There is up to $100,000 of Federal Deposit Insurance Corporation (FDIC) insurance coverage of this investment. The secondary market for CDs can vary and calls for some review prior to making an investment. A more restrictive CD may require an early-withdrawal penalty.

- *Commercial paper.* Larger corporations issue short-term notes that carry higher yields than on government debt issuances. There is also an active secondary market for them, so there is usually no problem with liquidity. Commercial paper is generally not secured; however, staying with the commercial paper issued by "blue chip" organizations minimizes the risk of default. Most commercial paper matures in 30 days or less, and rarely matures in greater than 270 days, in order to avoid the registration requirements of the Securities and Exchange Commission (SEC). Commercial paper is issued at a discount, with the face value being paid at maturity.

- *Money market fund.* This is a package of government instruments, usually composed of Treasury bills, notes, and bonds, that is assembled by a fund management company. The investment is highly liquid, with many investors putting in funds for as little as a day. There are varying levels of risk between different money market funds, since some funds are more active in trying to outperform the market (with an attendant increase in risk).

- *Repurchase agreement.* This is a package of securities (frequently government debt) that an investor buys from a financial institution, under the agreement that the institution will buy it back at a specific price on a specific date. It is most commonly used for the overnight investment of excess cash from a company's cash concentration account, which can be automatically handled by the company's primary bank. The typical interest rate earned on this investment is equal to or less than the money market rate, since the financial institution takes a transaction fee that cuts into the rate earned.

- *U.S. Treasury issuances.* The United States government issues a variety of notes with maturity dates that range from less than a year (U.S. Treasury certificates) through several years (notes) to more than five years (bonds). The wide range of maturity dates gives one a broad range of investment options. Also, there is a strong secondary market for these issuances, so they can be liquidated in short order. U.S. government debts of all types are considered to be risk free, and so have lower yields than other forms of investment. At times, the demand for these issuances has been so strong that yields have been essentially zero.

The summary table in Exhibit 8.1 shows the key features of each of the above types of investments.

When any of the preceding investments are initially issued to an investor or dealer, this is considered a *primary market transaction*. It is quite likely that many of these investments will be subsequently resold to a series of investors, depending on the duration of the investment. These subsequent transactions are considered to be trading in the *secondary market*.

Exhibit 8.1 Investment Comparison

Investment Type	Maturity	Issued By	Interest Rate	Interest Paid	Secured	Capital Access Prior to Maturity
Bankers' acceptances	Less than 1 year	Banks	Fixed	Discount to face value	Yes	Secondary market available
Bonds near maturity date	Multiyear	Corporations and governments	Fixed	Coupon	No	Secondary market available
Certificates of deposit	1 day to 2 years	Banks	Mostly fixed, variable available	On maturity	FDIC only	Secondary market available
Commercial paper	Overnight to 270 days	Corporations	Fixed	Discount to face value	No	Secondary market available
Money market fund	Weighted average of 90 days or less	Assemblage of federal government issuances	Variable	Periodic	No	Secondary market available
Repurchase agreement	Negotiable	Corporations and banks	Negotiable	On maturity	Yes	Negotiable
U.S. Treasury issuances	Varies	Federal government	Fixed	On maturity	No	Secondary market available

Many of the secondary market transactions pass through the hands of dealers, who add a small markup to the price of each investment that they then sell to an investor. However, it is possible to deal directly with the United States Treasury to buy government debt. The government has set up the www.publicdebt.treas.gov web site. A company can use the site to create a TreasuryDirect account for making electronic purchases of debt. Though the intent of the site is to sell debt that is held to maturity, one can request a debt sale through the Federal Reserve Bank of Chicago via the Treasury's Sell Direct system; the government will then sell one's debt investments on the open market in exchange for a small fee per security sold. The usual investment will be in Treasury bills, since they have the shortest term to maturity and can therefore liquidate prior to any need for a commissionable sale to a broker or reseller. More information about this service is available by downloading the Treasury Direct Investor Kit from the aforementioned web site.

INVESTMENT STRATEGIES

The treasurer should develop a standard methodology for investing funds. This goes beyond the selection of a type of investment, and enters the ream of strategies that can range from being passive (and requiring no attention) to those that are quite active and call for continuing decision making. This section describes a range of possible investment strategies.

At the most minimal level of investment strategy, the treasurer can do nothing and leave idle balances in the corporate bank accounts. This is essentially an *earnings credit strategy*, since the bank uses the earnings from these idle balances to offset its service fees. If a company has minimal cash balances, then this is not an entirely bad strategy—the earnings credit can be the equivalent of a modest rate of return, and if there is not enough cash to plan for more substantive investments, leaving the cash alone is a reasonable alternative.

A *matching strategy* simply matches the maturity date of an investment to the cash flow availability dates listed on the cash forecast. For example, ABC Company's cash forecast indicates that $80,000 will be available for investment immediately, but must be used in two months for a capital project. The treasurer can invest the funds in a two-month instrument, such that its maturity date is just prior to when the funds will be needed. This is a very simple investment strategy that is more concerned with short-term liquidity than return on investment, and is most commonly used by firms having minimal excess cash.

A *laddering strategy* involves creating a set of investments that have a series of consecutive maturity dates. For example, ABC Company's cash forecast indicates that $150,000 of excess cash will be available for the foreseeable future, and its investment policy forbids any investments having a duration of greater than three months. The treasurer could invest the entire amount in a three-month instrument, since this takes advantage of the presumably somewhat higher interest rates that are available on longer-term investments. However, there is always a risk that some portion of the cash will be needed sooner. In order to keep the investment more liquid while still taking advantage of the higher interest rates available through longer-term investments, the treasurer breaks the available cash into thirds, and invests $50,000 in a one-month instrument, another $50,000 in a two-month instrument, and the final $50,000 in a three-month instrument. As each investment matures, the treasurer reinvests it into a three-month instrument. By doing so, ABC always has $50,000 of the invested amount coming due within one month or less. This improves liquidity, while still taking advantage of longer-term interest rates.

A *tranched cash flow strategy* requires the treasurer to determine what cash is available for short, medium, and long-term investment, and to then adopt different investment criteria for each of these investment tranches. The exact investment criteria will vary based on a company's individual needs, but here is a sample of how the tranches might be arranged:

- The short-term tranche is treated as cash that may be needed for operational requirements on a moment's notice. This means that cash flows into and out of this tranche can be strongly positive or negative. Thus, return on investment is not a key criterion—instead, the treasurer focuses on very high levels of liquidity. The return should be the lowest of the three tranches, but should also be relatively steady.

- The medium-term tranche includes cash that may be required for use within the next 3 to 12 months, and usually only for highly predictable events, such as periodic tax or dividend payments, or capital expenditures that can be planned well in advance. Given the much higher level of predictability in this tranche, the treasurer can accept longer-term maturities with moderate levels of volatility that have somewhat higher returns on investment.

- The long-term tranche includes cash for which there is no planned operational use, and which the treasurer feels can be safely invested for at least one year. The priority for this tranche shifts more in favor of a higher return on investment, with an attendant potential for higher levels of volatility and perhaps short-term capital loss, with a reduction in the level of liquidity.

Portrayed graphically, the tranches would appear as noted in Exhibit 8.2. The corporate cash balance should rarely decline into the long-term tranche, with occasional forays into the medium-term tranche, while the cash level will vary considerably within the short-term tranche.

Exhibit 8.2   Investments by Cash Flow Tranches

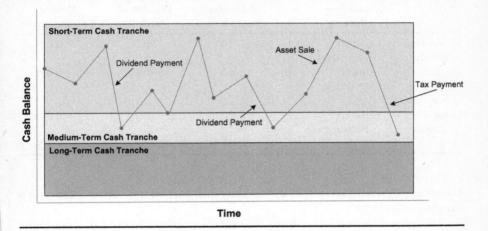

An example of the numerical result of a tranched cashflow strategy is shown in Exhibit 8.3, which assumes a baseline return to be the return on one-month Treasuries, with a target of increased basis points (BPs) above that standard for the medium-term and long-term tranches.

To engage in the tranched cash flow strategy, the treasurer should regularly review the cash forecast, and adjust the amounts of cash needed in each of the three tranches. Inattention to these adjustments could result in an unanticipated cash requirement when the cash in the company's long-term tranche is tied up in excessively long-term, illiquid investments.

The preceding strategies were mechanical; the treasurer analyzes cash flows and engages in investments based on cash availability. The next two strategies are more speculative, since the treasurer is guessing at the possible direction of future yields.

Riding the yield curve is a strategy of buying longer-term securities and selling them prior to their maturity dates. This strategy works when interest rates on short-term securities are lower than the rates on longer-term securities, which is normally the case. An example of an upward-sloping yield curve is shown in Exhibit 8.4, which is based on the Constant Maturity Treasury rates in May 2009. In such an environment, the longer-term securities with their higher interest rates that are held by the company will increase in value over time. For example, ABC Company has $75,000 of cash available for investment for a three-month period of time. The treasurer invests in a six-month security and sells it after three months, achieving a higher-than-usual rate of return. However, if the yield curve had changed during the interim, so that short-term rates were higher than long-term rates, then

Exhibit 8.3 Returns from Tranched Cash Flow Strategy

	Baseline Return	+	Additional Basis Points	Percent of Portfolio	Return Enhancement
Short-term tranche	1-month Treasuries	+	0	50%	0 BPs
Medium-term tranche	1-month Treasuries	+	15	40%	+6 BPs
Long-term tranche	1-month Treasuries	+	60	10%	+6 BPs
			Total Incremental Return		+12 BPs

the treasurer would have sold the security and earned a below-market return on the investment.

Under a *credit-rating strategy*, the treasurer buys the debt of a company that may be on the verge of having its credit rating upgraded. By doing so, the investment ends up earning a higher interest rate than would other investments with a comparable credit rating. This strategy works best when the treasurer is very familiar with the debt issuer and has some confidence in his credit assessment. However, the company's stated investment policy may prevent the treasurer from buying debt below a fairly high credit rating, which eliminates this strategy from consideration. Also, it is difficult to time a possible credit-rating upgrade to be within the term of an investment. And finally, delving into lower-grade debt increases the risk of an outright default on payments by the debtor.

For all of the investment strategies noted here, the treasurer must closely monitor the credit rating of the debt issuer. A credit downgrade can result in a substantially lower return to the company if the treasurer needs to sell the debt prior to its maturity date.

The strategies outlined here involve a broad range of ongoing investment activities; the more active ones call for additional staffing that a treasury department may not have available. If so, outsourcing investment management, as noted in the next section, may be a viable alternative.

OUTSOURCED INVESTMENT MANAGEMENT

A treasurer may conclude that investment management is not a core competency, or have little funding for a professional in-house investment staff. If so, it is possible to shift cash into a separate account that is managed by outside investment advisors. Under this arrangement, the outside firm invests the cash under the terms of a customized investment agreement with the company. The company can choose from a variety of possible investment strategies, as well as restrict investments to certain classes of assets.

Exhibit 8.4   Upward Sloping Yield Curve

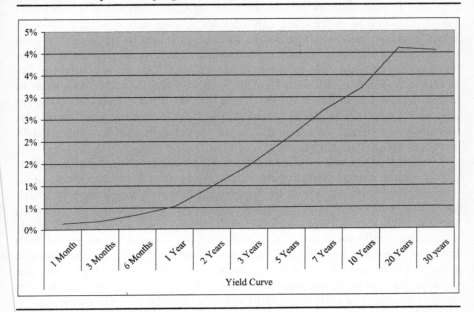

Yield Curve

This approach gives the company access to an experienced group of investment managers that presumably uses strong systems of control when initiating and tracking transactions. The fees a company incurs through an outsourcing arrangement can be quite competitive in comparison to the cost of maintaining a similarly experienced in-house staff.

RISK-REDUCTION STRATEGIES

A simple risk-reduction strategy is to avoid investments in the securities of any single entity, in favor of investments solely in one or more money market funds. These funds provide instant diversification across a multitude of issuers, with the attendant risk being constantly reviewed by a staff of risk management professionals. The use of money market funds is especially cost-effective for smaller treasury departments that cannot afford the services of an in-house investment manager.

The FDIC insures a bank customer's deposits at the bank against the failure of the bank, up to a maximum reimbursement of $100,000; types of deposits covered by the insurance include certificates of deposit, checking accounts, and money market accounts. This protection is minimal for the deposits of all but the smallest companies; however, it is possible to place a much larger amount of funds with the Certificate of Deposit Account Registry Service (located at www.cdars.com), which maintains the FDIC coverage on up to $50 million of deposits. It achieves this coverage by splitting larger deposits into amounts of just under $100,000, and spreading the deposits over a network of more than 2,000 banks. Under this system, customers select a single bank in the network as their primary bank, which in turn issues them a statement listing each holding. There is no depositor fee for this service, though the network banks pay CDARS to be listed in the network. A possible risk with CDARS is that, if the primary bank were to fail, a depositor's funds could be tied up by the FDIC during its recovery period. Of course, a treasurer could simply shop for a large number of CDs with different banks, and manually track the investments, but the CDARS system is simpler to administer.

In order to invest funds, cash must be physically shifted out of a company's cash concentration account (see Chapter 4) and into the investment. This physical shift is required by the Federal Reserve's Regulation Q, which prohibits banks from paying interest on demand deposits. A common method to circumvent this restriction is to create a *sweep account*, where funds are automatically swept out of the concentration account at the end of each business day and moved into an interest-earning account. The interest earned is less than what may be available from other investments, since the bank charges a sweeping fee. However, a sweep is still a good option for smaller amounts of cash that would not otherwise be actively managed.

The overnight sweep can be set up as a *one-to-one sweep*, where the company's funds are used to buy a specific asset. An alternative is for the bank to pool funds from multiple customers and buy an asset in the bank's name, which it liquidates in the morning and apportions back to its customers. This is called a *one-to-many sweep*. The one-to-one sweep is safer for the company if its bank enters bankruptcy, since the asset was purchased in the company's name, and the company therefore has title to the asset. The one-to-many sweep is more risky in the event of a bankruptcy, since the asset was purchased in the name of the bank, which leaves the company having a claim to the asset, along with all other creditors.

This section noted three risk-reduction strategies. Using the inherent diversification of money market funds is the simplest means for reducing risk. Setting up a CDARS account can greatly improve the amount of FDIC insurance coverage of a company's investments, while the use of one-to-one sweeps provides extra protection in the event of a bank's bankruptcy.

ACCOUNTING FOR INVESTMENTS

A company will normally invest in *marketable securities*, so that it can more easily liquidate its investments. Marketable securities are investments that can be easily liquidated through an organized exchange, such as the New York Stock Exchange. For accounting purposes, marketable securities must be grouped into one of the following three categories at the time of purchase and reevaluated periodically to see if they still belong in the designated categories:

1. *Available for sale.* This category includes both debt and equity securities. It contains those securities that do not readily fall into either of the following two categories. These securities are reported on the balance sheet at their fair value, while unrealized gains and losses are charged to an equity account and reported in other comprehensive income in the current period. The balance in the equity account is only eliminated upon sale of the underlying securities. If a permanent reduction in the value of an individual security occurs, the unrealized loss is charged against earnings, resulting in a new and lower cost basis in the remaining investment. Any subsequent increase in the value of such an investment above the new cost basis cannot be formally recognized in earnings until the related security is sold, and so the interim gains will be temporarily "parked" in the unrealized gains account in the equity section of the balance sheet.

   All interest, realized gains or losses, and debt amortization are recognized within the continuing operations section of the income statement. The listing of these securities on the balance sheet under either current or long-term assets is dependent upon their ability to be liquidated in the short term and to be available for disposition within that time frame, unencumbered by any obligations.

2. *Held to maturity.* This category includes only debt securities for which the company has both the intent and ability to hold them until their time of maturity. Their amortized cost is recorded on the balance sheet. These securities are likely to be listed on the balance sheet as long-term assets.

   If marketable securities are shifted into the held-to-maturity category from debt securities in the available-for-sale category, their unrealized holding gain or loss should continue to be stored in the equity section, while being gradually amortized down to zero over the remaining life of each security.

3. *Trading securities.* This category includes both debt and equity securities that the company intends to sell in the short term for a profit. They are recorded on the balance sheet at their fair value. This type of marketable security is always positioned in the balance sheet as a current asset.

No matter how an investment is categorized, a material decline in its fair value subsequent to the balance sheet date but prior to the release of the financial statements should be disclosed. Further, clear evidence of permanent impairment in the value of available-for-sale securities prior to the release date of the financial statements is grounds for restatement to recognize permanent impairment of the investment.

Example

Available-for-Sale Transactions

The Arabian Knights Security Company has purchased $100,000 of equity securities, which it does not intend to sell in the short term for profit, and therefore designates as available for sale. Its initial entry to record the transaction is as follows:

	Debit	Credit
Investments—available for sale	$100,000	
Cash		$100,000

After a month, the fair market value of the securities drops by $15,000, but management considers the loss to be a temporary decline, and so does not record a loss in current earnings. However, it must still alter the value of the investment on the balance sheet to show its fair value, and report the loss in Other Comprehensive Income, which requires the following entry:

	Debit	Credit
Unrealized loss on security investment (reported in Other Comprehensive Income)	$15,000	
Investments—available for sale		$15,000

Management then obtains additional information indicating that the loss is likely to be a permanent one, so it then recognizes the loss with the following entry:

	Debit	Credit
Loss on equity securities	$15,000	
Unrealized loss on security investment (reported in Other Comprehensive Income)		$15,000

Another month passes by and the fair value of the investment rises by $3,500. Since this gain exceeds the value of the newly written-down investment, management cannot recognize it, even though the new value of the investment would still be less than its original amount. Instead, the following entry is used to adjust the investment value on the balance sheet:

	Debit	Credit
Investments—available for sale	$3,500	
Unrealized gain on security investment (recorded in Other Comprehensive Income)		$3,500

Example

Trading Transactions

The Arabian Knights Security Company purchases $50,000 of equity securities that it intends to trade for a profit in the short term. Given its intentions, these securities are added to the corporate portfolio of trading securities with the following entry:

	Debit	Credit
Investments—held for trading	$50,000	
Cash		$50,000

After two months, the fair value of these trading securities declines by $3,500. The company recognizes the change in current earnings with the following entry:

	Debit	Credit
Loss on security investment	$3,500	
Investments—held for trading		$3,500

Later in the year, the fair value of the securities experiences a sudden surge, resulting in a value increase of $5,750. The company records the change with the following entry:

	Debit	Credit
Investments—held for trading	$5,750	
Gain on security investments		$5,750

Transfers between Available-for-Sale and Trading Investments

An investment designated as a trading security can be shifted into the available for sale portfolio of investments with no recognition of a gain or loss on the value of the investment, since this type of investment should have been adjusted to its fair value in each reporting period already. If a gain or loss has arisen since the last adjustment to fair value, this amount should be recognized at the time of the designation change.

If an investment designated as an available-for-sale security is shifted into the trading portfolio of investments, any gain or loss required to immediately adjust its value to fair value should be made at once. This entry should include an adjustment from any prior write-down in value that may have occurred when securities were classified as available for sale.

Example

Transfer from the Trading Portfolio to the Available-for-Sale Portfolio

The Arabian Knights Security Company owns $17,500 of equity securities that it had originally intended to sell for a profit in the short term, and so had classified the investment in its trading portfolio. Its intent has now changed, and it wishes to hold the securities for a considerably longer period, so it must shift the securities into the available-for-sale account. It had marked the securities to market one month previously, but now the securities have lost $350 of value. The company records the following entry to reclassify the security and recognize the additional loss:

	Debit	Credit
Investments—available for sale	$17,150	
Loss on equity securities	350	
Investments—held for trading		$17,500

Example

Transfer from the Available-for-Sale Portfolio to the Trading Portfolio

The Arabian Knights Security Company finds that it must liquidate $250,000 of its available-for-sale portfolio in the short term. This investment had previously been marked down to $250,000 from an initial investment value of $275,000, and its value has since risen by $12,000. The incremental gain must now be recognized in current income. The entry is as follows:

	Debit	Credit
Investments—held for trading	$262,000	
Investments—available for sale		$250,000
Gain on security investments		12,000

Accounting for Investments in Debt Securities

A debt security can be classified as either held for trading or available for sale (as previously defined for equity securities), or as held to maturity. The held-to-maturity portfolio is intended for any debt securities for which a company has the intent and ability to retain the security for its full term until maturity is reached. An investment held in the held-to-maturity portfolio is recorded at its historical cost, which is not changed at any time during the holding period, unless it is shifted into a different investment portfolio. The only exceptions to this rule are (1) the periodic amortization of any discount or premium from the face value of a debt instrument, depending on the initial purchase price; and (2) clear evidence of a permanent reduction in the value of the investment.

Example

Held-to-maturity transactions

The Arabian Knights Security Company purchases $82,000 of debt securities at face value. The company has both the intent and ability to hold the securities to maturity. Given its intentions, these securities are added to the corporate portfolio of held-to-maturity securities with the following entry:

	Debit	Credit
Investment in debt securities—held to maturity	$82,000	
Cash		$82,000

The fair value of the investment subsequently declines by $11,000. There is no entry to be made, since the investment is recorded at its historical cost. However, the company receives additional information that the debt issuer has filed for bankruptcy and intends to repay debtholders at 50 cents on the dollar. Since management considers this to be a permanent reduction, a charge of $41,000 is recorded in current income with the following entry:

	Debit	Credit
Loss on debt investment	$41,000	
Investment in debt securities—held to maturity		$41,000

The company subsequently learns that the debt issuer is instead able to pay 75 cents on the dollar. This increase in value of $20,500 is not recorded in a journal entry, since it is a recovery of value, but is instead recorded in a footnote accompanying the financial statements.

Transfers of Debt Securities among Portfolios

The accounting for transfers between debt securities portfolios varies based on the portfolio from which the accounts are being shifted, with the basic principle being that transfers are recorded at the fair market value of the security on the date of the transfer. The treatment of gains or losses on all possible transfers is noted in Exhibit 8.5.

Exhibit 8.5 Accounting Treatment of Debt Transfers between Portfolios

"From" Portfolio	"To" Portfolio	Accounting Treatment
Trading	Available for sale	No entry (assumes gains and losses have already been recorded)
Trading	Held to maturity	No entry (assumes gains and losses have already been recorded)
Available for sale	Trading	Shift any previously recorded gain or loss shown in Other Comprehensive Income to operating income.
Available for sale	Held to maturity	Amortize to income over the remaining period to debt maturity any previously recorded gain or loss shown in Other Comprehensive Income, using the effective interest method.
Held to maturity	Trading	Record the unrealized gain or loss in operating income.
Held to maturity	Available for sale	Record the unrealized gain or loss in the Other Comprehensive Income section of the income statement.

The offsetting entry for any gain or loss reported in the Other Comprehensive Income section of the income statement goes to a contra account, which is used to offset the investment account on the balance sheet, thereby revealing the extent of changes in the trading securities from their purchased cost.

The flowchart shown in Exhibit 8.6 shows the decision tree for how gains and losses are handled for different types of securities portfolios. The decision flow begins in the upper left corner. For example, if a security is designated as available-for-sale and there is a change in its fair value, then the decision tree moves to the right, asking if there is a permanent value impairment. If so, the proper treatment matches that of a loss for a held-for-trading security; if not, the proper treatment is listed as being reported in the Other Comprehensive Income section of the income statement.

Recognition of Deferred Tax Effects on Changes in Investment Valuations

A deferred tax benefit or tax liability should be recognized alongside the recognition of any change in the fair value of an investment listed in either a trading or available-for-sale portfolio or of a permanent decline in the value of a debt security being held to maturity. The tax impact varies by investment type, and is noted as follows:

Exhibit 8.6 Accounting for Gains or Losses on Securities

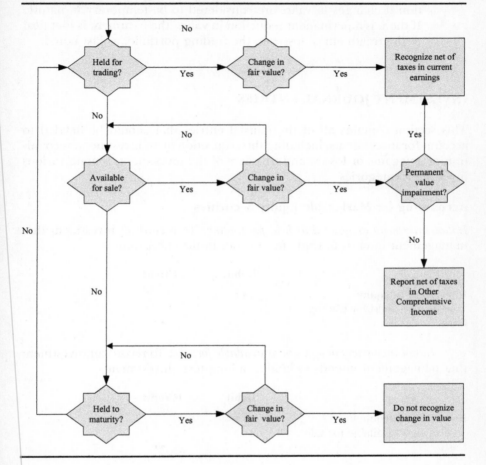

- *Gains or losses on the trading portfolio.* The deferred tax effect is recognized in the income statement. If there is a loss in value, then debit the deferred tax benefit account and credit the provision for income taxes account. If there is a gain in value, then debit the provision for income taxes account and credit the deferred tax liability account.

- *Gains or losses on the available-for-sale portfolio.* The same treatment as noted for gains or losses on the trading portfolio, except that taxes are noted in the Other Comprehensive Income section of the income statement.

- *Gains or losses on the held-to-maturity portfolio.* There is no tax recognition if changes in value are considered to be temporary in nature. If there is a permanent reduction in value, the treatment is identical to the treatment of losses in the trading portfolio, as just noted.

INVESTMENT JOURNAL ENTRIES

This section contains all of the journal entries that should be needed to account for investments, including the acquisition of an investment, recognition of any gains or losses, and transfers of the investments among various investment categories.

Accounting for Marketable Equity Securities

Initial investment designated as held for trading: To record an investment that management intends to trade for a profit in the short term.

	Debit	Credit
Investment in equity securities—held for trading	••	
Cash		••

Initial investment designated as available for sale: To record an investment that management intends to hold as a long-term investment.

	Debit	Credit
Investment in equity securities—available for sale	••	
Cash		••

Gain or loss on investment designated as held for trading: The first entry shows the immediate recognition in the current period of a loss due to a drop in the value of an investment designated as a trading security, as well as the related tax effect. The second entry shows the immediate recognition in the current period of a gain due to an increase in the value of an investment designated as a trading security, as well as the related tax effect.

	Debit	Credit
Loss on equity security investment	••	
Deferred tax benefit	••	
Investment in equity securities—held for trading		••
Provision for income taxes		••

	Debit	Credit
Investment in equity securities—held for trading	••	
Provision for income taxes	••	
Gain on equity security investments		••
Deferred tax liability		••

Gain or loss on investment designated as available-for-sale: The first entry shows an unrealized loss in the other comprehensive income account on an investment designated as available for sale, as well as the related tax effect. The second entry shows an unrealized gain in the other comprehensive income account on an investment designated as available for sale, as well as the related tax effect. In both cases, the tax effect is netted against the investment account, rather than a provision for income taxes account).

	Debit	Credit
Unrealized loss on equity security investment	••	
Deferred tax benefit	••	
Investments in equity securities—available for sale		••
Investment in equity securities—available for sale	••	
Unrealized gain on equity security investment		••
Deferred tax liability		••

Impairment in value of equity investments classified as available-for-sale: When a drop in the value of an available-for-sale investment is judged to be other than temporary, the first journal entry should be used to recognize the drop in value. The entry includes the initial recognition of a related income tax benefit on the transaction. If one had previously recognized an income tax benefit associated with the loss but prior to its classification as a permanent decline in value, the offset to the deferred tax benefit would have been the investment account itself. If so, shift the offset from the investment account to an income tax liability account, as shown in the second journal entry.

	Debit	Credit
Loss on equity securities	••	
Deferred tax benefit	••	
Unrealized loss on available-for-sale securities		••
Provision for income taxes		••
Loss on equity securities	••	
Unrealized loss on available-for-sale securities		••
Provision for income taxes		••

Transfers of Equity Securities between Available-for-Sale and Trading Portfolios

Shift investment designation from a trading security to an available-for-sale security: To shift the designation of a security currently recorded as a trading security to that of an available-for-sale security. The journal entry includes provisions for the recognition of any gains or losses on the fair value of the securities transferred since they were last marked to market.

	Debit	Credit
Investments—available for sale	••	
Loss on equity securities	••	
Investments—held for trading		••
Gain on equity securities		••

Shift investment designation from an available-for-sale security to a trading security: To shift the designation of a security currently recorded as an available-for-sale security to that of a trading security, which requires the recognition of all unrealized gains or losses. The first entry assumes the recognition of unrealized losses on securities, while the second entry assumes the recognition of unrealized gains.

	Debit	Credit
Investments—held for trading	••	
Loss on equity securities	••	
Investments—available for sale		••
Unrealized loss on available for sale securities		••
Investments—held for trading	••	
Unrealized gain on available-for-sale securities	••	
Investments—available-for-sale		••
Gain on equity securities		••

Accounting for Investments in Debt Securities

Initial investment designated as held for trading: To record an investment in debt securities that management intends to trade for a profit in the short term.

	Debit	Credit
Investment in debt securities—held for trading	••	
Cash		••

Initial investment designated as available-for-sale: To record an investment in debt securities that management intends to hold as a long-term investment.

	Debit	Credit
Investment in debt securities— available for sale	••	
Cash		••

Initial investment designated as held-to-maturity: To record an investment in debt securities that management has the intent and ability to hold to the debt maturity date.

	Debit	Credit
Investment in debt securities— held to maturity	••	
Cash		••

Gain or loss on debt investment designated as held for trading: The first journal entry records the immediate recognition in the current period of a loss due to a drop in the value of a debt investment designated as a trading security. The second journal entry records the immediate recognition of a gain due to an increase in the value of a debt investment designated as a trading security.

	Debit	Credit
Loss on debt security investment	••	
Investment in debt securities— held for trading		••
Investment in debt securities— held for trading	••	
Gain on debt securities—held for trading		••

Gain or loss on debt investment designated as available for sale: The first journal entry records the immediate recognition in the current period of a loss due to a drop in the value of a debt investment designated as an available-for-sale security, which is reported in the Other Comprehensive Income section of the income statement. The second journal entry records the immediate recognition of a gain due to an increase in the value of a debt investment designated as an available-for-sale security.

	Debit	Credit
Unrealized loss on debt security investment	••	
Deferred tax benefit	••	
Investments in debt securities— available for sale		••
Investment in debt securities— available for sale	••	

	Debit	Credit
Unrealized gain on debt security investment		••
Deferred tax liability		••

Impairment in value of debt investments classified as held to maturity: To record a loss on a held to maturity debt investment, which only occurs when management considers a drop in value to be permanent in nature.

	Debit	Credit
Loss on debt investment		••
Investment in debt securities— held to maturity	••	

Transfers of Debt Securities among Portfolios

Shift investment designation from the available-for-sale debt security portfolio to the trading debt security portfolio: Any debt security shifted from the available-for-sale portfolio to the trading portfolio must be recorded at its fair market value on the date of the transfer. The first journal entry records the recognition of a loss on the transfer date, while the second entry records a gain.

	Debit	Credit
Investment in debt securities— held for trading	••	
Loss on debt securities	••	
Investment in debt securities— available for sale		••
Unrealized loss on debt securities—available for sale		••
Investment in debt securities— held for trading	••	
Unrealized gain on debt securities—available for sale	••	
Investment in debt securities— available for sale		••
Gain on holding debt securities		••

Shift investment designation from the available-for-sale debt security portfolio to the held-to-maturity debt security portfolio: Any debt security shifted from the available-for-sale portfolio to the held-to-maturity portfolio must be recorded at its fair market value on the date of the transfer. The first journal entry records the recognition of a loss on the transfer date, while the second entry records a gain.

	Debit	Credit
Investment in debt securities— held to maturity	••	
Loss on debt securities	••	
Investment in debt securities— available for sale		••
Unrealized loss on debt securities—available for sale		••
Investment in debt securities— held to maturity	••	
Unrealized gain on debt securities—available for sale	••	
Investment in debt securities— available for sale		••
Gain on holding debt securities		••

Shift investment designation from the held-to-maturity debt security portfolio to the available-for-sale debt security portfolio: To record any accumulated gain or loss on a held-to-maturity debt security being transferred into the available-for-sale portfolio, which is recorded in other comprehensive income. The first entry records a loss on the transaction, while the second entry records a gain.

	Debit	Credit
Investment in debt securities— available for sale	••	
Unrealized loss on holding debt securities	••	
Investment in debt securities— held to maturity		••
Investment in debt securities— —available for sale	••	
Investment in debt securities— held to maturity		••
Unrealized gain on holding debt securities		••

Shift investment designation from the held-to-maturity debt security portfolio to the held-for-trading debt security portfolio: To record any accumulated gain or loss on a held-to-maturity debt security being transferred into the held-for-trading portfolio, which is recorded in earnings. The first entry records a loss on the transaction, while the second entry records a gain. There are no unrealized gains or losses to recognize, since no gains or losses are recognized for held-to-maturity debt investments.

	Debit	Credit
Investment in debt securities—held for trading	••	
Loss on holding debt securities	••	
Investment in debt securities—held to maturity		••
Investment in debt securities—held for trading	••	
Investment in debt securities—held to maturity		••
Gain on holding debt securities		••

INVESTMENT REPORTING

It is useful to have a summary-level report itemizing the investment, current market value and return on investment for each investment made. An example is shown in Exhibit 8.7, where all investments are in equity. This approach yields a quick view of a company's overall level of investment and the results thereof.

If the investment portfolio includes debt, then the report could be expanded to include either individual or average maturity dates.

INVESTMENT MANAGEMENT CONTROLS

The process of issuing funds for an investment is unique in that every step in the process is a control point. Without regard to controls, the only step required to make an investment is for an authorized person to create and sign an investment authorization form (itself a control point) and deliver it to the bank, which invests the company's funds in the designated investment. However, as shown in the flowchart in Exhibit 8.8, there are a number of additional steps, all designed to ensure that there is an appropriate level of control over the size and duration of the investment, and that the earnings from the investment vehicle are maximized.

The controls noted in the flowchart are described at greater length as follows, in sequence from the top of the flowchart to the bottom:

- *Create and approve a cash forecast.* There must be some basis for both the size and duration of an investment. Otherwise, a mismatch can develop between the need for cash and its availability, resulting in liquidity problems or an excessive amount of underutilized cash. By requiring that a cash forecast be completed and approved by an authorized person, there is less risk of these problems occurring.

Exhibit 8.7   Report on Investment Position

Security	Number of Shares	Market Value	Purchase Price	Rate of Return	Total Dividends Y-T-D
1. ABC Corporation	500	$37,000	$31,000	5.2%	$ 800
2. Atlas Construction	100	2,400	2,400	6.3	75
3. National Co.	1,000	30,000	31,000	6.5	1,000
4. USA Corporation	1,000	65,500	64,000	7.8	2,000
5. JPC Corporation	100	1,900	1,875	7.5	70
6. Security Co.	500	42,000	38,000	5.3	1,000
Total or average		$178,800	$168,275	6.5%	$4,945

- *Record proposed investment and duration on the cash forecast.* Though the cash forecast alone should be a sufficient control over the determination of the correct size and duration of an investment, it helps to also formally write this information directly on the cash forecast, so there is no question about the details of the proposed investment.

- *Obtain approval of investment recommendation.* A manager should sign off on the proposed investment. By placing the approval signature line directly on the cash forecast, the approver can review the accuracy of the forecast as well as the resulting investment recommendation, giving sufficient information for the approver to determine if the recommendation is correct.

- *Obtain and document ___ quotes for each investment.* An investment officer may have a favorite bank and will continue to invest with it, even if its rates are not competitive. It is also common for the investment staff to not want to go to the effort of obtaining multiple quotes on a regular basis. By requiring them to complete a quotation sheet, this control ensures that the best investment rate is obtained.

- *Issue a signed investment authorization form to the issuer.* Banks will not invest funds without a signed investment authorization form from the company. From the company's perspective, a signed authorization also ensures that the appropriate level of management has approved the investment.

- *Match authorization form to transaction report.* The bank may unintentionally invest funds incorrectly or neglect to invest at all. By matching the signed authorization form to any investment transaction report issued by the bank, the company can verify what action the bank took as a result of the authorization.

Exhibit 8.8   The System of Controls for Investments

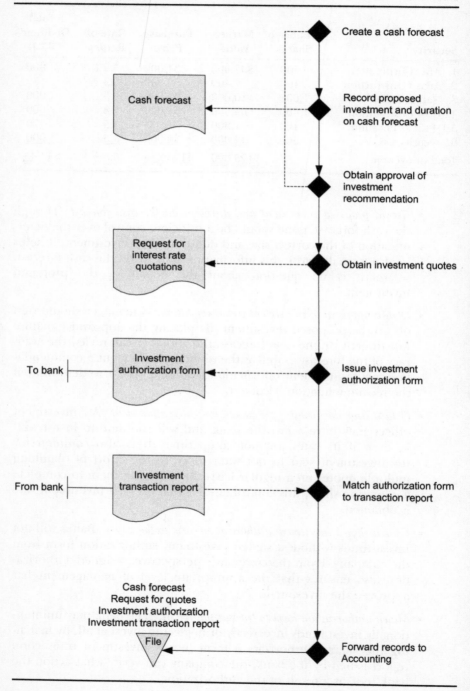

- *Forward records to accounting for storage.* There is some risk that a person in the investment department will alter investment authorization documents after the fact to hide evidence of inappropriate investments. To reduce this risk, require them to immediately forward a set of supporting documents to the accounting department for storage in a locked location. The accounting staff should stamp the receipt date on each set of documents received, which the internal auditors can use to determine if any documents were inappropriately delayed.

In addition to the basic process flow just noted, the following controls are also useful for ensuring that the documented investments were actually obtained and stored:

- *Periodically match the approved cash forecast, quote sheets, and investment authorization to actual investments completed.* Though all the supporting paperwork may be in order, it is still possible for an investment officer to shift funds to some other, unauthorized form of investment. To detect such transactions, the internal audit department should periodically match all supporting documents to the actual investments made, as reported by the issuing entities.

- *Assign securities custody to independent party.* It is not common for a company to physically control securities; instead, they are more commonly stored by a third-party custodian, which represents a higher level of control. If some securities must be stored on-site, then ensure that the person responsible for their physical security is not also responsible for recording the securities in the accounting records.

The controls noted here assume that a company is investing in simpler investments, such as CDs, that are handled through a bank. It will be necessary to expand these controls for more complex investments that are not routed through banks.

INVESTMENT MANAGEMENT POLICIES

An investment policy is used to define the level of risk that a company is willing to tolerate and defines the exact types of investment vehicles to be used (or not used). Such a policy should cover the level of allowable liquidity. For example, the policy may state that all investments must be capable of total liquidation upon notification or that some proportion of investments must be in this class of liquidity. Thus, the policy could state that 75 percent of all investments must be capable of immediate liquidation (which rules out real estate holdings!), or that any investments over a base level of $50 million can be invested in less liquid instruments. Generally speaking, the policy should severely restrict the use of any investments that cannot be liquidated within a short period of time, since this gives a company maximum use of the money in case of special opportunities (such as an acquisition) or emergencies (such as a natural disaster destroying a facility). Such careful delineation of investment liquidity will leave a small number of investments that a treasurer can safely use.

The second policy criterion is risk. Many companies have decided that they are not in the business of making investments, and so they avoid all risk, even though they may be losing a significant amount of investment income by putting all excess cash in U.S. government securities. Other companies take the opposite tack and attempt to derive a significant proportion of their profits from investment income. No matter which direction a company takes, it is necessary to delineate which kinds of investments are to be used, thereby keeping the treasurer focused on a specific set of investment options.

The final policy criterion is return on investment. For the purposes of a company's short-term investments, this should be the least of the three investment criteria; it is much more important for a company to achieve high levels of liquidity and risk minimization than it is to achieve a high rate of return. If a company is willing to rebalance the three criteria in favor of a greater return, then it should at least consider making return on investment a lesser factor for its short-term investments, since they have less time to recover from the vagaries of the financial market.

The investment policy should be closely aligned with the investment strategy. For example, if the treasurer elects to divide available cash into short-term, medium-term, and long-term tranches, then the policy should allow for long-term investments that approximate the amounts and durations to be used in the long-term tranche. Similarly, if the treasurer plans to aggressively anticipate interest rates, then the policy should allow for some degree of speculation. Conversely, if the board of directors specifically does *not* allow certain activities, then this limits the treasurer's available strategies.

There are a multitude of possible investment policies that a treasury can adopt; some are designed to restrict its choices of possible investments, while others are needed to account for investments. The following policy possibilities are sorted into the categories for funds investment, designations of types of investments, transfers of investments among different portfolio designations, and investment accounting. A more comprehensive sample investment policy is shown at the end of this section.

Funds Investment

- *At least $___ shall be invested in overnight investments and in negotiable marketable obligations of major U.S. issuers.* This policy forces the treasury staff to attain a minimum level of liquidity. The fixed dollar amount used in the policy should be regularly reviewed to match upcoming budgeted working capital requirements.

- *No more than ___ percent of the total portfolio shall be invested in time deposits or other investments with a lack of liquidity.* This policy is similar to the preceding one, except that it ignores a fixed liquidity requirement, focusing instead on a maximum proportion of the total portfolio that must be retained for short-term requirements. This policy tends to require less periodic updating.

- *The average maturity of the investment portfolio shall be limited to ___ years.* This policy is designed to keep a company from investing in excessively long maturities. The policy can be broken down into more specific maturity limitations for different types of investments, such as 5 years for any U.S. government obligations, 1 year for bank CDs, and 270 days for commercial paper.

- *Investments in foreign commercial paper shall be limited to those unconditionally guaranteed by a prime U.S. issuer and fully hedged.* This policy is designed to lower the risk of default on investments in securities issued by foreign entities.

- *Investments in commercial paper shall be limited to those of companies having long-term senior debt ratings of A or better.* This policy is designed to limit the risk of default on commercial paper investments by focusing investments on only the highest-grade commercial paper. The policy can be expanded to require the sale of any commercial paper when the debt rating is adjusted downward below the minimum rating level.

- *Investments in bank certificates of deposit shall be limited to those banks with capital accounts exceeding $1 billion.* This policy is designed to limit the risk of default on certificates of deposit, on the assumption that large capital accounts equate to minimal risk of bank failure.

- *Investments shall only be made in investments backed by U.S. government debt obligations.* This policy can be used in place of the preceding ones that specify allowable investments in nongovernment investments. This policy tends to be used by highly risk-averse companies who place less emphasis on the return generated from their investments.

- *Securities physically held by the company shall be stored with an accredited third party.* This policy improves the physical control over securities.

- *If an employee is responsible for the physical security of securities held by the company, then this person cannot also be responsible for recording the securities in the accounting records.* This policy prevents an employee from removing securities and then eliminating evidence of the securities from the accounting records.

Investment in Debt Securities Accounting

- *The unrecognized amount of gains or losses on held-to-maturity securities shall be regularly reported to the board of directors.* Management may designate poor-performing debt securities as held-to-maturity, in which case any changes in their fair value will not be recognized. This policy is designed to reveal any gains or losses that would be recognized if these securities were to have any other portfolio designation, so the Board is aware of any "hanging" gains or losses.

- *Debt securities shall not be classified as held to maturity unless sufficient investments are already on hand to cover all budgeted short-term cash requirements.* Generally accepted accounting principles (GAAP) already requires that debt securities not be classified as held to maturity if a company does not have the ability to hold the securities for the required time period—this policy is more specific in stating that all anticipated cash flows be fully covered by other investments before any debt securities receive the held-to-maturity classification. The policy makes it more likely that a company will not be forced to prematurely liquidate its held-to-maturity debt portfolio.

Investment Portfolios, Transfer Between

- *The board of directors shall be notified of the reasons for any significant shift in the designation of securities among the held-to-maturity, available-for-sale, and trading portfolios, and the approximate impact on different categories of income.* This policy is designed to require management to justify its actions in shifting securities between portfolios, which is likely to reduce the amount of shifting, while also keeping the board informed of any likely movements of gains or losses between the Operating Income and Other Comprehensive Income parts of the income statement.

Investment Portfolios, Transfer of Debt Securities Among

- *The board of directors must authorize all shifts in investment designation out of the held-to-maturity portfolio.* There are specific accounting instances where the transfer of securities out of the held-to-maturity portfolio will preclude a company's subsequent use of the held-to-maturity portfolio. Accordingly, the board of directors should be notified of the reasons for such a designation and give its formal approval before the designation change can be made.

Marketable Equity Securities Accounting

- *All securities purchases shall be designated as trading securities at the time of purchase.* This policy is intended to avoid the designation of an investment as "available for sale," which would allow management to avoid recording short-term changes in the fair value of the investment in reported earnings. The policy removes the ability of management to alter financial results by shifting the designation of an investment.

- *All losses on securities designated as available for sale shall be considered permanent.* Accounting rules allow one to avoid recognizing losses on available-for-sale securities by assuming that the losses are temporary. By using this policy to require an immediate write-down on all losses, management no longer has the ability to manipulate earnings by making assumptions that losses are temporary in nature.

- *Available-for-sale securities shall not be sold solely to recognize related gains in their fair market value.* Accounting rules do not allow ongoing recognition of gains in the value of available-for-sale securities in earnings until they have been sold, so there is a natural temptation to manage earnings by timing their sale. This policy is designed to set an ethical standard for management to prevent such actions from taking place. In reality, this is a difficult policy to enforce, since management can find reasonable excuses for selling securities when their unrecognized gains are needed for bookkeeping purposes.

A sample investment policy that selectively incorporates some of the preceding policies is shown in Exhibit 8.9.

A company may find that its investment policy, while appearing to be reasonable on paper, does not match the realities of the marketplace, resulting in a suboptimal investment portfolio. To bring the investment policy into better alignment with the market, use *backtesting* with the company's historical investment records to see what various changes to the policy would have done to the company's investment profile. This can yield suggestions for fine-tuning the investment policy, especially if performed at regular intervals to account for ongoing changes in the marketplace.

INVESTMENT MANAGEMENT PROCEDURES

The detailed procedures used for initiating an investment, as well as for transferring investments between portfolios, are shown in this section. The investment procedure is noted in Exhibit 8.10.

Exhibit 8.9 Sample Investment Policy

Objective: To invest excess cash in only top-quality short-term investments, for optimum total return, commensurate with corporate liquidity requirements.

Liquidity: Liquidity shall be provided by minimum and maximum limits as follows:

1. At least $80 million shall be invested in the overnight investments and in negotiable marketable obligations of major U.S. issuers.

2. No more than 50% of the total portfolio shall be invested in time deposits or other investments with a lack of liquidity such as commercial paper for which only the dealer and issuer make a market.

Diversification: Diversification shall be provided through a limit on each non-government issuer (as listed next). These are general limits, and in each case quality review may result in elimination of a lower limit for the issuer. Overnight or repurchase investments must meet quality criteria but are not subject to limits on the amount invested.

1. U.S. Government and agencies—no limit.

2. Domestic bank certificates of deposit, time deposits and banker's acceptances—$30 million limit for banks with capital accounts in excess of $800 million (top 10 banks); $20 million for banks with capital accounts of $350 to $800 million (second 11 banks); $5 million for all other banks with capital accounts in excess of $250 million (11 banks).

3. U.S. dollar (or fully hedged foreign currency) obligations of foreign banks, each with capital accounts exceeding $500 million—limited to $15 million each for Canadian banks and $10 million each for other foreign banks, subject to an aggregate limit of $75 million for non-Canadian foreign banks.

4. Domestic commercial paper with P-1/A-1 rating only—$20 million limit for issuers with long-term senior debt rating of Aa or better; $10 million for issuers with a debt rating of A; and $10 million for commercial bank holding companies with capital amounts in excess of $500 million, within the overall limit of the flagship bank described in item 2 above.

5. Foreign commercial paper unconditionally guaranteed by a prime U.S. issuer and fully hedged, subject to the guarantor's issuer limit described in item 4 above.

Operating procedure: Payments shall be made only against delivery of a security to a custodian bank. Securities shall be delivered from custody only against payment. Due bills by a bank will be accepted for delivery only under exceptional conditions. No due bills issued by a dealer will be accepted.

Maturity limits: The average maturity of the entire fund shall be limited to an average of two years. The maximum maturity for each category is as follows:

U.S. Government	5 years
Municipal obligations	2 years
Bank certificates of deposit	1 year
Banker's acceptances	1 year
Bank time deposits	90 days
Commercial paper	270 days

External investment management. On an annual basis, the treasurer shall examine the cost-effectiveness and risk management benefits associated with outsourcing the company's investment management function, and report on the results of this analysis to the board of directors.

Reporting: The investment portfolio shall be marked to market at the end of each calendar quarter. The resulting changes in valuation, including a clear statement of gains and losses, shall be reported to the CEO, CFO, and treasurer.

Exhibit 8.10   Investment Procedure

Procedure Statement   Retrieval No.: TREASURY-04

Subject: Determination of investment amount and type, and investment execution

1. PURPOSE AND SCOPE

This procedure is used by the treasury staff to invest funds in accordance with the corporate investment policy.

2. PROCEDURES

2.1 Create a Cash Forecast (Treasury Staff)

1. Create a cash forecast covering the next __ weeks, including standard cash inflows and outflows, and also incorporating expected capital expenditures and special adjustments.
2. Compare the new forecast to the forecast developed for the preceding week to see if there are any large variances in the weekly cash results; investigate and adjust as necessary.

2.2 Record Proposed Investment on Cash Forecast (Treasury Staff)

1. Based on the amount of excess funds projected to be available, note below each week on the forecast the proposed amount of funds to invest, the type of investment, and the duration of each proposed investment. The type of investment should be based on the approved corporate investment policy.
2. Create a copy of the forecast and file it.
3. Send the original cash forecast to the Treasurer.

2.3 Approve Investment Recommendation (Treasurer)

1. Upon receipt of the cash forecast, review it in general for errors and omissions. Have the financial analyst revise the forecast as necessary.
2. Compare the proposed types of investments to the approved corporate investment policy to ensure that they are acceptable.
3. Verify that the proposed investment duration does not exceed the approved corporate investment duration policy.
4. Sign and date the forecast in the approval block.
5. Forward the cash forecast to the treasury staff.

2.4 Obtain Investment Quotes (Treasury Staff)

1. Upon receipt of the latest approved cash forecast, print the latest Request for Interest Rate Quotations form (see Exhibit 8.11).
2. Verify that the banks listed on the form are approved for investments by the company.
3. Contact the banks for rate quotes on the investment type, duration, and amount noted on the cash forecast, and enter the quotes on the form.
4. Sign in the "Quotes compiled by" field in the "Approvals" block of the form.
5. Review the quotes with the treasurer and enter the actual investment to be made in the "Final Investment" block of the form.
6. The treasurer signs in the "Approved by" field in the "Approvals" block of the form.
7. Forward the form to the Investment Manager for investment placement.
8. File the cash forecast.

2.5 Issue Investment Authorization Form (Investment Manager)

1. Extract a copy of the investment form from the forms cabinet and fill it out, entering the investment type, amount, and duration noted in the "Final Investment" block of the Request for Interest Rate Quotations form.
2. Sign the investment form.
3. Fax the form to the bank quoting the highest rate on the Interest Rate Quotations form.
4. Call the firm to verify receipt of the fax.
5. Sign in the "Investment placed by" field in the "Approvals" block of the Request for Interest Rate Quotations form.

6. Create two copies of the Request for Interest Rate Quotations form and investment form, and file both copies.
7. Forward the original versions of both the Request for Interest Rate Quotations form and investment form to the Treasury Clerk.

2.6 Match Authorization to Transaction Report (Treasury Staff)
Upon receipt of an investment transaction report from the bank, match its terms to those listed on the investment form and Request for Interest Rate Quotations form. If there are discrepancies, contact the bank to determine why, and forward this information to the Treasurer.

2.7 Forward Records to Accounting (Treasury Staff)

1. Assemble the cash forecast, Request for Interest Rate Quotations, investment form, and investment transaction report into a single packet.
2. Create a copy of the packet and file it by date.
3. Forward the original version of the packet to the general ledger accountant, to be recorded in the accounting system.

2.8 Record Investment Transaction (Accounting Staff)

1. Upon receipt of the approved investment packet, record a credit to the cash account and a debit to the investments account.
2. If the investment is into bonds, update the Bond Ledger Report (see Exhibit 8.12).
3. If the investment is into stocks, update the Stock Ledger Report (see Exhibit 8.13).
4. Stamp the investment packet as having been entered, and file the packet.

The procedure used to shift investments between investment portfolios is shown in Exhibit 8.14.

SUMMARY

Investing cash is a key role of the treasurer, and this chapter provided a great deal of guidance for doing so. In sorting through the large number of strategies, controls, policies, and accounting issues related to investment, the treasurer should particularly keep in mind the following three items:

1. *Investment policy is critical.* If there is a large quantity of cash to be invested, then there is a correspondingly large risk of losing it through inappropriate investments. To mitigate this risk, absolutely have a detailed investment policy that is regularly updated to match the changing needs of the company and the investment environment.

Exhibit 8.11 Request for Interest Rate Quotations

Request for Interest Rate Quotations   **Date:** _____

Funding Available: $_____

Approved Institution	Approved Investment Vehicles			
	Term Deposits	Treasury Bills	Bankers' Acceptance	Other _____
Bank Name #1 Address Address Phone Contact Name	Days ----- Rate 30 _____ 60 _____ 90 _____	Days ----- Rate 30 _____ 60 _____ 90 _____	Days ----- Rate 30 _____ 60 _____ 90 _____	Days ----- Rate 30 _____ 60 _____ 90 _____
Bank Name #2 Address Address Phone Contact Name	Days ----- Rate 30 _____ 60 _____ 90 _____	Days ----- Rate 30 _____ 60 _____ 90 _____	Days ----- Rate 30 _____ 60 _____ 90 _____	Days ----- Rate 30 _____ 60 _____ 90 _____
Bank Name #3 Address Address Phone Contact Name	Days ----- Rate 30 _____ 60 _____ 90 _____	Days ----- Rate 30 _____ 60 _____ 90 _____	Days ----- Rate 30 _____ 60 _____ 90 _____	Days ----- Rate 30 _____ 60 _____ 90 _____
Bank Name #4 Address Address Phone Contact Name	Days ----- Rate 30 _____ 60 _____ 90 _____	Days ----- Rate 30 _____ 60 _____ 90 _____	Days ----- Rate 30 _____ 60 _____ 90 _____	Days ----- Rate 30 _____ 60 _____ 90 _____

	Start Date	$ Amount	Maturity	Rate
Final Investment	/ /	$		%

Approvals

Quotes compiled by: _____   Date: _____

Investment placed by: _____   Date: _____

Approved by: _____   Date: _____

Exhibit 8.12 Bond Ledger Report

Bond Name: ABC Coal Mining Co.

Nominal Rate __7%__
Actual Rate __6.3%__

Purchased
Through __ABC Bond Sales__

Description:
Numbers: __B1676, B1677__
Denomination: __$5,000__
Where Payable: __Third Trust, Chicago__
Trustee: __Third Trust, Chicago__

Dated: __1/1/2010__
When Due: __12/31/2027__
Interest Payable: __6/30, 12/31__
Redeemable: __Yes__

Date	Pieces	Memo	Price	Debit	Credit	Balance	Profit or Loss	Due Date	Interest Amount	Paid Date
4/1/2010	2	ABC Bond	$107.5	$10,750		$10,750				
6/30/2010		Premium			$50	$10,700		6/30/2010	$500	6/30/2010
12/31/2010		Premium			$100	$10,600		12/31/2010	$500	12/31/2010
6/30/2011		Premium			$100	$10,500		6/30/2011	$500	6/30/2011
7/1/2011	1	Denver National	$107.0		$5,200	$5,250	$100			

Exhibit 8.13 Stock Ledger Report

Stock Ledger Report

Issued by: ___ABC Coal Mining Co.___

Class: ___Common___   Par Value: ___$1.00___

Bought				Sold					Balance		
Date	No. of Shares	Price	Cost*	Date	No. of Shares	Price	Total Received*	Profit or Loss	No. of Shares	Average Price	Cost
1/30/2010	100	$30	$3,020						100	$30.20	$3,020
				9/30/2010	25	$36	$890	$135	75	$30.20	$2,265
10/3/2010	50	$35	$1,770						125	$32.28	$4,035
				11/15/2010	25	$38	$940	$133	100	$32.28	$3,228

* Includes commission

Exhibit 8.14   Investment Transfer Procedure

Procedure Statement   Retrieval No.: TREASURY-05

Subject: Steps required to transfer investments between investment portfolios

1. PURPOSE AND SCOPE
   This procedure is used by the accounting staff to not only specify the correct accounting transactions for a shift between the available-for-sale and trading portfolios, but also to ensure that justification for the change has been documented and approved.

2. PROCEDURES

   2.1 Document Reason for Transfer (Assistant Controller)

   1. Document the reason for the shift between portfolios, and summarize the total impact of gains or losses to be recognized in current income as a result of the change, including the tax impact.
   2. If the impact on current earnings is significant, notify the board of directors of the prospective change, if required by company policy.

   2.2 Record Change in Portfolios (General Ledger Accountant)

   1. Create a journal entry to shift funds between the available-for-sale and trading portfolios, including the recognition of any gains or losses required to bring the recorded value of the securities to their fair market value as of the transaction date. Log the entry into the accounting system.
   2. Store all documentation of the shift in portfolios, including documentation of board notification and the related journal entry, in the journal entry binder.

---

2. *Return is least important.* Do *not* let return on investment become the key criterion for an investment strategy, or else the attendant increase in risk could result in a significant loss of principal.

3. *Use all controls.* Because of the large volumes of cash involved, there is a risk of investment fraud, as well as of inadvertently making incorrect investments. Strong controls mitigate this risk.

In short, the treasurer's primary goal in investment management is to guard the principal; a respectable return is nice, but not as critical as ensuring that no cash is lost. The investment strategy should be built around this key underlying goal.

PART THREE

RISK MANAGEMENT

9

Foreign Exchange Risk Management

When a company accepts foreign currency in payment for its goods or services, it accepts some level of foreign exchange risk, since the value of that currency in comparison to the company's home currency may fluctuate enough between the beginning of the contract and receipt of funds to seriously erode the underlying profit on the sale. This is becoming more of an issue over time because global competition is making it more likely that a company *must* accept payment in a foreign currency.

When dealing in foreign currencies, a company must determine its level of exposure, create a plan for how to mitigate that risk, engage in daily activities to implement the plan, and properly account for each transaction. Each of these steps is covered in the following sections.

FOREIGN EXCHANGE QUOTE TERMINOLOGY

Before delving into foreign exchange risk, it is useful to understand the terminology used in the foreign exchange quotation process. When comparing the price of one currency to another, the *base currency* is the unit of currency that does not fluctuate in amount, while the *quoted currency* or *price currency* does fluctuate. The U.S. dollar is most commonly used as the base currency. For example, if the dollar is the base currency and $1 is worth 0.7194 euros, then this quote is called the *indirect quote* of presenting a quote for euros. However, if the euro is used as the base currency, the same quote becomes $1.39 per euro (and is calculated as 1 / 0.7194), and is referred to as a *direct quote*. The direct quote is the inverse of the indirect quote. If neither the base currency nor the quoted currency is the U.S. dollar, then the exchange rate between the two currencies is called a *cross rate*.

As an example of an indirect quote, the U.S. dollar is listed first, and the currency it is being paired with is listed second. Thus, a USD/EUR quote (dollars/euros) means that $1 equals 0.7194 euros. Conversely, a EUR/USD (euros/dollars) quote is a direct quote, and means that one euro equals

208   Foreign Exchange Risk Management

$1.3900. The key factor to remember with any quote pairing is that the first currency referenced always has a unit value of one.

Most exchange rates are quoted to four decimals, since the sums involved in currency transactions are so large that the extra few decimals can have a meaningful impact on payments. A *point* is a change of one digit at the fourth decimal place of a quote.

A foreign exchange dealer will quote both *bid* and *offer* foreign exchange prices. The bid price is the price at which the dealer will purchase a currency, while the ask price is the price at which the dealer will sell a currency.

The current exchange rate between any two currencies is known as the *spot rate*. When two parties to a foreign exchange transaction exchange funds, this is on the *delivery date* or *value date*. When a company requires foreign exchange immediately, it engages in a *spot settlement*, though there is actually a one-to-two day delay in final settlement of the transaction.

Example

Toledo Toolmakers learns from its bank on June 1 that it has just received 50,000 euros. Toledo's treasurer wants to convert these funds into dollars, and so calls its bank and requests the U.S. dollar exchange rate in euros. The bank quotes him an exchange rate of $1.3900 per euro. The treasurer immediately sells the euros at the rate of $1.3900. Settlement is completed two working days later, on the delivery date of June 3, when Toledo will receive $35,971.

THE NATURE OF FOREIGN EXCHANGE RISK

We will assume that a company's home currency is the U.S. dollar. If, during the interval when a customer is obligated to pay the company, the dollar appreciates against the customer's currency, then the customer is paying with a reduced-value currency, which causes the company to record a foreign exchange loss once it is paid.

Example

Toledo Toolmakers sells goods to an Italian company for 100,000 euros. At the time of sale, one euro is worth $1.39079 at the spot rate, which is a total sale price of $139,079. The customer is not obligated to pay until 90 days have passed; upon receipt of the euro payment in 90 days, the value in dollars will be based on the spot rate at the time of receipt. On the day when payment is received, the spot rate has dropped to $1.3630, which reduces the value of the payment to $136,300, resulting in a decline of $2,779 or 2 percent. Toledo must record this reduction as a loss.

There is also a possibility that exchange rates will move in the opposite direction, which creates a gain for the selling company. Smaller firms that do not engage in much foreign currency trade are more likely to accept the gains and losses from changes in the spot rate. However, this can cause wild swings in the profitability of larger firms with substantial multicountry trading activity. These firms are more likely to seek a solution that reduces their earnings volatility. Hedging is the solution, and a broad array of possible solutions will be covered later in this chapter.

Before considering hedging solutions, a treasurer needs to know if there is any currency risk that requires such a solution—and that is not always a simple matter to determine. The next section discusses this problem.

DATA COLLECTION FOR FOREIGN EXCHANGE RISK MANAGEMENT

Determining the extent of a company's currency risk can be a frustrating exercise for the foreign exchange specialist, who is often at the receiving end of a flood of disorganized information arriving from the accounting, budgeting, tax, and treasury departments. The specialist must somehow aggregate this information, not only into a current statement of currency positions, but also into a reliable forecast of where currency positions are expected to be in the near to medium term. This information is then used as the foundation for a hedging strategy.

A large firm with an enterprise resources planning (ERP) system can automatically accumulate its existing net currency exposures from the ERP system, but such is not the case for a company with more distributed accounting systems; its staff will likely accumulate the information manually from each subsidiary and load it into an electronic spreadsheet in order to net out the positions of each subsidiary and determine the level of currency exposure. Obviously, those with an ERP system have a significant advantage in determining the amount of this *booked exposure*.

The currency forecast can be unusually difficult to formulate, because a company may have many subsidiaries, each of which has some level of exposure in multiple currencies that varies continually. Ideally, there should be a forecast for each currency, which can result in a multitude of forecasts. To manage the forecasting workload, the foreign exchange specialist usually only constructs forecasts for those currencies in which the company is most heavily committed, and ignores currencies where the company generally has minimal currency positions. The resulting *forecasted exposure* estimates the most likely size of currency transactions that will occur in the near term and medium term, so that hedging plans can be made to mitigate these exposures.

Booked exposure, especially when derived from ERP information, should be quite accurate. However, forecasted exposure is only moderately accurate in the near term, and its accuracy declines rapidly within a year. This reduced accuracy strongly impacts the amount of hedging that a company may be willing to engage in, as discussed in the next section.

FOREIGN EXCHANGE HEDGING STRATEGIES

There are a variety of foreign exchange hedging strategies noted in this section. The main strategy groupings are:

- To not hedge the exposure
- To hedge the exposure through business practices
- To hedge the exposure with a derivative

Also, within the third category, a treasurer must decide on what level of exposure to hedge. One possible strategy could be to hedge 100 percent of booked exposures, 50 percent of forecasted exposures over the next rolling 12-month period, and 25 percent of forecasted exposures over the following 12-month period. This gradually declining *benchmark hedge ratio* for longer forecast periods is justifiable on the assumption that the level of forecast accuracy declines over time, so that one should hedge against the minimum amount of exposure that will almost certainly occur.

Example

The treasurer of Toledo Toolmakers compares her trailing 6-month stream of euro-denominated cash flows (in thousands) to the original forecast, which appears in Exhibit 9.A.

The forecasted cash flow is consistently higher than the actual cash flow by 5 percent to 10 percent, which is a very high level of forecasting accuracy and is indicative of mature and stable cash flows. In this case, the treasurer can safely adopt a 90 percent benchmark hedge ratio, which should hedge nearly all of the forecasted exposure. However, what if a company has more difficulty in predicting its cash flows? Exhibit 9.B reveals a considerably more variable cash flow situation.

In this more difficult forecasting environment, the average variance of actual cash flows from the forecast is 21 percent, but also lower than the forecast by 41 percent in half of the reporting periods. In this case, the treasurer may well feel justified in adopting a benchmark hedge ratio of only 60 percent, in order to hedge only that portion of cash flows that is most likely to occur.

Exhibit 9.A   Sample Forecasted and Actual Cash Flow Stream (Stable)

	Jan	Feb	Mar	Apr	May	Jun
Forecast	€3,051	€3,293	€4,011	€3,982	€3,854	€3,702
Actual	2,715	3,015	3,742	3,800	3,750	3,509
€ Variance	−336	−278	−269	−182	−104	−193
% Variance	−11%	−8%	−7%	−5%	−3%	−5%

Exhibit 9.B   Sample Forecasted and Actual Cash Flow Stream (Unstable)

	Jan	Feb	Mar	Apr	May	Jun
Forecast	€3,051	€3,293	€4,011	€3,982	€3,854	€3,702
Actual	2,142	3,409	4,000	1,862	3,915	2,274
€ Variance	−909	116	−11	−2,120	61	−1,428
% Variance	−30%	4%	0%	−53%	2%	−39%

The benchmark hedge ratio does not need to be consistent across the entire currency portfolio. There may be significant differences in the level of forecasting accuracy by currency, so a high-confidence currency forecast with little expected volatility can be matched with a higher benchmark hedge ratio, while a questionable forecast may justify a much lower ratio. Introducing this higher degree of granularity into the hedging strategy allows for better matching of hedging activity to foreign exchange risk.

The benchmark hedge ratio is also important from the perspective of the availability of hedge accounting. If the benchmark hedge ratio can be proven to cause a "high probability" of hedging effectiveness, then hedge accounting (which can delay the recognition of hedging gains and losses) can be used. Consequently, an ongoing analysis of the most appropriate benchmark hedge ratio would leave open the option of using hedge accounting.

Accept the Risk

Not hedging the exposure is the simplest strategy of all. A company can accept the foreign exchange risk, and record any gains or losses on changes in the spot rate as they occur. The size of a company's currency exposure may dictate whether to hedge. For a smaller currency position, the expense associated with setting up and monitoring a hedge may be greater than any likely loss from a decline in the spot rate. Conversely, as a company's currency positions increase in size, the risk also increases, and makes this strategy less palatable.

The next seven strategies are all internal business practices that reduce currency exposure.

Insist on Home Currency Payment

It is possible to insist on being paid in the company's home currency, so that the foreign exchange risk shifts entirely to the customer. This is a likely strategy for a company that is dominant in its industry and can therefore impose terms on its customers. However, smaller firms will find that they have a modest competitive advantage if they allow customers to pay in their own currencies.

The worst option is to offer a customer a choice of currencies in which to make a payment, since it will invariably use the one having the more favorable exchange rate; the company essentially bears the downside risk in this scenario, with no upside potential.

Currency Surcharges

If a customer will not pay in a company's home currency, then a related option is to bill the customer a currency surcharge if the company incurs a foreign exchange loss between the time of billing and payment. The surcharge may not be billed for minor changes in the exchange rate (to avoid paperwork), but is triggered by a significant decline in the exchange rate. Customers are rarely happy about this, since they are taking on the foreign exchange risk, and they cannot budget for the amount of the surcharge. It is also hardly a competitive advantage for a company to impose this practice on its customers.

Get Paid on Time

When a company deals with a counterparty in another country, the payment terms may be quite long, due to longer delivery schedules, border-crossing delays, or simply because of longer customary payment intervals in the other country. If a payment period is unusually prolonged, then the company is exposed to changes in the spot rate to a much greater extent than would be the case if the payment interval were compressed. Consequently, it behooves a company's sales staff to constantly strive toward sales agreements with shorter payment terms, while the collections staff should be unusually aggressive in collecting from foreign customers.

Foreign Currency Loans

It is possible to offset a foreign currency risk exposure by creating a counter liability, such as a loan. To do so, a company can borrow an amount of money in the foreign currency that matches the amount of the receivable. When the customer pays off the receivable, the company uses the proceeds to pay off the loan—all in the same currency. This is an especially attractive option if foreign interest rates on debt are low, or if there are tax advantages peculiar to the foreign tax location, of which the company can take advantage.

Sourcing Changes

If there is a large amount of foreign currency cash flows coming from a specific country, then one way to hedge this risk is to start using suppliers located in the same country. By doing so, the company can find a ready use for the incoming currency, by turning it around and sending it right back to the same country. A more permanent possibility is to either buy or build a facility in that country, which will require currency not only for the initial capital investment, but also to fund continuing operations. This is a particularly favorable option if there are local government subsidies that give the company additional cost savings. However, local sourcing is not a good option if it will interrupt a smoothly operating supply chain.

Foreign Currency Accounts

If a company regularly receives and pays out funds in a particular foreign currency, it may make sense to open a foreign exchange account, in which it maintains a sufficient currency balance to meet its operational needs. This approach can be cost-effective, because the company would otherwise have to buy the foreign currency in order to pay those suppliers requiring payment in that currency, and then separately sell the same currency upon receipt of customer payments. While the company is still accepting the risk of loss on fluctuations in the exchange rate, it is eliminating the cost of continually buying and selling the currency.

Such a bank account does not necessarily have to be held in the country where the currency originates. It is also possible, and likely more efficient, to maintain a variety of currency accounts in a single major currency center, such as New York, London, or Amsterdam.

Unilateral, Bilateral, and Multilateral Netting Arrangements

A company that regularly conducts business in multiple countries must spend a considerable amount of time settling foreign exchange transactions. It may buy and sell the same currencies many times over as it processes individual payables and receivables. There are three ways to reduce the volume of these transactions, depending on the number of parties involved. They are:

1. *Unilateral netting.* A company can aggregate the cash flows among its various subsidiaries, to determine if any foreign exchange payments between the subsidiaries can be netted, with only the (presumably) smaller residual balances being physically shifted. This reduces the volume of foreign exchange cash flows, and therefore the associated foreign exchange risk.

2. *Bilateral spreadsheet netting.* If two companies located in different countries transact a great deal of business with each other, then they can track the payables owed to each other and net out the balances at the end of each month, and one party pays the other the net remaining balance.

3. *Multilateral centralized netting.* When there are multiple parties wishing to net transactions, it becomes much too complex to manage with a spreadsheet. Instead, the common approach is to net transactions through a centralized exchange, such as Arizona-based EuroNetting (www.euronetting.com). Under a centralized netting system, each participant enters its payables into a centralized database through an Internet browser or some other file upload system, after which the netting service converts each participant's net cash flows to an equivalent amount in each participant's base currency, and then uses actual traded exchange rates to determine the final net position of each participant. The exchange operator then pays or receives each participant's net position, and uses the proceeds to offset the required foreign exchange trades.

Each type of netting arrangement can involve a broad array of payment types, covering such areas as products, services, royalties, dividends, interest, loans, and hedging contracts.

When bilateral or multilateral netting is used, the parties usually sign a master agreement that itemizes the types of netting to be performed, as well as which contracts or purchase orders are to be included in the arrangement.

Though netting can be a highly effective way to reduce foreign exchange transaction costs, some governments do not recognize the enforceability of netting arrangements, because they can undermine the payment rights of third-party creditors. Consequently, consult a qualified attorney prior to entering into a netting arrangement.

The remaining strategies in this section involve the use of derivatives to hedge foreign exchange risk.

Forward Exchange Contracts

Under a forward exchange contract, which is the most commonly used foreign exchange hedge, a company agrees to purchase a fixed amount of a foreign currency on a specific date, and at a predetermined rate. This allows it to lock in the rate of exchange up front for settlement at a specified date in the future. The counterparty is typically a bank, which requires a deposit to secure the contract, with a final payment due in time to be cleared by the settlement date. If the company has a credit facility with the bank acting as its counterparty, then the bank can allocate a portion of that line to any outstanding forward exchange contracts and release the allocation once the contracts have been settled. The forward exchange contract is

considered to be an over-the-counter transaction, because there is no centralized trading location, and customized transactions are created directly
between parties.

Example

Toledo Toolmakers has a 100,000 euro receivable at a spot rate of 1.39079.
Toledo can enter into a forward foreign exchange (FX) contract with a bank
for 100,000 euros at a forward rate of 1.3900, so that Toledo receives a fixed
amount of $139,000 on the maturity date of the receivable. When Toledo
receives the 100,000-euro payment, it transfers the funds to the bank acting
as counterparty on the forward FX contract and receives $139,000 from the
bank. Thus, Toledo has achieved its original receivable amount of $139,000,
even if the spot rate has declined during the interval.

The price of a currency on the maturity date (its forward price) is
composed of the spot price, plus a transaction fee, plus or minus points that
represent the interest rate differential between the two currencies. The
combination of the spot rate and the forward points is known as the *all-in
forward rate*. The interest rate differential is calculated in accordance with
these two rules:

1. The currency of the country having a higher interest rate trades at
   a discount.
2. The currency of the country having a lower interest rate trades at
   a premium.

For example, if the domestic interest rate is higher than that of the
foreign currency, then forward points are deducted from the spot rate,
which makes the foreign currency less expensive in the forward market. The
result of this pricing is that the forward price should make the buyer indif-
ferent to taking delivery immediately or at some future date. Thus, if the
spot price of euros per dollar were 0.7194 and there was a discount of 40
points for forwards having a one-year maturity, then the all-in forward rate
would be 0.7154.

The calculation of the discount or premium points follows this formula:

$$\text{Premium/Discount} = \text{Exchange Rate} \times \text{Interest Rate Differential}$$

$$\times \frac{\text{Days of Contract Duration}}{360}$$

Example

The six-month U.S. dollar money market rate is 2.50 percent and the six-month euro money market rate is 3.75 percent. The USD/EUR exchange rate is 0.7194. The number of days in the forward exchange contract is 181. Because the euro interest rate exceeds the dollar interest rate, the dollar is at a premium to the euro. Thus, the USD/EUR forward exchange rate exceeds the spot rate. The premium is calculated as:

$$0.7194 \text{ Spot Rate} \times .0125 \text{ Interest Differential} \times (181/365 \text{ Days})$$
$$= .0045 \text{ Premium}$$

The premium is therefore 45 points, which results in a USD/EUR forward exchange rate of 0.7194 + 0.0045, or 0.7239.

There are a few problems with forward exchange contracts to be aware of. First, because they are special transactions between two parties, it can be difficult to sell them to a third party. Also, the transaction premium offered may not be competitive.

Another problem is that the arrangement relies on the customer's paying the company on or before the date when the forward FX contract matures. To continue using Toledo Toolmakers in an example, its terms to a European Union customer may require payment in 60 days, so it enters into a forward contract to expire in 63 days, which factors in an allowance of 3 extra days for the customer to pay. If the customer does not pay within 63 days, then Toledo still has to deliver euros on that date to fulfill its side of the forward contract.

It is possible to mitigate this problem with the variability of customer payments by entering into a *forward window contract*. This contract has a range of settlement dates during which the company can settle the outstanding contract at the currency rate noted in the contract. This contract is slightly more expensive than a standard forward exchange contract but makes it much easier to match incoming customer payments to the terms of the contract.

A related problem is when a company enters into a forward exchange contract to hedge an anticipated cash flow but the cash never happens at all, perhaps because a sale was canceled. In this case, the treasurer can enter into an offsetting forward exchange contract to negate the initial contract.

Example

Toledo Toolmakers learns on July 15 that a Belgian customer has financial difficulties and has defaulted on a payment of 250,000 euros that Toledo expected to receive on October 15. Unfortunately, Toledo already sold this amount through a forward exchange contract having a EUR/USD exchange rate of 1.3900, with a settlement date of October 15. Since it now has an obligation to deliver currency that will not be available on October 15, it needs to enter into an offsetting agreement to buy 250,000 euros on the same date.

Since the date of the original contract, the exchange rate has worsened, so that Toledo now enters into a three-month forward exchange contract having a EUR/USD rate of 1.3850. On the settlement date, Toledo buys 250,000 euros for $346,250 (250,000 × $1.3850) and sells them for $347,500 (250,000 × $1.3900), thereby incurring a loss of $1,250.

A variation on the forward contract is the *nondeliverable forward*. Under this arrangement, the only payment made between the parties is the difference between the spot rate and the forward rate. This net-cash solution can greatly reduce the total gross amount of funds being transferred.

Currency Futures

A currency future is the same as a forward exchange contract, except that it trades on an exchange. Each contract has a standardized size, expiry date, and settlement rules. The primary currency futures center with substantial volume is the Chicago Mercantile Exchange (CME). The CME offers futures trading between the major currencies, as well as some of the emerging market currencies; however, the volume of contracts in the emerging market currencies is quite low.

These contracts are normally handled through a broker, who charges a commission. There is also a margin requirement, so that the buyer may be called on to submit additional funds over time, if the underlying futures contract declines in value. Part of this margin is an initial deposit whose size is based on the contract size and the type of position being acquired. All futures contracts are marked to market daily, with the underlying margin accounts being credited or debited with the day's gains or losses. If the balance of the margin account drops too far, then the contract buyer must contribute more funds to the margin account. If the buyer does not update his margin account as required, then it is possible that the position will be closed out.

Since currency futures have standard sizes and expiry dates, it is quite likely that a futures hedging strategy will not exactly match the underlying currency activity. For example, if a company needs to hedge a projected receipt of 375,000 euros, and the related futures contract trades only in units of 100,000 euros, then the company has the choice of selling either three or four contracts, totaling 300,000 and 400,000 euros, respectively. Further, if the projected currency receipt date varies from the standard futures contract expiry date, then the company will be subject to some foreign exchange risk for a few days. Thus, the standardized nature of currency futures contracts result in an imperfect hedge for users.

Example

Toledo Toolmakers ships product to a German customer in February and expects to receive a payment of 425,000 euros on June 12. Toledo's treasurer elects to hedge the transaction by selling a futures contract on the CME. The standard contract size for the EUR/USD pairing is 100,000 euros, so Toledo sells four contracts to hedge its expected receipt of 425,000 euros. This contract always expires on Fridays; the nearest Friday following the expected receipt date of the euros is on June 15, so Toledo enters into contracts having that expiry date. Because the standardized futures contracts do not exactly fit Toledo's transaction, Toledo is electing not to hedge 25,000 euros of the expected receipt, and it will also retain the risk of exchange rate fluctuations between its currency receipt date of June 12 and its currency sale date of June 15.

Currency Options

A foreign currency option requires the payment of a premium in exchange for a right to use one currency to buy another currency at a specified price on or before a specified date. A *call option* permits the buyer to buy the underlying currency at the strike price, while a *put option* allows the buyer to sell the underlying currency at the strike price.

An option is easier to manage than a forward exchange contract because a company can choose not to exercise its option to sell currency if a customer does not pay it. Not exercising an option is also useful when it becomes apparent that a company can realize a gain on changes in the exchange rate, which would not have been the case if it were tied into a forward exchange contract.

Options are especially useful for those companies interested in bidding on contracts that will be paid in a foreign currency. If they do not win the bid, they can simply let the option expire, without any obligation to purchase currency. If they win the bid, then they have the option of taking advantage of the exchange rate that they locked in at the time they formulated the bid. Thus, options allow a company to realize the original margin that they quoted to a customer, rather than potentially having the margin erode due to exchange risk.

In an option agreement, the cost to the buyer is fixed up front, while the cost to the seller is potentially unlimited—which tends to increase the cost of the option to the point where the seller is willing to take on the risk associated with the contract. From the seller's perspective, the amount of an option premium is based on the strike price, time to expiration, and the volatility of the underlying currency. If the currency is highly volatile, then it is more likely that the buyer will exercise the option, which increases the risk for the seller. Thus, an option for a nonvolatile currency is less expensive, since it is unlikely to be exercised.

Currency options are both available over the counter and are traded on exchanges. Those traded on exchanges are known as *listed options*. The contract value, term, and strike price of a listed option is standardized, whereas these terms are customized for an over-the-counter option.

Within an option agreement, the *strike price* states the exchange rate at which the underlying currency can be bought or sold, the *notional contract amount* is the amount of currency that can be bought or sold at the option of the buyer, and the *expiry date* is the date when the contract will expire, if not previously exercised. If the option is *in the money*, then the buyer can exercise it at a better price than the current exchange rate. If the option is *at the money*, then the buyer can exercise it at the current market price, while it is considered to be *out of the money* if the buyer can exercise it only at an exchange rate that is worse than the market rate. A *European-style option* is only exercisable on the expiry date, while an *American-style option* can be exercised at any time prior to and including the expiry date.

The problem with an option is that it requires the payment of an upfront premium to purchase the option, so not exercising the option means that the fee is lost. This may be fine if a gain from currency appreciation offsets the fee, but is an outright loss if the nonexercise was caused by the customer's not paying on time.

Example

Toledo Toolmakers buys a 90-day option to buy 100,000 euros at $1.3900 for a fee of $4,000, which it plans to use as a hedge against a 100,000-euro payment from a customer that is due in 90 days. At the end of the option contract, the spot rate is $1.4350. Toledo elects to not exercise the option, thereby receiving 100,000 euros from its customer that can be exchanged at the spot price of $1.4350 for a total of $143,500. Thus, Toledo has gained $4,500 on the differential in the spot price, less $4,000 for the cost of the option, for a net profit of $500.

A more complicated version of the option is the *foreign exchange collar*. Under this strategy, a company buys one option and sells another at the same time, using the same expiry date and the same currencies. Doing so establishes an exchange rate range for a company. The upper limit of the exchange rate is established by the option the company buys, while the lower limit is established by the option that the company sells. If the exchange rate remains within the upper and lower price points of the collar, then neither option is exercised. By accepting a moderate range of acceptable prices, a company can offset the cost of the premium paid for the purchased option with the premium from the option that is sold. The options are usually European-style, so they are only exercised on the expiry date.

Example

Toledo Toolmakers is contractually obligated to pay a French supplier 500,000 euros in three months. The current EUR/USD exchange rate is 1.3900. Toledo's treasurer does not want to pay an option premium. The three-month EUR/USD forward exchange rate is 1.3950, and the treasurer is willing to accept a variation of 0.02 both above and below this rate, which means that the acceptable currency range is from 1.3750 to 1.4150. The option premium for selling euros at 1.4150 is 0.10, while Toledo can also earn the same premium for buying euros at 1.3750. Thus, the cost of one option is exactly offset by the earnings from the other option, resulting in a net option cost of zero.

The actual exchange rate on the settlement date is 1.4300, so the treasurer exercises the option to sell 500,000 euros at 1.4150, thereby avoiding an incremental loss of $7,500, which Toledo would otherwise have incurred if it had been forced to sell euros at 1.4300.

Another issue with options is that they must be marked to market at the end of every reporting period, with the gain or loss recorded in the company's financial statements. This is addressed more fully in the Hedge Accounting section.

Currency Swaps

A currency swap is a spot transaction on the over-the-counter market that is executed at the same time as a forward transaction, with currencies being exchanged at both the spot date and the forward date. One currency is bought at the spot rate and date, while the transaction is reversed at the forward date and rate. Thus, once the swap expires, both parties return to their original positions. The currency swap acts as an investment in one currency and a loan in another. The amount of a foreign exchange swap usually begins at $5 million, so this is not an option for smaller foreign exchange cash positions.

The exchange rates of both transactions are set at the time of the initial transaction, so the difference between the two rates is caused by the interest differential between the two currencies over the duration of the swap.

Example

Toledo Toolmakers has excess euros that it will need in nine months to pay for a capital project in Europe. In the interim, its treasurer wants to invest the euros in a short-term instrument, while also obtaining use of the funds in U.S. dollars to cover its operating cash flow needs. To do so, Toledo engages in a foreign exchange swap with its bank, under which it buys $10 million at a 0.7194 USD/EUR exchange rate, and sells 7,194,000 euros. Simultaneously, Toledo agrees to sell back $10 million of U.S. dollars in nine months at a rate of 0.7163 and buy back 7,163,000 euros. The difference between the spot rate and forward rate of 0.0031 represents the interest rate differential between euros and U.S. dollars over the nine months spanned by the swap agreement, or $31,000. Toledo earns the extra interest, because it has chosen to invest in the currency having the higher interest rate.

The currency swap is useful when a company forecasts a short-term liquidity shortfall in a specific currency, and has sufficient funds in a different currency to effect a swap into the currency where funds are needed. In addition, the company offsets what is likely to be a high interest rate on the short-term debt with the lower interest rate that it was earning on funds in a different currency.

Example

Toledo Toolmakers has a short-term negative euro account balance of 500,000 euros, which it expects will continue for the next six months. During that time, Toledo must pay its bank the London Interbank Offered Rate (LIBOR) plus 2 percent for the current account deficit. At the current LIBOR rate of 3.5% and EUR/USD spot rate of 1.3900, this represents an interest expense of $19,113, which is calculated as follows:

$$\$19{,}113 = C500{,}000 \times 1.3900 \text{ Exchange Rate}$$
$$\times 5.5\% \text{ Interest Rate} \times (180/360 \text{ Days})$$

Toledo has several million U.S. dollars available, so it engages in a six-month swap of dollars for euros, thereby eliminating the negative account balance. The interest rates in Europe and the United States are identical, so there is no premium or discount between the currencies. Toledo was earning the LIBOR rate on its short-term investments. The interest income that it gave up by engaging in the swap was $12,163, which is calculated as follows:

$12,163 = €500,000 × 1.3900 Exchange Rate
× 3.5% Interest Rate × (180/360 Days)

Thus, by using a swap to use low-interest investments to offset higher-cost debt, Toledo saves $6,950.

The currency swap is also useful when a foreign currency cash flow is delayed, and a company would normally be obligated to sell the currency on the expected receipt date, as per the terms of a forward exchange contract. To meet this contractually obligated payment, a company can swap its other currency reserves into the currency that must be sold, and reverse the transaction later, when the expected cash flow eventually arrives.

Proxy Hedging

If a company elects to receive a currency that is not actively traded, then it may have a difficult time locating a hedge in the same currency. However, changes in the value of the currencies of a large economic area, such as Southeast Asia, tend to be closely correlated with each other. If the treasurer feels that this correlation will continue, then it may make sense to instead hedge through a highly correlated currency. However, just because the respective values of a currency pair were highly correlated in the past does not mean that they will continue to be in the future, since a multitude of political and economic issues can break the correlation.

Summary of Strategies

Forward exchange contracts are the most heavily used form of hedging, for two reasons. First, they are very inexpensive, having a modest transactional cost. Second, they are an over-the-counter product, and so can be precisely tailored to a company's individual needs. However, they firmly lock a company into the current spot rate, giving them no opportunity to participate in any future favorable price movements. While a company could use partial hedging to give itself some upside potential, this is also a two-way street, with increased risk of loss if exchange rates move in the wrong direction.

Currency futures are more easily entered into and sold off, since they are standardized products that trade through a formal exchange system. However, these conveniences present a problem, since a company's hedging requirements cannot precisely fit the amount or timing of available futures contracts. Futures also suffer from the same problem as forward exchange contracts—they leave no room to participate in any future favorable price movements.

Currency options have a clear advantage over the preceding two strategies in that they allow a buyer to exercise an option or let it lapse, thereby allowing a treasurer to take advantage of favorable price movements. Against this major benefit is ranged the biggest problem with options—the premium imposed by the option seller. In practice, treasurers tend to buy options that are relatively far out of the money, since these options are less expensive, but doing so means that they must retain some foreign exchange risk. Because of the premium, options appear to be the most expensive alternative; however, one must also factor in the opportunity cost of using forward exchange contracts or currency futures where one cannot take advantage of favorable price swings. When netted against the option premium, the cost of options does not appear to be so prohibitive. Options also require closer monitoring than other strategies, since one must judge exactly when to exercise them.

In summary, forward exchange contracts and currency futures are easier and less expensive to engage in than options, and so are favored by organizations with simpler treasury operations and conservative risk profiles. Options are more expensive in the short-term and require closer monitoring, but can be financially rewarding to more aggressive treasury departments.

HEDGE ACCOUNTING[1]

There are complex hedging rules that permit a company to elect to obtain special accounting treatment relative to foreign currency risks. These rules include the establishment, at inception, of criteria for measuring hedge effectiveness and ineffectiveness. Periodically, each hedge must be evaluated for effectiveness, using the preestablished criteria, and the gains or losses associated with hedge ineffectiveness must be reported currently in earnings, and not deferred to future periods.

In the instance of foreign currency hedges, companies must exclude from their assessments of hedge effectiveness the portions of the fair value of forward contracts attributable to spot-forward differences (i.e., differences between the spot exchange rate and the forward exchange rate).

In practice, this means that companies must estimate the cash flows on forecasted transactions based on the current spot exchange rate, appropriately discounted for time value. Effectiveness is then assessed by comparing the changes in fair values of the forward contracts attributable to changes in the dollar spot price of the pertinent foreign currency to the changes in the present values of the forecasted cash flows based on the current spot exchange rate(s).

---

[1] Adapted with permission from the *2009 Wiley GAAP Guide*, John Wiley & Sons, Chapter 23.

On October 1, 2009, Toledo Toolmakers orders from its European supplier, Gemutlichkeit GmbH, a machine that is to be delivered and paid for on March 31, 2010. The price is 4 million euros. Although Toledo will not make the payment until the planned delivery date, it has immediately entered into a firm commitment to make this purchase and to pay 4 million euros upon delivery. This creates a euro liability exposure to foreign exchange risk; thus, if the euro appreciates over the intervening six months, the dollar cost of the equipment will increase.

To reduce or eliminate this uncertainty, Toledo desires to lock in the purchase cost in euros by entering into a six-month forward contract to purchase euros on the date when the purchase order is issued to and accepted by Gemutlichkeit. The spot rate on October 1, 2009, is $1.40 per euro and the forward rate for March 31, 2010 settlement is $1.44 per euro. Toledo enters into a forward contract on October 1, 2009, with the First Intergalactic Bank to pay US$5,760,000 in exchange for the receipt of 4 million euros on March 31, 2010, which can then be used to pay Gemutlichkeit. No premium is received or paid at the inception of this forward contract.

Assume the relevant time value of money is measured at 0.5 percent per month (a nominal 6 percent annual rate). The spot rate for euros at December 31, 2009, is $1.45, and at March 31, 2010, it is $1.48. The forward rate as of December 31 for March 31 settlement is $1.46.

Entries to reflect the foregoing scenario are as follows:

10/1/09	*No entries, since neither the forward contract nor the firm commitment have value on this date*		
12/31/09	Forward currency contract	78,818	
	Gain on forward contract		78,818

To record present value (at 0.5 percent monthly rate) of change in value of forward contract [= change in forward rate (1.46 − 1.44) × €4,000,000 = $80,000 to be received in three months, discounted at 6 percent per annum]

	Loss on firm purchase commitment	197,044	
	Firm commitment obligation		197,044

To record present value (at 0.5 percent monthly rate) of change in amount of firm commitment [= change in spot rate (1.45 − 1.40) × €4,000,000 = $200,000 to be paid in three months, discounted at 6% per annum]

	Gain on forward contract	78,818	
	Loss on firm purchase commitment		197,044
	P&L summary (then to retained earnings)	118,226	

To close the gain and loss accounts to net income and thus to retained earnings

3/31/10	Forward currency contract	81,182	
	Gain on forward contract		81,182

To record change in value of forward contract {[= (1.48 − 1.44) × €4,000,000 = $160,000] − gain previously recognized ($78,818)}

Loss on firm commitment	122,956	
Firm commitment obligation		122,956

To record change in amount of firm commitment {[= (1.48 − 1.40) × €4,000,000] less loss previously recognized ($197,044)}

Firm commitment obligation	320,000	
Machinery and equipment	5,600,000	
Cash		5,920,000

To record purchase of machinery based on spot exchange rate as of date of contractual commitment (1.40) and close out the firm commitment obligation (representing effect of change in spot rate during commitment period)

Cash	160,000	
Forward contract		160,000

To record collection of cash on net settlement of forward contract [= (1.48 − 1.44) × €4,000,000]

Gain on forward contract	81,182	
P&L summary (then to retained earnings)	41,774	
Loss on firm purchase commitment		122,956

To close the gain and loss accounts to net income and thus to retained earnings

With respect to fair value hedges of firm purchase commitments denominated in a foreign currency, the change in value of the contract related to the changes in the differences between the spot price and the forward or futures price would be excluded from the assessment of hedge effectiveness. As applied to the foregoing example, therefore, the net credit to income in 2009 ($118,226) can be further analyzed into two constituent elements: the amount arising from the change in the difference between the spot price and the forward price, and the amount resulting from hedge ineffectiveness.

The former item, not attributed to ineffectiveness, arose because the spread between spot and forward price at hedge inception, (1.44 − 1.40) = .04, fell to (1.46 − 1.45) = .01 by December 31, for an impact amounting to (.04 − .01) = .03 × 4,000,000 = $120,000, which, reduced to present value terms, equaled $118,227. The net credit to earnings in December 2009, ($78,818 + 118,226) = $197,044, relates to the spread between the spot and forward rates on December 31 and is identifiable with hedge ineffectiveness.

Forward Exchange Contract Accounting

Foreign currency transaction gains and losses on assets and liabilities that are denominated in a currency other than the home currency can be hedged if a U.S. company enters into a forward exchange contract. The following example shows how a forward exchange contract can be used as a hedge, first against a firm commitment and then, following delivery date, as a hedge against a recognized liability.

A general rule for estimating the fair value of forward exchange rates is to use the changes in the forward exchange rates, and discount those estimated future cash flows to a present-value basis. An entity will need to consider the time value of money if significant in the circumstances for these contracts. The following example does not apply discounting of the future cash flows from the forward contracts, in order to focus on the relationships between the forward contract and the foreign currency denominated payable.

Example

Toledo Toolmakers enters into a firm commitment with Dempsey Inc., Inc. of Germany, on October 1, 2009, to purchase a computerized robotic system for 6 million euros. The system will be delivered on March 1, 2010, with payment due 60 days after delivery (April 30, 2010). Toledo decides to hedge this foreign currency firm commitment and enters into a forward exchange contract on the firm commitment date to receive 6 million euros on the payment date. The applicable exchange rates are shown in the table below.

Date	Spot Rates	Forward Rates for April 30, 2009
October 1, 2009	€1 = $1.55	€1 = $1.570
December 31, 2009	€1 = $1.58	€1 = $1.589
March 1, 2010	€1 = $1.58	€1 = $1.585
April 30, 2010	€1 = $1.60	

The example continues on the following pages, and separately presents both the forward contract receivable and the dollars payable liability in order to show all aspects of the forward contract. For financial reporting purposes, most companies present just the net fair value of the forward contract that would be the difference between the current value of the forward contract receivable and the dollars payable liability. Note that the foreign currency hedges in the illustration are not perfectly effective. However, for this example, the degree of ineffectiveness is not deemed to be sufficient to trigger income statement recognition.

The transactions that reflect the forward exchange contract, the firm commitment, and the acquisition of the asset and retirement of the related liability appear below. The net fair value of the forward contract is shown below each set of entries for the forward exchange contract.

Unnumbered Exhibit 9A   Net Fair Value

Forward contract entries   *Hedge against firm commitment entries*

(1) 10/1/08 (forward
      rate for 4/30/09
      €1 = $1.57)

| Forward contract receivable | 9,420,000 | |
| Dollars payable | | 9,420,000 |

This entry recognizes the existence of the forward exchange contract using the gross method. Under the net method, this entry would not appear at all, since the fair value of the forward contract is zero when the contract is initiated. The amount is calculated using the 10/1/08 forward rate for 4/30/09 (€6,000,000 × $1.57 = $9,420,000).

Net fair value of the forward contract = $0

Note that the net fair value of the forward exchange contact on 10/1/08 is zero because there is an exact amount offset of the forward contract receivable of $9,420,000 with the dollars payable liability of $9,420,000. Many companies present only the net fair value of the forward contract on their balance sheets, and therefore, they would have no net amount reported for the forward contract at its inception.

Forward contract entries

Hedge against firm commitment entries

(2) 12/31/08
    (forward rate
    for 4/30/09
    €1 = $1.589)

| Forward contract receivable | 114,000 | |
| Gain on hedge activity | | 114,000 |

(3) 12/31/08

| Loss on hedge activity | 114,000 | |
| Firm commitment | | 114,000 |

The dollar values for this entry reflect, among other things, the change in the forward rate from 10/1/08 to 12/31/08. However, the actual amount recorded as gain or loss (gain in this case) is determined by all market factors.

Net increase in fair value of the forward contract = (1.589 − 1.57 = .019 × €6,000,000 = $114,000).

The increase in the net fair value of the forward exchange contract on 12/31/08 is $114,000 for the difference between the $7,134,000 ($7,020,000 plus $114,000) in the forward contract receivable and the $7,020,000 for the dollars payable liability. Many companies present only the net fair value on their balance sheet, in this case as an asset. And, this $114,000 is the amount that would be discounted to present value, if interest is significant, to recognize the time value of the future cash flow from the forward contract.

The dollar values for this entry are identical to those in entry (2), reflecting the fact that the hedge is highly effective (100%) and also the fact that the market recognizes the same factors in this transaction as for entry (2). This entry reflects the first use of the firm commitment account, a temporary liability account pending the receipt of the asset against which the firm commitment has been hedged.

(4) 3/1/09 (forward
    rate for 4/30/09
    €1 = $1.585)

| Loss on hedge activity | 24,000 | |
| Forward contract receivable | | 24,000 |

(5) 3/1/09

| Firm commitment | 24,000 | |
| Gain on hedge activity | | 24,000 |

These entries again will be driven by market factors, and they are calculated the same way as entries (2) and (3) above. Note that the decline in the forward rate from 12/31/08 to 3/1/09 resulted in a loss against the forward contract receivable and a gain against the firm commitment [1.585 − 1.589 = (.004) × €6,000,000 = ($24,000)].

Forward contract entries

Net fair value of the forward contract = $90,000

The net fair value of the forward exchange contract on 3/1/09 is $90,000 for the difference between the $9,510,000 ($9,420,000 plus 114,000 minus $24,000) in the forward contract receivable and the $9,420,000 for the dollars payable liability. Another way of computing the net fair value is to determine the change in the forward contract rate from the initial date of the contract, 10/1/08, which is $1.585 − $1.57 = $.015 × €6,000,000 = $90,000. Also note that the amount in the firm commitment temporary liability account is equal to the net fair value of the forward contract on the date the equipment is received.

(7) 4/30/09
     (spot rate
     €1 = $1.60)

Forward contract receivable	90,000	
Gain on forward contract		90,000

The gain or loss (gain in this case) on the forward contract is calculated using the change in the forward to the spot rate from 3/1/09 to 4/30/09 [€6,000,000 × ($1.60 − $1.585) = $90,000]

Net fair value of the forward contract = $180,000

Hedge against a recognized liability entries

(6) 3/1/09 (spot rate
     €1 = $1.58)

Equipment	9,390,000	
Firm commitment	90,000	
Accounts payable (€)		9,480,000

This entry records the receipt of the equipment, the elimination of the temporary liability account (firm commitment), and the recognition of the payable, calculated using the spot rate on the date of receipt (€6,000,000 × $1.58 = $9,480,000).

(8) 4/30/09

Transaction loss	120,000	
Accounts payable (€)		120,000

The transaction loss related to the accounts payable reflects only the change in the spot rates and ignores the accrual of interest. [€6,000,000 × ($1.60 − $1.58) = $120,000]

The net fair value of the forward exchange contract on 4/30/09 is $180,000 for the difference between the $9,600,000 ($9,510,000 plus $90,000) in the forward contract receivable and the $9,420,000 for the dollars payable liability. The net fair value of the forward contract at its terminal date of 4/30/09 is based on the difference between the contract forward rate of €1 = $1.57 and the spot rate on 4/30/09 of €1 = $1.60. The forward contract receivable has reached its maturity and the contract is completed on this date at the forward rate of €1 = $1.57 as contracted on 10/1/08. If the entity recognizes an interest factor in the forward contract over the life of the contract, then interest is recognized at this time on the forward contract, but no separate accrual of interest is required for the accounts payable in euros.

(9) 4/30/09		
Dollars payable	9,420,000	
Cash		9,420,000
Foreign currency units (€)	9,600,000	
Forward contract receivable		9,600,000

This entry reflects the settlement of the forward contract at the 10/1/08 contracted forward rate (€6,000,000 × $1.17 = $7,020,000) and the receipt of foreign currency units valued at the spot rate (€6,000,000 × $1.20 = $7,200,000).

(10) 4/30/09		
Accounts payable (€)	9,600,000	
Foreign currency units (€)		9,600,000

This entry reflects the use of the foreign currency units to retire the account payable.

Foreign Currency Investment Hedge Accounting

A company can invest in a subsidiary located in another country, and issue a loan to act as a hedge against the investment in the subsidiary. This loan can be designated as a hedge. The gain or loss from the designated hedge to the extent that it is effective is reported as a translation adjustment.

Example

Toledo Toolmakers has invested $15 million in a subsidiary in Germany, and for which the euro is the functional currency. The initial exchange rate is €1.2:$1, so the initial investment is worth 18 million euros. Toledo issues a debt instrument for 12 million euros and designates it as a hedge of the German investment. Toledo's strategy is that any change in the fair value of the loan attributable to foreign exchange risk should offset any translation gain or loss on two-thirds of Toledo's German investment.

At the end of the year, the exchange rate changes to €0.8:$1. Toledo uses the following calculation to determine the translation gain on its net investment:

$$€18,000,000/\$0.8 = \$22,500,000 - €18,000,000/\$1.2$$
$$= \$15,000,000 = \$7,500,000$$

Toledo uses the following calculation to determine the translation loss on its euro-denominated debt:

$$€12,000,000/\$0.8 = \$15,000,000 - €12,000,000/\$1.2$$
$$= \$10,000,000 = \$5,000,000$$

Toledo creates the following entries to record changes in the value of the translation gain on its investment and translation loss in its debt, respectively:

Investment in subsidiary	7,500,000	
Cumulative translation adjustment (equity)		7,500,000
Cumulative translation adjustment (equity)	5,000,000	
Euro-denominated debt		5,000,000

The net effect of these translation adjustments is a net increase in Toledo's investment of $2.5 million. In the following year, the exchange rates do not change, and Toledo sells its subsidiary for $17.5 million. Toledo's tax rate is 30 percent. Its reported annual gains and losses follow:

	Year 1	Year 2
Net income:		
Gain on sale of investment in ABC Company		$2,500,000
Income tax expense		(750,000)
Net gain realized in net income		1,750,000
Other comprehensive income:		
Foreign currency translation adjustment, net of tax	$1,750,000	
Reclassification adjustment, net of tax		(1,750,000)
Other comprehensive income net gain/ (loss)	$1,750,000	$(1,750,000)

If a company is hedging only its booked exposure, it may make sense from a paperwork perspective to not attempt to use hedge accounting, since its positions are necessarily short, and will not benefit from any recognition deferral. However, if a company chooses to hedge its forecasted position, which may cover a considerably longer time period, then its primary challenge is to prove that the hedge can be matched to a pool of exposures having the same time horizon as the hedge. A simple way to do this is to hedge only a portion of the total exposure, so that the full amount of the hedge can always be matched against some portion of the exposure.

FOREIGN EXCHANGE HEDGE CONTROLS

There are a variety of controls that the treasury department can implement in order to reduce the risk profile of its hedging activities. These controls are divided into ones related to hedging authorizations, contracts, hedge accounting, and risk assessment.

Authorization Controls

- *Define dealing responsibilities.* Management should define the authorizations and responsibilities of all treasury staff engaged in foreign exchange transactions, including the position titles authorized to deal, the instruments they are allowed to deal in, and limits on open positions.

- *Issue an updated signatory list to counterparties at least once a year.* Schedule a periodic distribution of the company's authorized derivative contract signers to all counterparties, to keep unauthorized transactions from taking place, as well as whenever someone is dropped from the list. This should be a written notification, followed by a call to verify receipt.

- *Centralize foreign exchange trading operations.* Centralization makes it easier to maintain control over a company's trading activities.

Contractual Controls

- *Verify contract terms and signatory.* It is possible that a company may have difficulty forcing a counterparty to pay for its obligations under an over-the-counter contract if the counterparty did not correctly fill out the contract or if the signatory to the agreement was not authorized to do so. The company's legal department can follow up on these issues whenever a new contract is signed.

- *Confirm all hedging transactions.* As soon as a hedging deal is concluded, a different person than the transaction originator should confirm the details of the deal. This should be a matching of the company's transaction details to those of the counterparty or exchange, which may involve a written or electronic message (such as an email or SWIFT MT300).

- *Use standardized master agreements.* By using the master agreements provided by such organizations as the International Swaps and Derivatives Association, a company can avoid entering into contracts having inadequate coverage that may leave it at risk.

Hedge Accounting Controls

- *Include in the hedging procedure a requirement for full documentation of each hedge.* Hedging transactions are allowed under generally accepted accounting principles (GAAP) only if they are fully documented at the inception of the hedge. One can ensure compliance by including the documentation requirement in an accounting procedure for creating hedges.

General Risk Assessment Controls

- *Determine counterparty creditworthiness.* In cases where a company expects to deal directly with a counterparty through an over-the-counter hedging transaction (as opposed to dealing with an exchange), the treasurer should determine the creditworthiness of the counterparty prior to entering into the contract. Otherwise, the company could be taking on a significant risk that the counterparty cannot meet its obligations under the contract. This control can be expanded to include specific procedures to follow in the event of a counterparty credit downgrade.

- *Full-risk modeling.* The treasury staff should periodically conduct full-risk modeling of its foreign exchange positions to determine the potential risk inherent in its unhedged portfolio, and to determine what the company's gain or loss would have been on a rolling historical basis if it had not engaged in hedging transactions.

- *Audit spreadsheet calculations and contents.* If a company is compiling its currency cash flows in spreadsheets, then there is a significant risk of spreadsheet error. A qualified auditor should review the spreadsheets at least annually, with a particular examination of formula ranges and totals. It is also possible that entire cash accounts or entities may not be included in the spreadsheets, so the auditor should be cognizant of missing information.

FOREIGN EXCHANGE HEDGE POLICIES

The following policies are divided into ones that introduce consistency into the accounting for hedges, create boundaries around the amounts and durations of hedging activities, and authorize the treasurer to engage in hedging.

Accounting Consistency Policies

- *The determination of hedge effectiveness shall always use the same method for similar types of hedges.* GAAP allows one to use different assessment techniques in determining whether a hedge is highly effective. However, changing methods, even when justified, allows the accounting staff room to alter effectiveness designations, which can yield variations in the level of reported earnings. Consequently, creating and consistently using a standard assessment method for each type of hedge eliminates the risk of assessment manipulation.

- A hedge shall be considered highly effective if the fair values of the hedging instrument and hedged item are at least ___ percent offset. GAAP does not quantitatively specify what constitutes a highly effective hedge, so a company should create a policy defining the number. A different hedging range can be used for different types of hedges.

Deal Boundaries

- *The benchmark hedge ratio shall be ___ percent for booked exposures, ___ percent for forecasted exposures over the next 12-month period, and ___ percent of forecasted exposures for the following ___-month period.* This staggered benchmark hedging policy gives the treasury staff firm guidance regarding the amount of hedging activity to engage in. The benchmark hedge ratio should decline over the three periods noted in the policy, to reflect the increased uncertainty of cash flows further in the future.

- *Review benchmark hedge ratio.* The treasury staff should periodically compare forecasted foreign currency cash flows to actual results, by currency, and determine if the benchmark hedge ratio is appropriate, based on the company's forecasting ability.

- All derivative transactions shall be limited to a time horizon of ___ months, and involve no more than $___ in aggregate and $___ individually. This policy is designed to put general boundaries around the use of derivatives, and can be expanded to include the authorized types of derivatives, and who can bind the company in derivatives transactions. It can even include the compensation for foreign exchange trader performance, since an excessive bonus plan can lead to risky trading behavior. If implemented, this policy must be updated regularly, since ongoing changes in a company's business may mandate different types of transactions or volumes.

Authorization Policies

- The treasurer is authorized to discontinue hedging transactions with those counterparties with whom the company has experienced ongoing or significant operational problems. This policy is deliberately vague, giving the treasurer authority to stop doing business with a counterparty for any number of reasons, such as improper contract completion, incorrect contract signatories, or difficulty in settling accounts.

- *Authorization to deal in foreign exchange hedging transactions shall be issued solely by the board of directors.* Not only does this policy tend to reduce the number of people authorized to deal in hedging transactions, but it is also a requirement of many banks that deal in such transactions.

- *All sales contracts not denominated in U.S. dollars must be approved in advance by the treasury department.* This policy not only gives the treasury staff advance notice of a forthcoming sale for which a hedge may be required, but may also give them some leverage to force a contract change, so that it is denominated in the company's home currency.

RECORD KEEPING FOR FOREIGN EXCHANGE
HEDGING ACTIVITIES

At the inception of a fair value hedge, GAAP requires documentation of the relationship between the hedging instrument and the hedged item, the risk management objectives of the hedging transaction, how the hedge is to be undertaken, the method to be used for gain or loss recognition, identification of the instrument used for the hedge, and how the effectiveness calculation is measured. Since hedge accounting cannot be used unless this documentation exists, it is important to store a complete set of documentation for each hedge for the duration not only of the hedge, but also through the audit following the hedge termination. It can then be included in the archives with accounting documentation for the year in which the transaction terminated.

FOREIGN EXCHANGE HEDGE PROCEDURES

The procedure shown in Exhibit 9.1 is a generic one designed to handle the basic steps in a foreign exchange hedging transaction.

Exhibit 9.1   Foreign Exchange Hedging Procedure

Procedure Statement   Retrieval No.: TREASURY-07

Subject: Steps required to create, monitor, and account for a foreign exchange hedging transaction.

1. PURPOSE AND SCOPE

   This procedure is used by the treasury, legal, and accounting staffs to set up, monitor, and account for a foreign exchange hedging transaction, incorporating key control points.

2. PROCEDURES

   2.1 Set Up Hedging Transaction (Assistant Treasurer)

   1. Ensure that the counterparty's credit rating equals or exceeds the company's minimum credit rating policy standard. Notify the treasurer if the counterparty exhibits a declining credit rating over the past two years.
   2. Calculate the level of hedging effectiveness of the proposed transaction, and document the calculation.
   3. Have the treasurer review and approve the transaction.
   4. Enter into the hedging transaction.
   5. Document the hedge, as required under hedge accounting standards. This includes documenting the relationship between the hedging instrument and liability, as well as the hedging strategy, risk management objectives, and how the effectiveness of the transaction shall be measured.
   6. Have the treasurer review and approve the hedge documentation.

   2.2 Confirm the Hedge (Treasury Clerk)

   1. Immediately upon notification of the deal, confirm it with the counterparty, either by email, orally, or by written notification. The confirmation should include all key terms of the deal, including the date of the transaction, the name and location of the counterparty, the rate, amount, currency, type and side of the deal, all relevant action dates, and the standard terms convention being used. *Note*: For transactions with short settlement periods, do not

wait for the counterparty's confirmation—send out your own confirmation instead.

2. If the confirmation sent by the counterparty contains incorrect information, then immediately call them back with correction information, and request a new version of the confirmation.
3. If the confirmation review process reveals an error that results in an open risk for either party, immediately close out the position.
4. Assemble the hedge contract, documentation, and confirmation into a package, and create a copy for distribution to the legal department. Retain the original documents.

2.3 Review the Contract Legality (Legal Staff)

1. Review the contract for completeness, and verify that the counterparty's signatory is authorized to approve such contracts.
2. Approve the contract if acceptable, and forward to the assistant controller. If not, return it to the treasurer with attached notes regarding problem areas. If there are problems, then retain a copy of the package, and follow up with the treasurer periodically regarding resolution of the indicated issues.

2.4 Account for the Hedge (Assistant Controller)

1. Determine the extent of hedge effectiveness, based on the ranges set forth in the corporate hedge effectiveness policy.
2. On an ongoing basis, charge to comprehensive income that portion of the hedge that is considered effective, for any gains or losses resulting from marking to market. At the same time, charge to earnings that portion of the hedge that is considered ineffective as a result of marking to market.
3. On a monthly basis, evaluate the nonrecoverability of hedge losses, and shift these losses from other comprehensive income to earnings.
4. On a monthly basis, evaluate if it has become probable that any forecasted cash flow transactions will not take place, and shift the associated gains or losses from other comprehensive income to earnings.

2.5 Reconcile the Hedge (Assistant Controller)

1. Match the internal account balances for the hedge to the statement received from the exchange or the over-the-counter counterparty. Report the reason for any significant differences to the treasurer and controller.
2. If the hedge is completed and settlement has occurred, reconcile the payment received or issued to internal records, and adjust for any differences.
3. If the reason for a reconciliation problem is not clear, or if the cause results in a variance of at least $_____, notify the treasurer and controller immediately.

2.6 Report on the Results of the Hedge (Assistant Controller)

1. Calculate the percentage of hedging achieved by the transaction and report this amount to the treasurer and controller.
2. Calculate the speed of confirmation matching, and the types of problems found during the reconciliation process, and report these metrics as key performance indicators to the treasurer and controller.

SUMMARY

Foreign exchange risk management can be used to reduce the volatility of a company's cash flows and earnings. If currency options are used aggressively by a well-trained and experienced treasury team, it can even generate additional profits. A treasurer should at least maximize the use of all internal hedging strategies, such as internal netting, sourcing changes, and prompt payment, which are all zero-cost alternatives. The next step up is to use a selection of forward exchange contracts, currency futures, or currency options to hedge any remaining foreign exchange risk.

This may seem to require a considerable amount of monitoring by the treasury staff. However, most multinational companies are not so far-flung that they need to track more than a dozen currencies. For such organizations, it is quite practical to aggregate currency positions across a relatively small number of subsidiaries, and then engage in one forward trade per month for each currency. Only companies trading in dozens of currencies need a more comprehensive and automated system to aggregate and forecast information, as well as a larger treasury team to measure risk and conduct trading activities.

The accounting for hedging is complex, requiring considerable documentation and a large volume of entries to record each transaction. Given the short-term nature of many currency hedging transactions, it may make more sense to ignore hedge accounting entirely and simply record hedging gains and losses as they occur. For longer-term hedges, a treasurer is more likely to opt for hedge accounting.

10

Interest Risk Management

Interest rate risk is the possibility of a change in interest rates that has a negative impact on a company's profits. A company incurs interest rate risk whenever it borrows or extends credit. This is a serious issue for companies with large amounts of outstanding debt, since a small hike in their interest expense could not only have a large negative impact on their profits, but possibly also violate several loan covenants, such as the interest coverage ratio. A less critical issue is when a company forecasts a certain amount of available cash in the coming year that will be available for investment purposes, but cannot reliably forecast the return on investment beyond the first few months of the year. In this situation, the company is forced to budget for some amount of interest income, but it has no way of knowing if the forecasted interest rate will be available throughout the year. In the first case, interest rate volatility can cause serious cash flow problems, and in the second case it can cause a company to miss its budgeted interest income.

Thus, it is important for a treasurer to define interest risk management objectives and implement strategies to mitigate the risk. This chapter addresses the management of interest risk, as well as associated accounting, controls, policies, and procedures.

INTEREST RISK MANAGEMENT OBJECTIVES

Does a treasurer care if interest rates change over time? After all, if a company acquires debt at a certain interest rate that subsequently varies, then rates over the long term should vary both above and below the benchmark of the initial rate. Thus, over the long term, interest rate fluctuations should cancel each other out. Right?

Not really. A company will attempt to borrow at the lowest possible interest rates, and may time its borrowing activities to take advantage of unusually low rates. This means that the initial benchmark is so low that subsequent interest rates are more likely to vary above this point than below it. Thus, one objective is to lock in exceptionally favorable interest rates. This is an especially important objective when a company is experiencing weak cash flows, and will violate interest coverage covenants if the floating interest rate rises too much beyond its current level. In such a case, locking in a favorable interest rate is an objective that could prevent the demise of a company.

It is only possible to lock in a low borrowing rate if the treasurer is allowed a considerable degree of flexibility regarding the amount of interest rate exposure that he is allowed to leave unhedged. The trouble is that, while waiting for the market to cycle down to a sufficiently low interest rate that can then be locked in with a hedge, there may be extended periods when a company is borrowing at much higher short-term interest rates; and given the higher rates, the treasurer may not elect to hedge them at all, on the grounds that they are unlikely to go much higher.

Another issue is that treasurers do not deal with multiyear timelines over which they can calmly accept large interest rate variations. Instead, they want to meet budgeted interest rates, either for borrowing or investments, and interest rates most certainly can vary during these shorter reporting intervals. Thus, another objective is to reduce or eliminate the volatility of interest rates, so that short-term budgeted financing targets can be met. This is a relatively easy hedge to create and maintain, since it requires no market timing, nor any ongoing monitoring of market conditions.

Thus, the objectives of interest risk management are to safeguard company profits, and to reduce the volatility of interest rates. We now move to the discussion of a variety of interest risk management strategies that can be used to accomplish these objectives.

INTEREST RISK MANAGEMENT STRATEGIES

There are a variety of strategies for managing interest risk. Before addressing methods that require interaction with outside parties, a treasurer should first explore a variety of available internal techniques. One possibility is *cash netting* across the company in order to avoid excess investments in one part of the company while a different subsidiary must borrow. Chapter 4 discussed the various methods for combining cash flows from different parts of a company. Another alternative is an *intercompany netting center* that reduces the number of payment transactions between related companies. This was discussed in Chapter 9, "Foreign Exchange Risk Management."

After the treasurer implements internal risk management strategies, the next alternative is to create hedges with external entities. However, before delving into specific techniques, a treasurer must determine the overall level of risk that the company is willing to accept. At the most conservative level of *full-cover hedging*, a company enters into hedging positions that completely eliminate all exposure. *Selective hedging* leaves room for some hedging activity, usually by the predetermined setting of minimum and maximum risk levels. The minimum amount of risk management is none at all, known as a *naked position*. A naked position may be intentional, based on management's assessment that hedging is not necessary, or through simple ignorance of how hedging can be used. Conversely, a company can engage in *speculative positions*, where it essentially reverses the underlying exposure. A speculative position is not recommended, since a company can place itself at considerable risk by doing so; also, this strategy establishes the presumption that the company is earning profits from its financing activities, rather than from its operations. Normally, financial activities are considered to be in support of operations, and therefore should never place those operations at risk.

The primary strategies for interest risk management are the use of forwards, futures, and options, and are described in the following subsections.

Forwards

A *forward rate agreement* (FRA) is an agreement between two parties to lock in an interest rate for a predetermined period of time. Under the FRA agreement, a borrower wants to guard against the cost of rising interest rates, while the counterparty wishes to protect against declining interest rates. The counterparty is usually a bank.

When a buyer engages in an FRA, and if interest rates rise, then it will be paid by the counterparty for the amount by which actual interest rates exceed the *reference rate* (typically based on an interbank rate such as the London Interbank Offered Rate [LIBOR] or Euribor) specified in the FRA. Assuming that the buyer was using the FRA to hedge the interest rate on its borrowings, it then pays its lender the increased interest rate, and offsets this added cost with the payment from the counterparty. Conversely, if interest rates decline, then the buyer pays the counterparty the difference between the reduced interest rate and the reference rate specified in the FRA, and adds this cost to the reduced interest rate that it pays its lender. Thus, the FRA buyer has locked in a fixed interest rate, irrespective of the direction in which actual interest rates subsequently move.

A number of date conventions are used in an FRA. The *contract date* is the start date of the agreement. The next sequential date in the agreement is the *expiry date*, which is when the difference between the market rate and the reference rate is determined. The *settlement date* is when the interest differential is paid; this is also the first day of the underlying period. Finally, the *maturity date* is the last day of the underlying FRA period. These dates are shown in the timeline example in Exhibit 10.1. In the exhibit, the FRA contract term is three months, running from January 1 to April 1. The underlying period is three months, from April 3 to July 3.

Exhibit 10.1   FRA Timeline

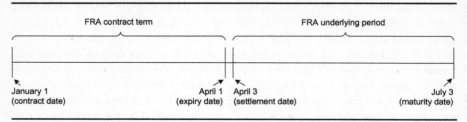

Exhibit 10.2   FRA Interest Payment Formula

Payment = Notional amount × (Day count fraction)
× (Reference rate – FRA rate)

Note: The day count fraction is the portion of a year over which rates are calculated, which is 360 days in Europe and the United States, though 365 days may be used elsewhere.

On the settlement date, one party pays the other, using a three-step process. First, they compare the contract interest rate on the contract date to the reference rate on the expiry date of the FRA. Second, they determine the difference between the two interest rates for the underlying period, multiplied by the notional amount of the contract. Thus, the parties only take a *notional position*, which means that one party only pays the other for the *incremental* change in interest rates. The formula under which incremental interest payments are made under an FRA is shown in Exhibit 10.2. Finally, the paying party discounts the amount of the payment against the reference rate, and pays this amount to the other party. The formula for discounting the payment to its net discounted present value is shown in Exhibit 10.3.

There are a broad range of time periods over which an FRA can be used. It is possible to enter into an FRA (for example) that begins in 9 months and expires in 12 months, or that begins in one year and expires in two years. Standard descriptive notation for the terms of a variety of possible FRAs is shown in Exhibit 10.4. In essence, the notation sets the effective (beginning) and termination dates of the FRA, with each date being the number of months from the present month.

A treasurer can also combine a sequential group of FRAs into an *FRA strip*, which provides a hedge for a longer interval.

Exhibit 10.3   Payment Discounting Formula

$$\text{Payment} = \frac{\text{Settlement Amount}}{1 + (\text{Days in FRA Underlying Period}/360 \text{ Days})}$$

Exhibit 10.4   Term Notation for a Forward Rate Agreement

FRA Term	Expanded Text of FRA Term	Effective Term
1×3	Effective 1 month from now, terminates 3 months from now	2 months
1×7	Effective 1 month from now, terminates 7 months from now	6 months
3×6	Effective 3 months from now, terminates 6 months from now	3 months
3×9	Effective 3 months from now, terminates 9 months from now	6 months
6×12	Effective 6 months from now, terminates 12 months from now	6 months
12×18	Effective 12 months from now, terminates 18 months from now	6 months

Example

Gulf Coast Petrochemical expects to borrow $25 million in one year's time to finance a new offshore drilling platform, and will need the funds for a period of one year. The current market interest rate is 5.00 percent, and Gulf Coast's treasurer anticipates that the rate will rise to 6.00 percent by the time the company needs the money. To lock in the 5.00 percent rate, he enters into a 12×24 FRA at 5.00 percent, where the reference rate is the LIBOR rate. The settlement amount of the FRA will depend on the 12-month LIBOR in 12 months. At that time, the reference rate has risen to 5.80 percent. Accordingly, the bank that was the counterparty to the FRA determines that (prior to discounting) it must pay $200,000 to Gulf Coast, which it calculates as:

$$\mathbf{\$200{,}000} = \$25{,}000{,}000 \times (360 \text{ Days in Contract}/360 \text{ Days in Year})$$
$$\times (.058 \text{ Reference Rate} - .050 \text{ Contract Rate})$$

The final step in the process is for the bank to calculate its discounted payment to Gulf Coast. The discounted payment is **$189,035.92**, which is calculated as $200,000 / (1 + (360/360 \times 5.80\%))$, in accordance with the formula in Exhibit 10.3, and using the 5.80 percent reference rate.

Example

The treasurer of Abbott Software wants to buy an FRA to hedge the risk of an interest rate increase in $30 million of debt that he plans to borrow in one month, extending for nine months. He plans to use a strip of consecutive three-month FRAs to construct this longer-term hedge. The FRA terms and rates are as follows:

FRA Term	FRA Rate
1 × 4 months	4.00%
5 × 7 months	4.20%
8 × 10 months	4.40%

The FRA rate gradually increases over time, since it is based on the yield curve (see Chapter 8), which is usually upward sloping. The treasurer buys the FRAs; the resulting reference (actual) rates are shown in the following table, along with the variance between the FRA and reference rates for each of the three FRAs.

FRA Term	Contract Rate	Reference Rate	Variance
1 × 4 months	4.00%	3.90%	−0.10%
5 × 7 months	4.20%	4.25%	0.05%
8 × 10 months	4.40%	4.50%	0.10%

For the 1 × 4 FRA, ABC pays the other party $7,500, which is calculated as:

$$-\$7,500 = \$30,000,000 \times (90/360) \times (.0390 - .0400)$$

Abbott's discounted payment to the other party is **$7,427.58**, which is calculated as $7,500 / (1 + (90/360 × 3.90%)), in accordance with the formula in Exhibit 10.3, and using the 3.90 percent reference rate for the 1 × 4 FRA.

For the 5 × 7 FRA, the other party pays Abbott $3,750, which is calculated as:

$$\$3,750 = \$30,000,000 \times (90/360) \times (.0425 - .0420)$$

Its discounted payment is **$3,710.58**, which is calculated as $3,750 / (1 + (90/360 × 4.25%)), in accordance with the formula in Exhibit 10.3, and using the 4.25% reference rate for the 5 × 7 FRA.

For the 8 × 10 FRA, the other party pays ABC $7,500, which is calculated as:

$$\$7,500 = \$30,000,000 \times (90/360) \times (.0450 - .0440)$$

Its discounted payment is **$7,416.56**, which is calculated as $7,500 / (1 + (90/360 × 4.50%)), in accordance with the formula in Exhibit 10.3, and using the 4.40 percent reference rate for the 8 × 10 FRA.

Thus, over the nine-month period, Abbott is paid a net total of $3,699.56 from its hedging activity, which it then uses to offset its increased borrowing cost.

Futures

An interest rate future is an exchange-traded forward contract that allows a company to lock in an interest rate for a future time period. Interest rate futures trade on the Chicago Mercantile Exchange (CME; www.cmegroup. com). The standard futures contract is in eurodollars, which are bank deposits comprised of U.S. dollars, and held outside the United States. However, the CME also offers futures contracts in a variety of other interest rate products, including 30-day federal funds, one-month LIBOR, and even Euroyen TIBOR (Tokyo Interbank Offered Rate). Most trading volume is in eurodollar contracts. Eurodollar contracts are available for as much as ten years into the future, though trading volumes drop off substantially after the first three years.

A eurodollar futures contract allows the buyer to lock in the interest rate on $1 million; if the buyer wishes to lock in the interest rate on a larger amount, then he must purchase additional contracts in $1 million increments. The quoted prices are derived from a baseline index of 100, and decline in amount for periods further in the future. The difference between the baseline index and the quoted price is the interest rate on the contract. For example, recent eurodollar rates traded on the CME were:

| March | 99.050 | September | 97.255 |
| June | 97.500 | December | 96.990 |

A company can buy a futures contract through a broker. The broker will charge a fee on the transaction, and also imposes margin requirements on the company that are used to ensure that the buyer or seller fulfills the futures contract's obligations. The initial margin requirement is calculated on the basis of the maximum likely volatility for one day. The initial margin varies from a low of one-sixteenth of a percent of the contract amount for three-month contracts, to 2 percent for ten-year Treasury bonds.

The futures position represented by a contract is *marked to market* (valued at market rates) every day; if the most recent valuation results in an incremental loss, then the margin account is reduced, and a *margin call* requires the contract holder to add more funds to the margin account to bring it up to the maintenance level. If the contract holder does not respond to the margin call, the broker can close out the futures position by offsetting the contract (at the contract holder's cost). Thus, the margin account keeps unrealized losses from accumulating, which might otherwise result in a contract default.

On the final day of the contract, the exchange prices the contract and makes a final cash settlement of the profit or loss due to or from the company.

An interest rate future is a standard contract, with a standard value, term, and underlying instrument; thus, its terms may vary somewhat from the amount of a company's borrowings. This means that there is likely to be an imperfect hedge, which means that the company utilizing a futures contract must still carry some amount of risk.

Example

The treasurer of Gulf Coast Petroleum decides to sell a three-month future with a contract term of six months. The current three-month LIBOR is 4.50 percent, and the 6 × 9 forward rate is 4.85 percent. Since the treasurer wishes to hedge a principal amount of $25 million, he sells 25 contracts of $1 million each. The future is now listed as 95.15, which is calculated as 100 minus the 4.85 percent forward rate. The future expires after six months; at that time, the forward rate has declined to 4.35 percent, which means that the future is now listed as 95.65 (derived from 100 minus the 4.35 percent forward rate). This means that Gulf Coast has earned a profit of $31,250, which is derived as follows:

$$\mathbf{\$31,250} = \$25,000,000 \times (90/360)$$
$$\times (.9565 \text{ ending price} - .9515 \text{ beginning price})$$

Interest Rate Swaps

The *interest rate swap* is an agreement between two parties (where one party is almost always a bank) to exchange interest payments in the same currency over a defined time period, which normally ranges from one to ten years. One of the parties is paying a fixed rate of interest, while the other is paying a variable rate. The variable interest rate is paid whenever a new coupon is set, which is typically once a quarter. Fixed interest is usually paid at the end of each year.

By engaging in a swap, a company can shift from fixed to variable payments, or vice versa. Thus, if a company uses a swap to shift from variable to fixed interest payments, it can better forecast its financing costs and avoid increased payments but loses the chance of reduced interest payments if rates were to decline. If it takes the opposite position and swaps fixed rates for variable rates, then it is essentially betting that it will benefit from a future decline in interest rates. An interest rate swap is especially useful for a company with a weak credit rating, since such entities must pay a premium to obtain fixed-rate debt. They may find it less expensive to obtain variable-rate debt, and then engage in an interest rate swap to secure what is essentially a fixed-rate payment schedule.

The parties to an interest rate swap deal directly with each other, rather than using a standard product that is traded over an exchange. They customarily use the standard master agreement that is maintained by the International Swaps and Derivatives Association (ISDA; www.isda.org). The ISDA represents participants in the privately negotiated derivatives industry, and maintains standard contracts for derivatives transactions. The parties commonly modify a variety of features within the agreement to suit their needs.

Example

ABC Company borrows $10 million. Under the terms of the agreement, ABC must make quarterly interest payments for the next three years that are based on LIBOR, which is reset once a quarter under the terms of the borrowing agreement. Since the interest payments are variable, the company will experience reduced interest payments if LIBOR declines, but will pay more if LIBOR increases. ABC's management is more concerned about the risk of LIBOR increasing, so it eliminates this risk by entering into an interest rate swap in which it agrees to pay interest for three years on $10 million at a fixed rate, while its counterparty agrees to make floating interest rate payments for three years on $10 million to ABC. The first-year payment stream for the transaction is shown in the following table, where the counterparty makes quarterly payments to ABC, which vary based on changes in LIBOR. ABC makes a single fixed interest rate payment to the counterparty at the end of year one. The result of these transactions is that ABC experiences a net reduction in its interest expense of $20,000 in the first year of the swap agreement.

Payment Date	Loan Fixed Rate	Applicable LIBOR Quarterly Rate	Payments from the Counterparty to ABC Company	Payments from ABC Company to the Counterparty
March 31	—	4.20%	$105,000	
June 30	—	4.35%	108,750	
September 30	—	4.60%	115,000	
December 31	4.25%	4.65%	116,250	$425,000
Totals			$445,000	$425,000

The treasurer should arrange for payments under an interest swap agreement to be as closely aligned as possible with the payment terms of the underlying debt agreement. Thus, it is not useful if a counterparty's payment to the company is scheduled to arrive several weeks after the company is scheduled to pay its bank under a loan agreement. Instead, the counterparty's payment should be scheduled to arrive just prior to the due date specified in the loan agreement, thereby better aligning the company's cash flows.

Another strategy is to use an *interest rate cap option*. The cap option allows a company to limit the extent of interest rate increases, while still retaining some of the benefit if interest rates subsequently decline. However, the cost of the rate cap will incrementally increase a company's borrowing cost. The cost of a rate cap option can be reduced by acquiring a more tailored solution called a *knockout cap*. Such a cap limits a company's debt service cost only so long as the baseline interest rate measurement does not exceed a certain interest rate. If the actual rate exceeds the upper boundary of the cap, then the company receives no protection at all.

Example

To use the same example, ABC Company buys a 6.00 percent interest rate cap, which keeps ABC's potential interest rate liability from exceeding 6.00 percent. Thus, if the interest rate were to actually reach 6.50 percent, the cap seller would pay ABC 0.50 percent, while ABC would pay its bank 6.50 percent interest on the loan, yielding a net interest rate of 6.00 percent.

Now, let's alter the example to assume that ABC's treasurer considers it likely that interest rates will only rise slightly. He wants to save on the cost of the interest rate cap, so he purchases a knockout cap that only provides protection up to 6.50 percent. The actual LIBOR rate jumps to 6.60 percent, thereby triggering the knockout. ABC must now pay the entire 6.60 percent interest on the loan, while the cap seller has no obligation to pay ABC.

Interest rate swaps work only if there are counterparties available who are willing to take on the company's perceived risk. However, when there is a general consensus that interest rates will increase, a greater volume of market participants will want to lock in their low borrowing rates with fixed interest rates, which tends to force the cost of a swap higher. The reverse situation arises when there is a general consensus that rates will decline; more companies shift into variable-rate debt in expectation of benefiting from lower rates, which makes it less expensive to create a swap for a fixed rate.

Example

ABC Company wants to exchange its variable rate payments for fixed rate payments for a period of three years. The benchmark government fixed rate yield for that time period is 5.50 percent, and a spread of .30 percent is added to the benchmark, which incorporates the supply and demand for a fixed rate swap. Thus, ABC must pay a fixed rate of 5.80 percent if it chooses to engage in an interest rate swap transaction.

If the parties to a swap agreement choose to terminate it prior to the contractual termination date, they determine the net present value of future payment obligations by each party. They then net the payments together to determine the net incremental payment to be made, which goes to whichever party is disadvantaged by terminating the swap. A variation on this approach is the *blend and extend*, where the closeout cost of the original swap agreement is incorporated into a new swap agreement.

It is also possible to assign the swap agreement to a third party, which is then obligated to make and receive payments until the contract maturity date. As part of the contract assignment, whichever party is assigning the swap will either pay to the new counterparty or receive from it a payment reflecting the net present value of cash flows remaining under the swap agreement.

One more alternative is to acquire a new swap agreement that offsets the payment streams of the original swap agreement.

There are several risks to be aware of when entering into swap agreements. They are:

- *Basis risk.* This is caused by the mismatch between the cash flows involved in a swap. For example, the reference rate may be tied to LIBOR, while the interest rate on a company's borrowing may be tied to some other index, such as an index of money market funds. Thus, if LIBOR increased by .5 percent and the basis for a company's debt increased by .6 percent, then the payments it receives through a swap arrangement would still leave the company with an unhedged .1 percent interest rate increase.

- *Counterparty risk.* One of the parties to a swap agreement may not meet its financial obligations. Accordingly, it is important for the counterparty to have excellent credit quality. If a bank or broker is acting as the intermediary between two parties, then it may assume the counterparty risk by charging a fee to both parties to the swap.

- *Legal risk.* One of the parties to an over-the-counter transaction may have incorrectly or incompletely filled out a contract, or the signer of it may not have been authorized to do so.

Debt Call Provisions

If a company is issuing its own debt, it can include a *call provision* in the debt instrument that allows the company to retire the debt at a predetermined price. A treasurer would take advantage of this provision if market rates were to decline subsequent to issuance of the debt, and could then refinance at a lower interest rate. The call provision typically incorporates higher prices for earlier calls, which gradually decline closer to par pricing further into the future. This higher initial price point compensates investors for the interest income they would otherwise have earned if the company had not called the debt. Also, a call provision limits a bond's potential price appreciation to the amount of its call price, since the issuer will then call the bond. Consequently, the call provision is useful to a company by allowing it to buy back expensive debt and reissue at lower rates, but only if the savings from doing so exceed the amount of the call price.

For example, ABC Company could issue bonds with a call provision that allows it to buy back the bonds at 105 percent of par value after two years, then again at 103 percent of par value after six years, and then at their par value after eight years.

Options

An options contract is a trade that gives the buyer the right to buy or sell an amount of futures contracts at some date in the future. The cost of this right is the *options premium*, and is paid to the counterparty at the beginning of the contract. This cost will vary based on such factors as the remaining term of an option, the strike price, and the volatility of the reference interest rate. If the option is entered into through an exchange, the exchange will ask for a deposit, which is refundable when the deal is completed.

In the options market, the party buying an option wants to reduce its risk, while the party selling an option is willing to be paid to accept the risk. Thus, the cost of an option is based on the comparative level of perceived risk. The options premium increases the borrowing cost of the party wishing to reduce its interest rate risk, so if the option is priced too high, a prospective hedger may elect to retain the risk.

A *call option* on interest rates protects the option buyer from rising interest rates, while a *put option* protects the option buyer from declining rates. Both types of options are benchmarked against a reference rate that is set forth in the option contract. Thus, if the reference rate is 5.00 percent, subsequent changes in the interest rate are measured in terms of their variation from 5.00 percent in determining potential benefits to option buyers. An interest rate option contract includes the following key components:

- A benchmark reference rate, as just described

- A strike price, which is the interest rate at which the option buyer can borrow or lend funds

- The amount of funds that can be borrowed or loaned

- How the contract may be settled, such as by cash payment or by delivery of the underlying asset

- The contract expiry date

It is possible to modify the above features to meet a company's specific needs by dealing in the over-the-counter market.

An interest rate option can be modified to include a *cap*; the buyer pays a premium in order to be protected from higher interest rates above the cap strike rate. At the expiry date of the option, the seller reimburses the buyer if the reference rate is above the cap strike rate and pays nothing if the reference rate is below the strike rate.

Example

ABC Company has $5 million of variable rate debt that resets every three months. ABC's treasurer buys a 3 × 6 interest rate cap with a strike price of 6.00 percent to cover its debt. The reference rate is the Euribor rate on the reset date. Subsequently, the reference rate increases to 6.30 percent. The seller must reimburse ABC for the difference between the cap strike price and the reference rate. The calculation of the payment is:

$$\$3,750 = \frac{\$5,000,000 \times (0.0630 - 0.0600) \times 90 \text{ days}}{360 \text{ days}}$$

In order to determine ABC Company's true savings, the cost of the option must be offset against the $3,750 payment from the option seller, so the net amount of the hedge does not entirely cover ABC's increased interest rate payment.

A company can engage in a longer-term cap by purchasing a strip of options with consecutive expiry dates and the same strike price for all options. The following table shows an option strip covering an 18-month period, where the principal was $1 million. The first few months are not included in the table, since the option for that period would expire at the beginning of the period, yielding a zero payout.

Option	Term	Strike Price	3-Month LIBOR Rate	(A) Payout Rate	(B) Principal	A × B × (90/360) Payment Calculation
1	3 × 6	4.50%	4.35%	0.00%	$1,000,000	—
2	6 × 9	4.50%	4.45%	0.00%	1,000,000	—
3	9 × 12	4.50%	4.55%	0.05%	1,000,000	$125
4	12 × 15	4.50%	4.60%	0.10%	1,000,000	250
5	15 × 18	4.50%	4.70%	0.20%	1,000,000	500
					Total	$875

In the example, the strike price at the expiry date of the first two options is higher than the reference rate, so the company does not trigger the option; this is not a concern to the treasurer, since the underlying debt payments that he is most concerned about have not increased, either. However, the reference rate is higher for the remaining three option periods, which triggers three payments to the company totaling $875. The treasurer then uses the payments from these options to offset the increased cost of his debt during the same time periods.

If a treasurer considers the cost of a cap to be too expensive, an alternative is to purchase a *collar* from a bank. This is composed of a purchased cap and a sold floor. The option that the treasurer sells (the floor) is used to take any profits from favorable interest rates and use them to pay for the cap. For this cost-offset method to work, the treasurer must align the time periods, reference rates, and exercise details of the cap and floor. If an option expires with the reference rate between the cap and floor rates, then neither side of the collar is exercised.

Example

The treasurer of the Alaskan Barrel Company anticipates that interest rates will fluctuate between 4.5 percent and 6.5 percent over the next two years, and is comfortable incurring interest expenses anywhere within that range. To avoid paying interest greater than 6.5 percent, he purchases a 6.5 percent cap and sells a 4.5 percent floor. If the interest rate stays between 4.5 percent and 6.5 percent, then neither the cap nor the floor is triggered. However, if interest rates rise to 7.0 percent, then the cap will pay for the 0.5 percent excess over the 6.5 percent cap. Also, if the interest rate falls below 4.5 percent, Alaskan must pay the difference between the reference rate and the floor of 4.5 percent, thereby effectively limiting its lowest possible interest rate to 4.5 percent.

Swaptions

A swaption is an option on an interest rate swap. The buyer of a swaption has the right, but not an obligation, to enter into an interest rate swap with predefined terms at the expiration of the option. In exchange for a premium payment, the buyer of a swaption can lock in either a fixed or variable interest rate. Thus, if a treasurer believes that interest rates will rise, he can enter into a swaption agreement, which he can later convert into an interest rate swap if interest rates do indeed go up.

Example

The Shapiro Pool Company needs to finance its construction of the pool complex for the Summer Olympic Games. It expects to do so at the floating LIBOR rate plus 1.5 percent in six months, with a duration of three years. To protect itself from rates increasing above 7.0 percent, Shapiro buys a swaption. The swaption agreement gives Shapiro the right, but not the obligation, to enter into an interest rate swap where it pays a fixed rate of 7.0 percent and receives LIBOR plus 1.5 percent. If the reference rate in nine months is above 7.0 percent, then Shapiro should exercise the option to enter into the swap.

A swaption can be a risky endeavor for a swaption seller, since the seller is taking on potentially substantial risk in exchange for a premium. Thus, the swaption buyer should carefully examine the credit risk of the swaption seller, both at the initiation of the transaction and throughout its term.

Counterparty Limits

There is a limit to the amount of the risk management strategies outlined here that a company can employ. The counterparty to FRAs, swaps, and collars are usually banks, and they will reduce their risk by setting up counterparty limits for each company doing business with them. Every time a company enters into one of these agreements with a bank, the bank reduces the available amount of the limit assigned to that company. Thus, it is possible that some of the risk strategies outlined here will not be available beyond a certain level of activity.

Summary of Interest Risk Management Strategies

Of the strategies presented here, forwards and futures are the most inflexible, because they do no more than lock a company into a set rate, and present an opportunity loss if rates turn in the opposite direction from the constructed hedge. Options are more flexible, since they can be tailored to provide payoffs that closely match a company's exposure, while also yielding benefits from a favorable market move.

A comparison of the various interest rate risk management strategies is shown in Exhibit 10.5.

ACCOUNTING FOR INTEREST RISK MANAGEMENT ACTIVITIES

The following discussion of accounting is targeted at derivative financial instruments, of which the two main forms of derivatives are option contracts and forward contracts. Within these main categories are interest rate caps

Exhibit 10.5   Interest Risk Management Strategy Comparison

	Forward Rate Agreements	Futures	Interest Rate Swaps	Options
Notional payments	Yes	Yes	Not necessarily	Yes
Agreement type	Customized	Standard	Customized	Standard or customized
Collateral requirement	None	Initial margin and margin calls	None	Initial margin and margin calls if originated on an exchange
Counterparty	A bank	An exchange	A bank	A bank or an exchange
Counterparty limits imposed	Yes	No	Yes	Yes
Method of exchange	Over the counter	Exchange traded	Over the counter	Exchange traded or over the counter
Settlement frequency	At expiry date	Daily	On coupon dates	Either daily or at expiry date

and floors, forward interest rate agreements, interest rate collars, futures, swaps, and swaptions.

Derivatives represent rights and obligations, and must be reported as assets and liabilities at their fair value. A gain or loss on a derivative that is not designated as a hedge must be recognized in earnings. If a derivative is designated as a hedge, then the accounting for it varies, depending on whether it is an effective hedge or an ineffective hedge.

A *fair value hedge* primarily relates to the hedging of fixed-interest balance sheet items, while *cash flow hedges* mean hedges against the risk associated with future interest payments from a variable-interest balance sheet transaction. Since this chapter is about the mitigation of risk associated with variable interest payments, the appropriate type of accounting is the cash flow hedge. Thus, the remainder of this section discusses the accounting for only a cash flow hedge.

To establish a valid cash flow hedge, one must document the relationship between the hedging instrument and an asset, liability, or forecasted transaction (including expected date of occurrence and amount). The documentation must also describe the hedging strategy, risk management objectives, and how the effectiveness of the transaction shall be measured. The method for effectiveness assessment must be defined at the time of hedge designation, and must be consistently maintained throughout the hedge period. Further, similar types of hedges should be documented and treated in the same manner, unless a different method can be reasonably justified.

In addition, the hedging relationship must be expected to be highly effective in producing offsetting cash flows, and evaluated at least quarterly to ensure that this is the case.

One must discontinue a cash flow hedge when the hedge criteria are no longer met, the hedging designation is canceled, or the derivative instruments used in the hedge are terminated. If any of these circumstances arise, a new hedging relationship can be documented with a different derivative instrument.

When reporting derivative gains and losses for a cash flow hedge, the effective portion of the gain or loss is reported in other comprehensive income, while any gains or losses attributable to the ineffective portion of the hedge are reported in earnings. For example, any differences in the key terms between a hedged item and the hedging instrument, such as notional amounts, maturities, quantities, or delivery dates would cause some amount of ineffectiveness, and the amount of that ineffective portion of the hedge would be included in earnings.

Whenever one expects a net loss from the hedging transaction, the amount not expected to be recovered must be shifted in the current period from other comprehensive income to earnings. Also, if a hedging relationship is established for a forecasted cash flow transaction and the transaction is deemed unlikely to occur, any gain or loss thus far recorded in other comprehensive income must be shifted to earnings in the current period.

Example

Accounting for an Interest Rate Swap[1]

On July 1, 2009, Abbott Corporation borrows $5 million with a fixed maturity (no prepayment option) of June 30, 2013, carrying interest at prime + 0.5 percent. Interest only is due semiannually. At the same date, it enters into a "plain vanilla"–type swap arrangement, calling for fixed payments at 8 percent and receipt of prime + 0.5 percent, on a notional amount of $5 million. At that date, prime is 7.5 percent, and there is no premium due on the swap arrangement.

This swap qualifies as a cash flow hedge, and it is appropriate to assume no ineffectiveness, since it fulfills all GAAP criteria.

NOTE: These criteria are that: the notional amount of the swap and the principal amount of the debt are equal; the fair value of the swap at inception is zero; the formula for computing net settlements under the swap is constant during its term; the debt may not be prepaid; all interest payments on the debt are designated as being hedged, and no payments beyond the term of the swap are so designated; there is no floor or cap on the variable rate of the

---

[1] The following two examples are taken with permission from the *2009 Wiley GAAP Guide* (Epstein, et. al.), Chapter 8.

debt that is not likewise designated for the swap; the repricing dates of the swap match those of the variable rate debt; and the same index is designated for the hedging instrument and the underlying obligation.

Accordingly, as rates change over the term of the debt and of the swap arrangement, changes in the value of the swap are reflected in other comprehensive income, and the swap will appear on the balance sheet as an asset or liability at fair value. As the maturity of the debt approaches, the value of the swap will converge on zero. Periodic interest expense in the income statement will be at the effective rate of 8 percent.

Assume that the prime rate over the four-year term of the loan, as of each interest payment date, is as follows, along with the fair value of the remaining term of the interest rate swap at those dates:

Date	Prime Rate (%)	Fair Value of Swap*
December 31, 2009	6.5	$-150,051
June 30, 2010	6.0	-196,580
December 31, 2010	6.5	-111,296
June 30, 2011	7.0	-45,374
December 31, 2011	7.5	0
June 30, 2012	8.0	23,576
December 31, 2012	8.5	24,038
June 30, 2013	8.0	0

*Fair values are determined as the present values of future cash flows resulting from expected interest rate differentials, based on the current prime rate, discounted at 8%.

Regarding the fair values presented in the foregoing table, it should be assumed that the fair values are precisely equal to the present value, at each valuation date (assumed to be the interest payment dates), of the differential future cash flows resulting from utilization of the swap. Future variable interest rates (prime + 0.5 percent) are assumed to be the same as the existing rates at each valuation date (i.e., there is no basis for any expectation of rate changes, and therefore the best estimate is that the current rate will persist over time). The discount rate, 8 percent, is assumed to be constant over time.

Thus, for example, the fair value of the swap at December 31, 2009, would be the present value of an annuity of seven payments (the number of remaining semiannual interest payments due) of $25,000 each (pay 8 percent, receive 7 percent, based on then-existing prime rate of 6.5 percent) to be made to the swap counterparty, discounted at an annual rate of 8 percent (using 4 percent for the semiannual discounting, which is a slight simplification). This computation yields a present value of a stream of seven $25,000 payments to the swap counterparty amounting to $150,051 at December 31, 2009, which is a liability to be reported by the entity at that date. The offset is a debit to other comprehensive income, since the hedge is (presumably) judged to be 100 percent effective in this case. Semiannual accounting entries will be as follows:

December 31, 2009

Interest expense	175,000	
Accrued interest (or cash)		175,000

To accrue or pay semiannual interest on the debt at the variable rate of prime + 0.5% (7.0%)

Interest expense	25,000	
Accrued interest (or cash)		25,000

To record net settlement on swap arrangement [8.0–7.0%]

Other comprehensive income	150,051	
Swap contract		150,051

To record the fair value of the swap contract as of this date (a net liability because fixed rate payable to counterparty of 8% exceeds floating rate receivable from counterparty of 7%)

June 30, 2010

Interest expense	162,500	
Accrued interest (or cash)		162,500

To accrue or pay semiannual interest on the debt at the variable rate of prime + 0.5% (6.5%)

Interest expense	37,500	
Accrued interest (or cash)		37,500

To record net settlement on swap arrangement [8.0–6.5%]

Other comprehensive income	46,529	
Swap contract		46,529

To record the fair value of the swap contract as of this date (increase in obligation because of further decline in prime rate)

December 31, 2010

Interest expense	175,000	
Accrued interest (or cash)		175,000

To accrue or pay semiannual interest on the debt at the variable rate of prime + 0.5% (7.0%)

Interest expense	25,000	
Accrued interest (or cash)		25,000

To record net settlement on swap arrangement [8.0–7.0%]

Other comprehensive income	150,051	
Swap contract		150,051

To record the fair value of the swap contract as of this date (decrease in obligation due to increase in prime rate

June 30, 2011

Interest expense	187,500	
Accrued interest (or cash)		187,500

To accrue or pay semiannual interest on the debt at the variable rate of prime + 0.5%
(7.5%)

Interest expense	12,500	
Accrued interest (or cash)		12,500

To record net settlement on swap arrangement [8.0–7.5%]

Swap contract	65,922	
Other comprehensive income		65,922

To record the fair value of the swap contract as of this date (decrease in obligation
due to further increase in prime rate)

December 31, 2011

Interest expense	200,000	
Accrued interest (or cash)		200,000

To accrue or pay semiannual interest on the debt at the variable rate of prime + 0.5%
(8.0%)

Interest expense	0	
Accrued interest (or cash)		0

To record net settlement on swap arrangement [8.0–8.0%]

Swap contract	45,374	
Other comprehensive income		45,374

To record the fair value of the swap contract as of this date (further increase in prime
rate to the original rate of inception of the hedge eliminates fair value of the
derivative)

June 30, 2012

Interest expense	212,500	
Accrued interest (or cash)		212,500

To accrue or pay semiannual interest on the debt at the variable rate of prime + 0.5%
(8.5%)

Receivable from counterparty (or cash)	12,500	
Interest expense		12,500

To record net settlement on swap arrangement [8.0–8.5%], counterparty remits
settlement

Swap contract	23,576	
Other comprehensive income		23,576

To record the fair value of the swap contract as of this date (increase in prime rate
creates net asset position for derivative)

December 31, 2012

Interest expense	225,000	
Accrued interest (or cash)		225,000

To accrue or pay semiannual interest on the debt at the variable rate of prime + 0.5% (9.0%)

Receivable from counterparty (or cash)	25,000	
Interest expense		25,000

To record net settlement on swap arrangement [8.0–9.0%], counterparty remits settlement

Swap contract	462	
Other comprehensive income		462

To record the fair value of the swap contract as of this date (increase in asset value due to further rise in prime rate)

June 30, 2013 (Maturity)

Interest expense	212,500	
Accrued interest (or cash)		212,500

To accrue or pay semiannual interest on the debt at the variable rate of prime + 0.5% (8.5%)

Receivable from counterparty (or cash)	12,500	
Interest expense		12,500
Other comprehensive income	24,038	
Swap contract		24,038

To record the fair value of the swap contract as of this date (value declines to zero as expiration date approaches)

Example

Accounting for a Swaption

The facts of this example are a variation on the previous example. Abbott Corporation anticipates as of June 30, 2009, that as of June 30, 2011, it will become a borrower of $5 million with a fixed maturity four years hence (June 30, 2015). Based on its current credit rating, it expects to be able to borrow at prime + 0.5%. As of June 30, 2009, it is able to purchase, for a single payment of $25,000, a "swaption" (an option on an interest rate swap), calling for fixed pay at 8 percent and variable receipt at prime + 0.5%, on a notional amount of $5 million, for a term of four years. The option will expire in two years. At June 30, 2009, prime is 7.5 percent.

NOTE: The interest rate behavior in this example differs somewhat from the prior example, to better illustrate the "one-sidedness" of options, versus the obligation under a swap arrangement or other futures and forwards.

It will be assumed that the time value of the swaption expires ratably over the two years.

This swaption qualifies as a cash flow hedge. However, while the change in fair value of the contract is an effective hedge of the cash flow variability of the prospective debt issuance, the premium paid is a reflection of the time value of money and is thus to be expensed ratably over the period that the swaption is outstanding.

The table below gives the prime rate at semiannual intervals including the two-year period prior to the debt issuance, plus the four years during which the forecasted debt (and the swap, if the option is exercised) will be outstanding, as well as the fair value of the swaption (and later the swap itself) at these points in time.

Date	Prime Rate (%)	Fair Value of Swaption/Swap*
December 31, 2009	7.5	$0
June 30, 2010	8.0	77,925
December 31, 2010	6.5	0
June 30, 2011	7.0	−84,159
December 31, 2011	7.5	0
June 30, 2012	8.0	65,527
December 31, 2012	8.5	111,296
June 30, 2013	8.0	45,374
December 31, 2013	8.0	34,689
June 30, 2014	7.5	0
December 31, 2014	7.5	0
June 30, 2015	7.0	0

*Fair value is determined as the present value of future expected interest rate differentials, based on the current prime rate, discounted at 8%. An "out-of-the-money" swaption is valued at zero, since the option does not have to be exercised. Since the option is exercised on June 30, 2011, the value at that date is recorded, although negative.

The value of the swaption contract is recorded (unless and until exercised, of course, at which point it becomes a contractually binding swap) only if it is positive, since if "out of the money" the holder would forgo exercise in most instances, and thus there is no liability by the holder to be reported. (This example is an illustration of the opposite, however, as despite having a negative value the option holder determines that exercise is advisable.) At June 30, 2010, for example, the swaption is an asset, since the reference variable rate (prime + 0.5 percent or 8.5 percent) is greater than the fixed swap rate of 8 percent, and thus the expectation is that the option will be exercised at expiration. This would, if present rates hold steady—which is the naïve assumption—result in a series of eight semiannual payments from the swap counterparty in the amount of $12,500. Discounting this at a nominal 8 percent, the present value as of the debt origination date (to be June 30, 2011) would be $84,159, which, when further discounted to June 30, 2010, yields a fair value of $77,925.

Note that the following period (December 31, 2010) prime drops to such an extent that the value of the swaption evaporates entirely (actually goes negative, which will not be reported since the holder is under no obligation to exercise it), and the carrying value is therefore eliminated. At expiration, the holder does (for this example) exercise, notwithstanding a negative fair value, and from that point forward the fair value of the swap will be reported, whether positive (an asset) or negative (a liability).

As previously noted, assume that, at the option expiration date, despite the fact that prime + 0.5 percent is below the fixed pay rate on the swap, the management of Abbott Corporation is convinced that rates will climb over the four-year term of the loan, and thus exercises the swaption at that date. Accounting journal entries over the six years are as follows:

June 30, 2009

Swaption contract	25,000	
Cash		25,000

To record purchase premium on swaption contract

December 31, 2009

Loss on hedging transaction	6,250	
Swaption contract		6,250

To record change in time value of swaption contract—charge premium to income since this represents payment for time value of money, which expires ratably over two-year term

June 30, 2010

Swaption contract	77,925	
Other comprehensive income		77,925

To record the fair value of the swaption contract as of this date

Loss on hedging transaction	6,250	
Swaption contract		6,250

To record change in time value of swaption contract—charge premium to income since this represents payment for time value of money, which expires ratably over two-year term

December 31, 2010

Other comprehensive income	77,925	
Swaption contract		77,925

To record the change in fair value of the swaption contract as of this date; since contract is "out of the money," it is not written down below zero (i.e., a net liability is not reported)

Loss on hedging transaction	6,250	
Swaption contract		6,250

To record change in time value of swaption contract—charge premium to income since this represents payment for time value of money, which expires ratably over two-year term

June 30, 2011

Other comprehensive income	84,159	
Swap contract		84,159

To record the fair value of the swap contract as of this date—a net liability is reported since swap option was exercised

Loss on hedging transaction	6,250	
Swaption contract		6,250

To record change in time value of swaption contract—charge premium to income since this represents payment for time value of money, which expires ratably over two-year term

December 31, 2011

Interest expense	200,000	
Accrued interest (or cash)		200,000

To accrue or pay interest on the debt at the variable rate of prime + 0.5% (8.0%)

Interest expense	0	
Accrued interest (or cash)		0

To record net settlement on swap arrangement [8.0–8.0%]

Swap contract	84,159	
Other comprehensive income		84,159

To record the change in the fair value of the swap contract as of this date

June 30, 2012

Interest expense	212,500	
Accrued interest (or cash)		212,500

To accrue or pay interest on the debt at the variable rate of prime + 0.5% (8.5%)

Receivable from counterparty (or cash)	12,500	
Interest expense		12,500

To record net settlement on swap arrangement [8.0–8.5%]

Swap contract	65,527	
Other comprehensive income		65,527

To record the fair value of the swap contract as of this date

December 31, 2012

Interest expense	225,000	
Accrued interest (or cash)		225,000

To accrue or pay interest on the debt at the variable rate of prime + 0.5% (9.0%)

Receivable from counterparty (or cash)	25,000	
Interest expense		25,000

To record net settlement on swap arrangement [8.0–9.0%]

Swap contract	45,769	
Other comprehensive income		45,769

To record the fair value of the swap contract as of this date

June 30, 2013

Interest expense	212,500	
Accrued interest (or cash)		212,500

To accrue or pay interest on the debt at the variable rate of prime + 0.5% (8.5%)

Receivable from counterparty (or cash)	12,500	
Interest expense		12,500

To record net settlement on swap arrangement [8.0–8.5%]

Other comprehensive income	65,922	
Swap contract		65,922

To record the change in fair value of the swap contract as of this date (declining prime rate causes swap to lose value)

December 31, 2013

Interest expense	212,500	
Accrued interest (or cash)		212,500

To accrue or pay interest on the debt at the variable rate of prime + 0.5% (8.5%)

Receivable from counterparty (or cash)	12,500	
Interest expense		12,500

To record net settlement on swap arrangement [8.0–8.5%]

Other comprehensive income	10,685	
Swap contract		10,685

To record the fair value of the swap contract as of this date (decline is due to passage of time, as the prime rate expectations have not changed from the earlier period)

June 30, 2014

Interest expense	200,000	
Accrued interest (or cash)		200,000

To accrue or pay interest on the debt at the variable rate of prime + 0.5% (8.0%)

Receivable from counterparty (or cash)	0	
Interest expense		0

To record net settlement on swap arrangement [8.0–8.0%]

Other comprehensive income	34,689	
Swap contract		34,689

To record the decline in the fair value of the swap contract to zero as of this date

December 31, 2014

Interest expense	200,000	
Accrued interest (or cash)		200,000

To accrue or pay interest on the debt at the variable rate of prime + 0.5% (8.0%)

Receivable from counterparty (or cash)	0	
Interest expense		0

To record net settlement on swap arrangement [8.0–8.0%]

Swap contract	0	
Other comprehensive income		0

No change to the zero fair value of the swap contract as of this date

June 30, 2015 (Maturity)

Interest expense	187,500	
Accrued interest (or cash)		187,500

To accrue or pay interest on the debt at the variable rate of prime + 0.5% (7.5%)

Interest expense	12,500	
Accrued interest (or cash)		12,500

To record net settlement on swap arrangement [8.0–7.5%]

Other comprehensive income	0	
Swap contract		0

No change to the zero fair value of the swap contract, which expires as of this date

Interest Risk Management Controls

There are a variety of controls that the treasury department can implement in order to reduce the risk profile of its hedging activities. These controls are divided into ones that can be used for all types of hedges, and those that apply specifically to cash flow hedges.

Hedges—General

- *Determine counterparty creditworthiness.* In cases where a company expects to deal directly with a counterparty through an over-the-counter hedging transaction (as opposed to dealing with an exchange), the treasurer should determine the creditworthiness of the counterparty prior to entering into the contract. Otherwise, the company could be taking on a significant risk that the counterparty cannot meet its obligations under the contract.

- *Verify contract terms and signatory.* It is possible that a company may have difficulty forcing a counterparty to pay for its obligations under an over-the-counter contract if the counterparty did not correctly fill out the contract or if the signatory to the agreement was not authorized to do so. The company's legal department can follow up on these issues whenever a new contract is signed.

- *Include in the hedging procedure a requirement for full documentation of each hedge.* Hedging transactions are only allowed under generally accepted accounting principles (GAAP) if they are fully documented at the inception of the hedge. One can ensure compliance by including the documentation requirement in an accounting procedure for creating hedges.

- *Confirm all hedging transactions.* As soon as a hedging deal is concluded, a different person than the transaction originator should confirm the details of the deal. This should be a matching of the company's transaction details to those of the counterparty or exchange, which may involve a written or electronic message (such as an email or SWIFT MT300).

- *Reconcile accounts.* The treasury staff should regularly reconcile all debt and investment accounts to counterparty account balances on a monthly basis. If there is a serious problem, then the control should provide for an immediate escalation of the issue to a higher level of management. This review can be supplemented by periodic unscheduled reconciliations by the internal audit staff.

- *Full-risk modeling.* The treasury staff should conduct full-risk modeling of its investments and debt on at least a quarterly basis, to determine the potential risk inherent in its unhedged portfolio, and also to determine what the company's gain or loss would have been on a rolling historical basis if it had not engaged in hedging transactions.

Cash Flow Hedges

- *Include in the monthly financial statement procedure a review of the recoverability of cash flow hedge losses.* GAAP requires that a nonrecoverable cash flow hedge loss be shifted in the current period from other comprehensive income to earnings. Since this can only result in a reduced level of earnings, accounting personnel tend not to conduct the review. Including the step in the monthly procedure is a good way to ensure prompt loss recognition.

- *Include in the monthly financial statement procedure a review of the likely occurrence of forecasted cash flow transactions.* GAAP requires that any accumulated gain or loss recorded in other comprehensive income be shifted into earnings as soon as it becomes probable that the forecasted cash flow transaction will not take place. Including a standard periodic review of forecasted transactions in the monthly procedure is a good way to ensure prompt inclusion of accumulated gains or losses in earnings.

- *Compare hedging effectiveness assessments to the corporate policy setting forth effectiveness ranges.* GAAP does not specify the exact amount by which hedging instruments and hedged items must offset each other in order to be deemed highly effective, so a corporate policy should be established (see the Policies section) to create such a standard. This control is intended to ensure that the policy is followed when making effectiveness assessments. Comparison to the corporate policy should be included in the assessment procedure.

INTEREST RISK MANAGEMENT POLICIES

The first two policies noted below are designed to introduce consistency into the accounting for hedges, so that the accounting department will be unable to take liberties with profit recognition. The final policy provides for a hard credit-rating floor, below which a company is not allowed to deal with a counterparty whose financial position may be weak. The final policy is a catchall authorization to avoid counterparties that are too hard to deal with. The policies are:

- *The determination of hedge effectiveness shall always use the same method for similar types of hedges.* GAAP allows one to use different assessment techniques in determining whether a hedge is highly effective. However, changing methods, even when justified, allows the accounting staff room to alter effectiveness designations, which can yield variations in the level of reported earnings. Consequently, creating and consistently using a standard assessment method for each type of hedge eliminates the risk of assessment manipulation.

- *A hedge shall be considered highly effective if the fair values of the hedging instrument and hedged item are at least ___ percent offset.* GAAP does not quantitatively specify what constitutes a highly effective hedge, so a company should create a policy defining the number. A different hedging range can be used for different types of hedges.

- *The company shall not deal with a counterparty having a credit rating of less than ___.* This policy is designed to mitigate the risk of a counterparty's failing to pay its obligations to the company under a hedging agreement. The underlying procedure can direct the attention of the treasury staff to changes in counterparty credit ratings from previous periods, so that those with declining ratings are watched more carefully.

- The treasurer is authorized to discontinue hedging transactions with those counterparties with whom the company has experienced ongoing or significant operational problems. This policy is deliberately vague, giving the treasurer authority to stop doing business with a counterparty for any number of reasons, such as improper contract completion, incorrect contract signatories, or difficulty in settling accounts.

RECORD KEEPING FOR INTEREST RATE RISK MANAGEMENT

At the inception of a hedge, GAAP requires documentation of the relationship between the hedging instrument and the hedged item, the risk management objectives of the hedging transaction, how the hedge is to be undertaken, the method to be used for gain or loss recognition, identification of the instrument used for the hedge, and how the effectiveness calculation is measured. Since hedge accounting cannot be used unless this documentation exists, it is important to store a complete set of documentation for each hedge for the duration not only of the hedge, but also through the audit following the hedge termination. It can then be included in the archives with accounting documentation for the year in which the transaction terminated.

INTEREST RISK MANAGEMENT PROCEDURES

The procedure shown in Exhibit 10.6 is a generic one designed to handle the basic steps in an interest hedging transaction.

SUMMARY

Interest risk management is useful for reducing the volatility of a company's cash flows and earnings, as well as for avoiding significant increases in interest costs that can seriously impact the financial well-being of a heavily leveraged company. There are a number of alternatives available to hedge against these risks, which a treasurer can take advantage of either at a minimal level, with selective hedging, or completely, with full-cover hedging. The extent to which hedging is used varies widely by company, and depends on the level of conservatism that each one practices in managing its funds. The accounting for hedging is complex, requiring considerable documentation and a large volume of entries to record each transaction.

Exhibit 10.6   Interest Hedging Procedure

Procedure Statement   Retrieval No.: TREASURY-06

Subject: Steps required to create, monitor, and account for an interest hedging transaction.

1. PURPOSE AND SCOPE

   This procedure is used by the treasury, legal, and accounting staffs to set up, monitor, and account for an interest hedging transaction, incorporating key control points.

2. PROCEDURES

   2.1 Set up Hedging Transaction (Assistant Treasurer)

   1. Ensure that the counterparty's credit rating equals or exceeds the company's minimum credit rating policy standard. Notify the treasurer if the counterparty exhibits a declining credit rating over the past two years.
   2. Calculate the level of hedging effectiveness of the proposed transaction, and document the calculation.
   3. Have the treasurer review and approve the transaction.
   4. Enter into the hedging transaction.
   5. Document the hedge, as required under hedge accounting standards. This includes documenting the relationship between the hedging instrument and liability, as well as the hedging strategy, risk management objectives, and how the effectiveness of the transaction shall be measured.
   6. Have the treasurer review and approve the hedge documentation.

   2.2 Confirm the Hedge (Treasury Clerk)

   1. Immediately upon notification of the deal, confirm it with the counterparty, either by email, orally, or by written notification. Confirmation should include all key terms of the deal.
   2. Assemble the hedge contract, documentation, and confirmation into a package, and create a copy for distribution to the legal department. Retain the original documents.

   2.3 Review the Contract Legality (Legal Staff)

   1. Review the contract for completeness, and verify that the counterparty's signatory is authorized to approve such contracts.
   2. Approve the contract if acceptable, and forward to the assistant controller. If not, return it to the treasurer with attached notes regarding problem areas. If there are problems, then retain a copy of the package, and follow up with the treasurer periodically regarding resolution of the indicated issues.

   2.4 Account for the Hedge (Assistant Controller)

   1. Determine the extent of hedge effectiveness, based on the ranges set forth in the corporate hedge effectiveness policy.

   2. On an ongoing basis, charge to comprehensive income that portion of the hedge that is considered effective, for any gains or losses resulting from marking to market. At the same time, charge to earnings that portion of the hedge that is considered ineffective as a result of marking to market.

   3. On a monthly basis, evaluate the nonrecoverability of hedge losses, and shift these losses from other comprehensive income to earnings.

   4. On a monthly basis, evaluate if it has become probable that any forecasted cash flow transactions will not take place, and shift the associated gains or losses from other comprehensive income to earnings.

2.5 Reconcile the Hedge (Assistant Controller)

   1. Match the internal account balances for the hedge to the statement received from the exchange or the over-the-counter counterparty. Report the reason for any significant differences to the treasurer and controller.

   2. If the hedge is completed and settlement has occurred, reconcile the payment received or issued to internal records, and adjust for any differences.

   3. If the reason for a reconciliation problem is not clear, or if the cause results in a variance of at least $_____, notify the treasurer and controller immediately.

2.6 Report on the Results of the Hedge (Assistant Controller)

   1. Calculate the percentage of hedging achieved by the transaction and report this amount to the treasurer and controller.

   2. Calculate the speed of confirmation matching, and the types of problems found during the reconciliation process, and report these metrics as key performance indicators to the treasurer and controller.

PART FOUR

TREASURY SYSTEMS

11

Clearing and
Settlement Systems

This chapter contains descriptions of a number of clearing and settlement systems that are used for both electronic and check payments within the United States, as well as a multicurrency clearing system. *Clearing* is all of the steps involved in transferring funds ownership from one party to another except for the final step, which is settlement. *Settlement* involves the finalization of a payment, so that a new party takes possession of transferred funds. The treasurer should be aware of these processes in order to understand the timing of payment transfers.

CHARACTERISTICS OF CLEARING AND SETTLEMENT SYSTEMS

In clearing and settlement systems, the banks of the payer and beneficiary exchange information regarding monetary transfers; the result of this exchange is payments between the banks.

OVERVIEW OF THE CLEARING AND SETTLEMENT PROCESS

The general concept of clearing and settlement is for the banks of the paying party (the payer) and the receiving party (the beneficiary) to exchange information regarding monetary transfers, resulting in the transfer of funds between the two banks. The banks, in turn, debit the account of the payer and credit the account of the beneficiary. Given the massive volume of such transactions, formal clearing and settlement systems have been installed to streamline the process.

Clearing and settlement systems are generally organized around individual countries or economic regions. Banks located within these areas can have an account with the local clearing and settlement institution; settlement takes place between the accounts of the banks held *at* the clearing institution. Banks located outside of these areas do not have such an account, and so must use a local bank as a correspondent bank that handles payment instructions on their behalf.

Settlement Types

Payments can be on a *gross basis*, where each bank pays the total amount owed. Payments handled through a gross settlement system are more likely to have a requirement for immediate execution, where payment instructions are processed separately for each individual transaction. The cost of gross settlement transactions is high, so individual transactions running through these systems tend to involve larger amounts of funds or be very time sensitive.

Payments can also be on a *net basis*, where a large number of transactions are accumulated and offset against each other, with only the net differential being transferred between banks. Payments handled through a net settlement system usually wait until the end of the day, when all transactions between the banks are summarized and offset against each other by a clearing institution; the clearing institution then sends the net transfer information to the settlement institution, which executes the transfer of funds between banks. The clearing institution normally completes its daily summarization process and transmits net transfer information to the settlement institution after the cutoff time of the settlement institution. This means that the transfer of funds to the account of the beneficiary bank will be delayed by one business day. A few clearing institutions compile net transfer information to settlement institutions not only before their cutoff times, but several times per day, which allows for settlement speeds similar to those of gross settlement systems. The cost of net settlement transactions is low, so lower-value transactions are usually settled through these systems.

Banks prefer to use net settlement systems because payments processed through them require greatly reduced funds transfers (and therefore considerably less liquidity) than gross settlement systems.

Transaction Types

Each clearing and settlement system is primarily designed to handle a certain type of transaction. One such type is the *high-value payment*, which must be executed immediately. Because of the time constraint, high-value payments cannot wait for end-of-day netting, and so are settled on a gross basis, with an immediate cash transfer between banks. Another payment type is the *low-value payment*, which does not require immediate execution and tends to be for smaller amounts. Because of the reduced need for immediate execution, these payments are handled through a net settlement system.

FEDWIRE

The Fedwire system is a gross settlement system that is operated by the U.S. Federal Reserve and processes large-value items with same-day, real-time settlement. Nearly all U.S. banks and the agencies of foreign banks participate in the Fedwire system. If a bank is sending funds through the Fedwire system on behalf of a client company, then the deadline for initiating such transfers is 6 P.M. eastern time. The fee for a Fedwire payment is relatively inexpensive.

The process flow for a Fedwire payment is for a paying company to transmit payment instructions to its bank, which debits the paying company's account and forwards the payment instructions on to the Federal Reserve (Fed). The Fed then debits the paying bank's account at the Fed and credits the account of the beneficiary bank at the Fed. Finally, the beneficiary's bank credits the account of the beneficiary. The process flow for a Fedwire payment is shown in Exhibit 11.1.

AUTOMATED CLEARING HOUSE (ACH) SYSTEM

The ACH system is the net settlement system used for electronic payments in the United States, and is used by most banks in the country. The ACH system is used for large-volume, low-value payments, such as payroll direct deposits, business-to-business payments, dividends, tax payments, and Social Security payments. The transfer of funds from the payer to the beneficiary can take several days, depending on the payer's payment instructions. This system is significantly more complex than the Fedwire system, since it comprises a network of bank associations and privately owned processing entities. The cost of an ACH payment is quite low, usually just a few cents per transaction.

The ACH process flow is for a company to submit an electronic file to its bank (also known as the *originating depository financial institution*), containing payment information; the bank lets these submissions accumulate until the end of the day. At that time, it directly pays any of the authorized items with a book transfer if the recipient has an account with the bank. If not, the bank batches and forwards the remaining payment authorizations to its designated ACH operator (usually a regional branch of the Federal Reserve, or the Electronic Payments Network). The ACH operator collects the ACH submissions from all of the banks in its region and calculates the net settlement amounts that they must pay to each other. The ACH operator then aggregates the remaining transactions involving banks outside of its region, subdivides them by ACH region, and transmits them to the ACH operators responsible for conducting similar processing for their regions. Payments are made to the beneficiary's banks (also known as *receiving depository financial institutions*), which in turn pay the beneficiaries. Payments between banks

Exhibit 11.1   Fedwire Process Flow

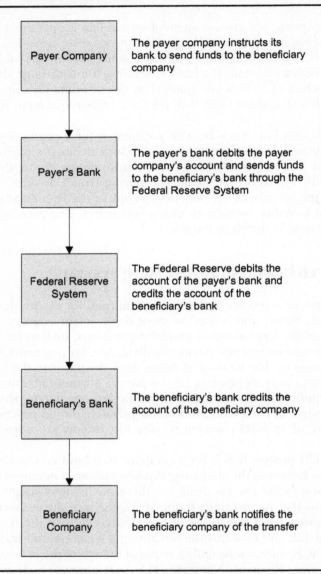

Payer Company	The payer company instructs its bank to send funds to the beneficiary company
Payer's Bank	The payer's bank debits the payer company's account and sends funds to the beneficiary's bank through the Federal Reserve System
Federal Reserve System	The Federal Reserve debits the account of the payer's bank and credits the account of the beneficiary's bank
Beneficiary's Bank	The beneficiary's bank credits the account of the beneficiary company
Beneficiary Company	The beneficiary's bank notifies the beneficiary company of the transfer

associated with different ACH operators are settled on a gross basis. The process flow for an ACH payment is shown in Exhibit 11.2.

Settlement timing is based on the payment date specified by the payer in the ACH file submitted to its bank. A company can deliver ACH debit instructions that are no earlier than one banking day prior to the settlement

Exhibit 11.2   ACH Process Flow

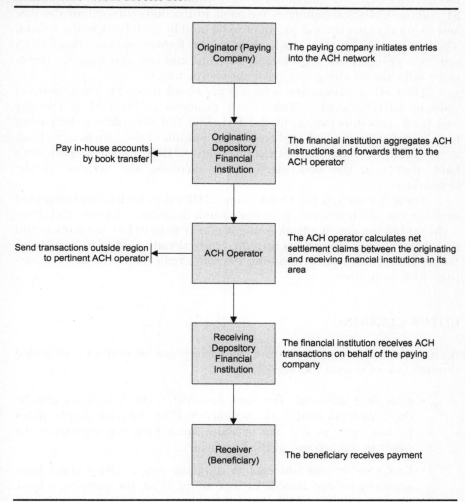

Originator (Paying Company)	The paying company initiates entries into the ACH network
Originating Depository Financial Institution	The financial institution aggregates ACH instructions and forwards them to the ACH operator
Pay in-house accounts by book transfer	
ACH Operator	The ACH operator calculates net settlement claims between the originating and receiving financial institutions in its area
Send transactions outside region to pertinent ACH operator	
Receiving Depository Financial Institution	The financial institution receives ACH transactions on behalf of the paying company
Receiver (Beneficiary)	The beneficiary receives payment

date, while ACH credits can be delivered no earlier than two banking days prior to the settlement date. If the ACH file is delivered too late to settle on the specified date, then the ACH operator will use the next business day as the settlement date.

CLEARING HOUSE INTERBANK PAYMENTS SYSTEM (CHIPS)

CHIPS is a net settlement system that is operated by the Clearing House in New York, which in turn is owned by a group of banks. It settles primarily foreign exchange and eurodollar trades, with total daily volume exceeding $1 trillion. CHIPS accumulates payment instructions throughout the day, and then calculates the net payment to be paid by each bank in the system. The net payment is then made through the Fedwire system. The CHIPS system is designed for high-value payments, and can also transmit remittance information along with payment instructions.

The CHIPS process flow is for a payer's bank to send payment instructions to CHIPS, which calculates net positions at the end of the day and sends this information to the Fed. The Fed then debits the paying bank's account at the Fed, and credits the account of the beneficiary's bank at the Fed. A separate instruction from CHIPS to the beneficiary's bank results in the beneficiary's bank crediting the account of the beneficiary.

There is some risk for a bank using CHIPS because it is not being paid until the end of the day but could make funds available to its customers *prior to* the end of the day; if a bank owing it money were to fail, the bank would then have no means of recovering the funds already paid to its customers. Banks control this risk by imposing intraday credit limits on their transactions with each other.

CHECK CLEARING

A check issued from a payer to a beneficiary can be cleared and settled through one of several routings. They are:

- *Same bank settlement.* The bank on which a check is drawn may be the same bank used by the beneficiary. If so, the bank simply makes a book entry to shift the in-house funds from the account of the payer to the account of the beneficiary.

- *Correspondent bank settlement.* A company may receive a check from an entity located outside of its country. If so, the company's bank sends the check to a correspondent bank in the originating country; clearing and settlement occurs in that country, and then the correspondent bank uses an electronic transfer to shift the funds back to the beneficiary's bank.

- *Check-clearing institution.* Checks are physically processed through the Federal Reserve System. The process flow is for the beneficiary (check recipient) to send the check to its bank, which in turn sends the check to the check-clearing institution (CCI), which is frequently the Fed. The CCI aggregates the information on all checks received and sends a payment instruction to the Fed. The Fed then debits the account of the payer's bank at the Fed and credits the account of the beneficiary's bank at the Fed. Meanwhile, the CCI has notified the banks of both the payer and beneficiary, who debit the payer's bank account and credit the beneficiary's account, respectively.

- *Electronic check presentment.* Either the recipient of a check or its bank can scan a check to create an electronic image, and then send the image to the CCI. Since no transport of actual checks occurs, the clearing process can be several days quicker than traditional paper check clearing. The process flow for an electronic check presentment is shown in Exhibit 11.3.

Exhibit 11.3   Electronic Check Presentment Process Flow

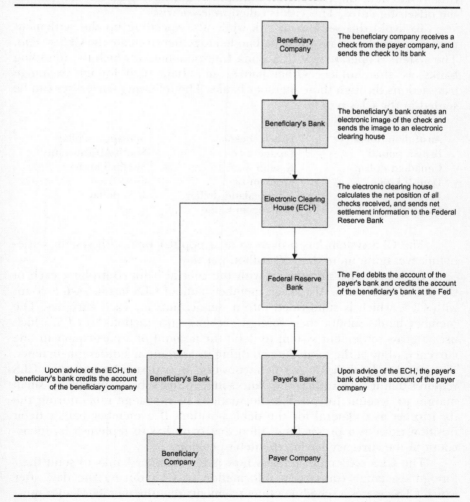

Beneficiary Company	The beneficiary company receives a check from the payer company, and sends the check to its bank
Beneficiary's Bank	The beneficiary's bank creates an electronic image of the check and sends the image to an electronic clearing house
Electronic Clearing House (ECH)	The electronic clearing house calculates the net position of all checks received, and sends net settlement information to the Federal Reserve Bank
Federal Reserve Bank	The Fed debits the account of the payer's bank and credits the account of the beneficiary's bank at the Fed

Upon advice of the ECH, the beneficiary's bank credits the account of the beneficiary company — Beneficiary's Bank / Payer's Bank — Upon advice of the ECH, the payer's bank debits the account of the payer company

Beneficiary Company / Payer Company

THE CONTINUOUS LINK SETTLEMENT (CLS) SYSTEM

Foreign exchange settlement presents a risk of one party's defaulting before a transaction has been completed because settlement takes place through accounts in the correspondent banks in the countries where the relevant currencies are issued. Because the various national payment systems are located in different time zones around the world, one side of a foreign exchange transaction will likely be settled before the other side of the transaction. For example, dollar payments are settled later than euro payments, which in turn are settled later than yen payments. Thus, someone buying in dollars and paying in euros will have settled the euro side of the payment before receiving any dollars. If the counterparty were to fail in the midst of this transaction, the transaction initiator would have paid dollars but lost the offsetting euros. This risk is called *settlement risk*.

To avoid this settlement risk while also speeding up the settlement process, a number of major banks banded together to create the CLS system. The system is operated by CLS Bank International, of which the founding banks are shareholders. Other banks can submit their foreign exchange transactions through these member banks. The following currencies can be settled in the CLS system:

Australian dollar	Israeli shekel	Singapore dollar
British pound	Japanese yen	South African rand
Canadian dollar	Korean won	Swedish krona
Danish krone	Mexican peso	Swiss franc
Euro	New Zealand dollar	U.S. dollar
Hong Kong dollar	Norwegian krone	

The CLS system has proven to be a popular one, with system settlements averaging more than $2 trillion per day.

CLS maintains an account with the central bank controlling each of the above currencies. Also, each member bank of CLS has its own account with CLS, which is subdivided into a sub-account for each currency. The member banks submit their foreign exchange transactions to CLS, which uses a gross settlement system to debit the account of a participant in one currency, while at the same time crediting its account in a different currency. If a member bank has a net debit position in a particular currency, CLS requires that it have sufficient balances in its other subaccounts (less a small margin to account for possible fluctuations in exchange rates during the day) to act as collateral for the debit position. If a member bank's debit position exceeds a preset limit, then that bank has to replenish its subaccount in the currency having the debit position.

The CLS settlement process flow is for member banks to send their foreign exchange transaction information to CLS during the day, after which CLS creates a schedule of net payments that the member banks must pay to CLS. CLS then processes both sides of each individual foreign exchange transaction, so that the account of one member bank is debited, while the account of another member bank is credited. CLS processes these transactions on a first-in, first-out basis. If, during the processing sequence, a member bank's cash position with CLS becomes too low, CLS will shunt aside and postpone its remaining transactions until additional funds are provided by the member bank.

After CLS has completed this process, it transfers the updated balances of the settlements back to the accounts that the member banks hold at the central banks in their home countries. Since these payments are the result of the aggregation of a multitude of smaller transactions, they are on a net basis. This processing period must be completed during a five-hour period that covers the overlapping business hours of the participating national settlement systems.

How does CLS impact the corporation? It gives the treasurer exact information about when settlements will occur in various currencies, which previously had been difficult to predict with precision. With better foreign exchange settlement information, the treasury staff can now optimize its short-term investment strategy.

SUMMARY

With the exception of the CLS system, this chapter has described only the clearing and settlement systems operating within the United States. Similar systems operate in other countries and economic regions, and also fall into the general categories of high-value, gross settlement systems or low-value, net settlement systems. Examples of such systems are TARGET2, Euro1, and STEP2 in Europe, BACS and CHAPS in the United Kingdom, and BOJ-NET and FXYCS in Japan. If a treasurer's company transacts significant business in regions outside of the United States, it may be worthwhile to research the process flows of the clearing and settlement systems used in those regions.

12

Treasury Systems

The treasurer requires information that is not normally available through a company's standard accounting systems, or even from its enterprise resources planning (ERP) systems. Even though an ERP system is designed to aggregate all of the information used in a modern corporation, the treasurer also requires information from a variety of external sources regarding investments, foreign exchange positions, interest rates, and so forth. Consequently, treasury systems are needed that integrate information from a variety of sources, yielding real-time information that the treasury staff can use to efficiently perform their tasks. This chapter describes the treasurer's technology needs, and whether to install a treasury management system.

TREASURER'S TECHNOLOGY NEEDS

The treasurer is in the difficult position of requiring information from many sources, most of which are not required by any other company manager. Since treasury is a relatively small department that may not command the resources of larger departments, it can be difficult to collect all of the required information. Consequently, the treasurer must frequently prioritize information needs. While priorities may vary by company, the following list establishes a reasonable set of priorities, in declining order:

1. *Cash position.* The treasurer's overriding obligation is to ensure that the company has adequate cash to fund its operations. Thus, the following technology needs are critical:
   - Cash book balance tracking
   - Multibank reporting of balance information
   - Cash pooling management

- Cash forecasting and reconciliation of actual to projected cash flows
- Funds transfer capability
- Investment management, including money market dealing
- Interest income calculation
- Debt management
- Interest expense calculation
- Payment processing
- Intercompany transaction settlement with notional accounts

2. *Foreign exchange transactions.*   Some companies have so little foreign business that foreign exchange transactions are negligible, but larger firms with established treasury operations will likely need the ongoing purchase and sale of multiple currencies. Thus, the following technology needs arise:

- Rate feeds from Bloomberg or Reuters
- Intercompany netting capability
- Foreign exchange forecasting and position analysis
- Foreign exchange bid summarization
- Foreign exchange deal-making capability
- Foreign exchange confirmation processing

3. *Hedging.*   For those companies that elect to hedge their interest rates or foreign exchange positions, consider the following technology requirements:

- Rate feeds from Bloomberg or Reuters
- Exposure modeling capability
- Hedge deal–making capability
- Hedge confirmation processing
- Hedge documentation capability for Statement of Financial Accounting Standards (SFAS) 133 requirements

In all cases, transactions generated by the treasury system should automatically create accounting entries that are interfaced directly into the corporate general ledger.

In addition to these three core areas, the treasurer also needs a reporting system that reveals the global cash position, investment portfolio, debt portfolio, cash forecast, and foreign exchange transactions. The system should also provide mark-to-market valuations, scenario analysis, and counterparty risk summaries. This information can be presented through a customized online dashboard that is updated in real time.

The treasurer's technology needs also extend to the efficiency of and control over treasury activities. Thus, the following requirements should be considered:

Efficiency Issues

- *Minimize data entry.* The system should never require the manual entry of a transaction into the system more than once, and preferably should involve automated data collection and posting, so that no manual entry is required at all.

- *Work flow processing.* If supervisory approval is required, the system should electronically route the pertinent transaction to the correct supervisor for approval.

Control Issues

- *Audit trail.* All treasury transactions should result in a clearly defined audit trail that identifies who made a transaction and the date, amount, and accounts impacted by the transaction.

- *Segregation of duties.* The system should limit access to certain modules and require approval of key transactions.

- *Warning indicators.* The system should automatically notify users if transaction confirmations have not been received, if hedging policies are being violated, if there are negative cash balances, and so on.

These treasury technology issues are applied in the next section, where we address the treasury management system.

TREASURY MANAGEMENT SYSTEM

All of the technology requirements noted in the last section are available in treasury management systems today. However, these systems are quite expensive, beginning in the six-figure range and comfortably exceeding $1 million for fully integrated systems. The difference in those systems located between the low and high ends of this price range is the amount of functionality and bank interfaces added to the treasury system—if a buyer wants every possible feature and must share data with a large number of financial suppliers, then the cost will be much closer to the top of the range. Thus, more banking relationships and users equate to a high price.

Given these costs, a treasury management system is generally not cost-effective for companies with sales volumes under $250 million, and many companies do not find them to be cost-effective unless their sales are substantially higher. Also, because of the large number of interfaces needed to connect the system to the data feeds of other entities, the installation time can exceed one year.

Why spend so much money and installation time on a treasury management system? Because it automates so many of the rote treasury tasks. For example, if an employee buys an investment and runs the transaction through this system, it will create a transaction for the settlement, one for the maturity, and another for the interest. It will then alter the cash forecast with this information, and create a wire transfer to send the money to the financial intermediary that is handling the purchase.

A treasury management system will be less expensive and easier to install if the treasurer reduces the number of outside banking relations that the company has, so that there are fewer customized interfaces to construct. Since it can take multiple months to unwind a banking relationship, this issue should be dealt with well before the system's scheduled installation date.

A key issue with a treasury management system is its complexity, which can be substantial. There is a significant risk that the system will not be fully utilized, since employees will gain expertise only in those specific functions that they were performing prior to the system installation. To avoid this issue, schedule thorough training for all affected personnel in *all* functions of the system, and also schedule an audit of system usage several months after installation, to determine which features are not being used. The likely result of this review will be targeted training for underutilized functionality.

What if a company cannot find a cost-beneficial way to acquire a treasury management system? One solution is to examine the cost of a failed manual system, such as a spreadsheet error. If such an error is discovered, its cost may be justification for acquiring a system. Another option is to enlist the internal auditors, who can argue that the risk of a transactional error may result in a Sarbanes-Oxley control breach that would have to be revealed in the company's public filings. A third alternative is to explore a third-party hosting solution, which substitutes the large up-front capital cost of a treasury management system for an ongoing monthly fee.

If none of these alternatives work, the treasurer should at least attempt to install those portions of a treasury management system that reduce the amount of data entry and repetitive work by the treasury staff, thereby giving them more time to work on such value-added activities as risk management, fund raising, and hedge analysis. As the size of the company gradually increases, it may then be possible to add to the functionality of the existing system.

SWIFT CONNECTIVITY

The Society for Worldwide Interbank Financial Telecommunication (SWIFT) operates a worldwide network that banks use to exchange standardized electronic messages that are known as SWIFT MT codes. The SWIFT network is highly secure and is designed strictly to transport messages between participants—it does not provide a clearing or settlement service.

Companies are now able to access the SWIFT network by any one of four methods, which are as follows:

- *Standardized corporate environment (SCORE)*. Under this approach, a company can communicate with all member banks in a closed user group. Companies allowed to use this method must be listed on selected stock exchanges in specific countries, which include most of western Europe, North America, and some countries in eastern Europe, Latin America, and Asia. SWIFT invoices companies directly for their message traffic. This is the most efficient method, because users have direct access to nearly all banks.

- *Member-administered closed user group (MA-CUG)*. A company can join a separate MA-CUG for each bank with which it wishes to communicate. Each MA-CUG is administered by a bank, rather than SWIFT. The bank running each CUG will invoice member companies for their message traffic. This approach may call for membership in multiple MA-CUGs, which is less convenient than the SCORE method. However, it is available to all types and sizes of companies.

- *Alliance lite*. SWIFT has made this method available to smaller companies having low transaction volumes. It allows them to use either a manual browser-based payment entry system or to integrate directly into their treasury management systems.

- *SWIFT bureaus*. Third-party providers have set up their own access to the SWIFT network and allow companies access through their systems for a per-transaction fee. This approach avoids the need for any in-house systems maintenance, but connectivity to any in-house treasury management systems is likely to be limited.

In none of the preceding access methodologies is a company allowed to deal directly with another corporation; it can only send messages through bank intermediaries.

Access to the SWIFT network is important for larger companies, because they can link their treasury management systems directly into the SWIFT network. By doing so, they avoid having to establish individual interfaces with the reporting systems of all the banks with which they do business, and instead can rely on a single standard messaging format to initiate transactions with and acquire information from bank accounts all over the world.

Each SWIFT MT code used to send messages within the SWIFT network contains a standard set of information fields. Thus, a different SWIFT MT code is used for each type of transaction. For example, a company can issue an MT 101 to move funds, an MT 104 to debit a debtor's account, an MT 300 for a foreign exchange confirmation, an MT 320 for a loan confirmation, and an MT 940 to request bank account information. Given the high degree of standardization, these messages can be automatically generated by a company's treasury management system and transmitted through SWIFT, while all incoming messages can also be dealt with by the treasury management system in a highly automated manner.

In summary, there are multiple ways available for a company to gain access to the SWIFT system, which it can then integrate into its treasury management system. Doing so streamlines a number of treasury transactions, which makes the entire system more cost-effective to operate.

SUMMARY

A company can subsist on spreadsheet-based systems if it engages in a trifling number of treasury transactions. However, it will soon find with increased volume that the amount of rote data entry labor and outright errors associated with such systems will eventually call for the implementation of formal treasury systems. These systems operate best if the treasurer insists on a high level of staff training, as well as some reduction in the number of external banking relationships. Also, the increased availability of the SWIFT network to corporations makes it possible to engage in a high degree of transactional automation, thereby giving the treasury staff more time for tasks that better utilize their skills.

Index